POPE FRANCIS'S
"Paradigm Shift"

JOSÉ ANTONIO URETA

POPE FRANCIS'S
"Paradigm Shift"

Continuity or Rupture in the Mission of the Church?

AN ASSESSMENT OF
HIS PONTIFICATE'S FIRST FIVE YEARS

Translated by José A. Schelini

The American Society for the
Defense of Tradition, Family and Property
Spring Grove, Penn.

First published as *Il "cambio di paradigma" di Papa Francesco: Continuità o rottura nella missione della Chiesa? Bilancio quinquennale del suo pontificato.*
Copyright © 2018 Instituto Plinio Corrêa de Oliveira
Rua Maranhão, 341
Bairro Higienópolis
São Paulo–SP
01240-001
Brazil
www.IPCO.org.br

English translation copyright © 2018 The American Society for the
Defense of Tradition, Family and Property®—TFP®
1358 Jefferson Road
Spring Grove, Penn. 17362
Tel.: (888) 317–5571
www.TFP.org

Free e-book versions of this work are available at:
English: http://www.tfp.org/ParadigmShift
Italian: https://www.atfp.it/il-cambio-di-paradigma-di-papa-francesco
Portuguese: https://ipco.org.br/a-mudanca-de-paradigma

The American Society for the Defense of Tradition, Family and Property®, TFP® is a registered name of The Foundation for a Christian Civilization, Inc., a 501(c)(3) tax-exempt organization.

Citations for Bible versions other than the Douay-Rheims are designated by their respective abbreviated prefix. Citations of Saint Thomas Aquinas and the Fathers of the Church are abbreviated in the footnotes with full entries in the Bibliography. Unless otherwise noted, all English translations from foreign language sources are the translator's.

ISBN (Softcover): 978-1-877905-56-8
ISBN (E-book): 978-1-877905-57-5

Library of Congress Catalogue Card No.: 2018958393

Printed in the United States of America

Cover image: © Maxim Kulemza | Dreamstime.com

Contents

List of Abbreviations
C – *The New Testament of Our Lord and Savior Jesus Christ*, Confraternity of Catholic Doctrine
KL – *The New Testament*, translated by James A. Kleist, SJ and Joseph L. Lilly, CM

INTRODUCTION

Last March, Pope Francis's pontificate reached its five-year milestone, a sufficient time span for historians, analysts, and scholars to make an initial assessment on his reign. Their perspectives vary, but all agree that this has been a period full of innovation. It was marked by his constant efforts to place the papacy in a new light. Some even speak of a *New Church of Francis.*[1]

The idea of a "New Church" comes through like a new paradigm in the debates now enveloping the Church founded by Our Lord Jesus Christ. It leads one to ask: Can a paradigm shift take place, concerning Her 2,000-year-old life and teachings?

In its traditional sense, a *paradigm* is an example or standard to follow.[2] Popularized in 1962, by physicist and philosopher Thomas S. Kuhn, the expression *paradigm shift* has come to mean a major change in the "conceptual or methodological model underlying the theories and practices of a science or discipline at a particular time; (hence) a generally accepted worldview."[3] For the layman, writer George Weigel says that a paradigm shift "signals a dramatic, sudden, and unexpected break in human understanding—and thus something of a new beginning."[4]

---

1. See, for example, *La nuova Chiesa di papa Francesco*, ed. J. M. Kraus (Rome: Moralia, 2013); the Mar. 14, 2013, headlines of *La Repubblica* (Rome), http://www.funize.com/images/frontpages/49f68a39ba42 f26173c991cc12df7c44.jpeg; Álvaro de Juana, "La nueva Iglesia del Papa Francisco," *La Razón*, Mar. 13, 2017, https://www.larazon.es/religion/la-nueva-iglesia-del-papa-Francis-EK14699739; Adam Littlestone-Luria, "How Pope Francis Has Fundamentally Reshaped the Catholic Church," *The Washington Post*, Sept. 24, 2017, https://www.washingtonpost.com/news/made-by-history/wp/2017/09/24/how-pope-francis-has -fundamentally-reshaped-the-catholic-church/?utm_term=.8f70db361778; Alexander M. Santora, "Five Years of Francis Framing a New Church," *NorthJersey.com*, Mar. 12, 2018, https://www.northjersey.com /story/opinion/contributors/2018/03/12/five-years-pope-francis-framing-new-church-opinion/417177002/.

2. "Example, pattern; *especially*: an outstandingly clear or typical example or archetype." "Paradigm," *Merriam-Webster.com*, accessed Jul. 8, 2018, https://www.merriam-webster.com/dictionary/paradigm.

3. "Paradigm, n.," OED Online, June 2018, Oxford University Press, accessed Jul. 18, 2018, http://www.oed.com/view/Entry/137329. See Thomas S. Kuhn, *Structure of Scientific Revolutions*, 4th ed. (Chicago: Chicago University Press, 2012).

4. George Weigel, "The Catholic Church Doesn't Do 'Paradigm Shifts,'" *First Things*, Jan. 31, 2018, https://www.firstthings.com/web-exclusives/2018/01/the-catholic-church-doesnt-do-paradigm-shifts. Andrea Lavazza writes in the same line in *Avvenire*, a daily owned by the Italian Bishops Conference: "The idea of a paradigm shift has come into common use. The expression was coined to indicate a radical change in the way of facing a scientific problem. At one stage, all researchers agree on a core of knowledge and methods and work with them smoothly, making little progress. However, when a series of anomalies appear in the dominant theory, it enters into crisis and one witnesses a revolutionary phase that leads to a shift in the paradigm hitherto shared." Andrea Lavazza, "Islam e occidente, diplomazia e realtà: Cambio di paradigma," *Avvenire*, Sept. 22, 2012, https://www.avvenire.it/opinioni/pagine/cambio-di-paradigma.

There have been and will be more sea changes in the history of science that can be aptly termed paradigm shifts.[5] But it is very rash, to say the least, to think of a new conceptual model for the Church founded by the Word Incarnate. This is because the Church is based upon Divine Revelation and an unchangeable deposit of faith that was made explicit by a constant and consistent magisterium over the course of twenty centuries. However, Pope Francis himself used the expression in the recent Apostolic Constitution *Veritatis Gaudium* on Catholic university teaching. In this papal document, he called for "a broad and generous effort at a radical paradigm shift, or rather—dare I say—at 'a bold cultural revolution.'"[6]

The terms "paradigm shift" and "cultural revolution" bring to mind the idea of rupture or discontinuity with previous models. Here, the concept is applied mainly to moral theology and one of its components, Catholic social doctrine.[7] It encompasses teachings of Catholicism regarding contemporary society in many fields, from science to economics, from politics to diplomacy. In the opinion of a large team of bishops and scholars, a paradigm shift is needed in all of these areas.

In this context, untold numbers of believers ask themselves: Where is the Church going? At the end of the first five years of this pontificate, they wonder about the future. Some voice their questions publicly, others ponder them in

---

5. Khun's applications of the paradigm shift concept are unacceptable, since he is a post-Darwinian Kantian relativist. For him, concepts of truth and error are valid, but only within a given paradigm. According to him, science would be incapable of attaining absolute truth in any field, because reality is unknowable. Like Kant, he "believed that without some sort of *a priori* paradigm the mind cannot impose order on sensory experience. But whereas Kant and Darwin each thought that we are all born with more or less the same, innate paradigm, Kuhn argued that our paradigms keep changing as our culture changes. 'Different groups, and the same group at different times,' Kuhn told me, 'can have different experiences, and therefore in some sense live in different worlds.' Obviously all humans share some responses to experience, simply because of their shared biological heritage, Kuhn added. But whatever is universal in human experience, whatever transcends culture and history, is also 'ineffable,' beyond the reach of language. Language, Kuhn said, 'is not a universal tool.' . . . But isn't mathematics a kind of universal language? I asked. Not really, Kuhn replied, since it has no meaning." John Horgan, "What Thomas Kuhn Really Thought About Scientific 'Truth,'" *Scientific American*, May 23, 2012, https://blogs.scientificamerican.com/cross-check/what-thomas-kuhn-really-thought-about-scientific-truth/. It is no surprise that his thinking was adopted by deconstructionist, anti-scientific, and absolutely relativistic postmodernism. See Marcel Kuntz, "The Postmodern Assault on Science: If All Truths Are Equal, Who Cares What Science Has to Say?" *EMBO Reports*, Sept. 18, 2012, https://www.ncbi.nlm.nih.gov/pmc/articles/PMC3463968/.

6. Francis, Apostolic Constitution *Veritatis Gaudium*, Dec. 8, 2017, no. 3, https://w2.vatican.va/content/francesco/en/apost_constitutions/documents/papa-francesco_costituzione-ap_20171208_veritatis-gaudium.html.

7. On how Catholic social doctrine derives from theology and especially moral theology, see John Paul II, Encyclical *Sollicitudo Rei Socialis,* Dec. 30, 1987, no. 41, http://w2.vatican.va/content/john-paul-ii/en/encyclicals/documents/hf_jp-ii_enc_30121987_sollicitudo-rei-socialis.html, and Encyclical *Centesimus Annus*, May 1, 1991, no. 55, http://w2.vatican.va/content/john-paul-ii/en/encyclicals/documents/hf_jp-ii_enc_01051991_centesimus-annus.html.

silence. There is widespread concern, however, that a paradigm shift may jeopardize one of the Church's marks: Her unity.

As will be seen later, the paradigm shift debate is indicative of a growing and profound division in Catholic circles. Fault lines are surfacing, notwithstanding all the talk within the Church about legitimate diversity, the multifaceted nature of ecclesial reality, dialogue, and listening. But, how are dialogue and listening even possible when the paradigm shift's "pastoral conversion of ecclesial language" radically changes the very meaning of words?[8]

While there are many studies, lectures, and articles on the topic, I highlight a single emblematic case that involved two prominent churchmen. Their pronouncements were made in the midst of the ongoing debate that erupted during the February 2014 consistory, when Cardinal Walter Kasper proposed that divorced and civilly "remarried" couples be allowed to receive Holy Communion.[9]

The first prelate is Chicago archbishop, Cardinal Blase Cupich. He delivered a lecture in Cambridge, England, that was expressively titled, "Pope Francis' Revolution of Mercy: Amoris Laetitia as a New Paradigm of Catholicity."

The second is the former prefect of the Congregation for the Doctrine of the Faith, Cardinal Gerhard Müller. Ten days after Cardinal Cupich's Cambridge lecture, he published an article in *First Things* with an equally significant title: "Development or Corruption? Can There Be 'Paradigm Shifts' in the Interpretation of the Deposit of the Faith?"

These texts are entirely contrary to one another.

The cardinal archbishop of Chicago advocates the need for a paradigm shift that is "nothing short [of] revolutionary" in the relationship between moral doctrine and pastoral *praxis*. This, he claims, is necessary to respond positively, as Pope Francis wishes, to the needs caused by the "situations" people face today. For the American cardinal, this "shift" consists above all in inverting the order of things: Doctrine and law must be subordinated to life as contemporary man lives it. The Church should not teach but should learn from social reality. She should accompany people in their different "situations," without seeking to impose on them "an abstract, isolated set of truths."[10] He claims that the paradigm shift also consists in understanding that God is present and reveals

8. Guido Vignelli, *A Pastoral Revolution: Six Talismanic Words in the Synodal Debate on the Family* (Spring Grove, Penn.: The American Society for the Defense of Tradition, Family, and Property, 2018), xiii, http://www.tfp.org/PastoralRevolution.

9. See Sandro Magister, "Kasper cambia el paradigma, Bergoglio aplaude," Mar. 1, 2014, *L'Espresso–Settimo Cielo*, http://chiesa.espresso.repubblica.it/articolo/1350729ffae.html?sp=y.

10. Blase Cupich, "Pope Francis's Revolution of Mercy: Amoris Laetitia as a New Paradigm of Catholicity," Von Hügel Institute Annual Lecture, Feb. 9, 2018, https://www.vhi.st-edmunds.cam.ac.uk/resources-folder /papers-presentations/cupich-annual-lecture-2018.

Himself even in "situations" that the Church previously defined as sinful.[11]

Many joined their voices to that of the Chicago archbishop. They welcomed the paradigm shift as an authentic and profound rebirth and reinterpretation of the Church; a rereading of Holy Writ; a new conception of the Church's salvific mission in light of what God is supposedly revealing to contemporary man through society's present "situations."

Opposing Cardinal Cupich's approach, are prelates and theologians who agree that a paradigm shift may occur legitimately in fields like science, politics, or economics. However, they find it unacceptable to apply the term to the interpretation of the substance of the truths of the Faith.

Cardinal Müller is among those who deny that a paradigm shift can take place within the Church's perennial teachings or disciplines. In the article cited above, he recalled that "'Jesus Christ is the same yesterday, today, and forever' (Heb. 13:8)—this is, in contrast, our paradigm, which we will not exchange for any other. 'For no other foundation can anyone lay than that which is laid, which is Jesus Christ' (1 Cor. 3:11)."

The German theologian explained that it is possible and even necessary to grow in the conceptual and intellectual understanding of the truths of the Faith. New explanations and insights are possible, but nothing of the Faith's substance can be changed. In his view, paradigm shift advocates fall into the errors of Modernism and even Gnosticism, "by introducing a novel principle of interpretation by which to give a completely different direction to all of Church teaching." This is done on the pretext of a pastoral about-face. In reality, however, it masks their surrender to the old temptation to adapt the Church to the world's prevailing mentality. Moreover, Cardinal Müller says, authentic growth in the understanding of God's Revelation "does not occur from any kind of natural necessity, and it has nothing to do with the liberal belief in progress."

The cardinal further recalled that "The authority of the papal magisterium rests on its continuity with the teachings of previous popes." Were this not so, he said, the authority of any pope and the Church's magisterium would lose all credibility. In fact, how could one guarantee that a paradigm shift implemented today would not be considered *passé* tomorrow, and therefore, no longer valid? Thus, the German cardinal categorically asserts, "Whoever speaks of a Copernican turn in moral theology, which turns a direct violation of God's commandments into a praiseworthy decision of conscience, quite evidently speaks against the Catholic faith." If this is the paradigm shift, he wrote, then "opposition is a duty of conscience" for the faithful, in keeping with the teaching of

---

11. See Luiz Sérgio Solimeo, "Cardinal Cupich's Modernist Concepts," *TFP.org*, Feb. 21, 2018, http://www.tfp.org/cardinal-cupichs-modernist-concepts/.

Saint Paul in his Epistle to the Galatians (2:11) and commentaries on this passage penned by Church Fathers and Doctors, like Saint Augustine and Saint Thomas Aquinas.[12]

The prominence of these two eminent exponents of the clashing viewpoints on a paradigm shift in Church moral theology and pastoral discipline helps demonstrate the importance of what is at stake.

However, those aware of the reality of Catholic life today know that such divergence goes far beyond Holy Communion being given to civilly "remarried" divorcees. The idea of a paradigm shift idea reverberates in controversies over the validity and priority of other Church teachings and practices, for example, the desire for a new, supposedly *responsible* rereading of the Encyclical *Humanae Vitae*. Some alleged pretexts for this reinterpretation are socio-demographic problems and caring for the planet.

The promotion of a paradigm shift within the Church has also inspired the rapid change through which, in just a few years, unnatural vice is increasingly becoming accepted within the Church. Initially, homosexuals received timid invitations to join Church activities. Today, the faithful are told to recognize the "mutual aid to the point of sacrifice"[13] supposedly found in their relationships. Similarly, paradigm shifters increasingly clamor for the approval of Church blessing ceremonies for same-sex couples and Catholic funeral services for unrepentant homosexuals!

Until five years ago, papal magisterium on these and other pressing issues was crystal clear. Some matters were "non-negotiable." These included:

- the protection of life at every stage, from conception to natural death
- the recognition and promotion of the natural structure of the family, based on marriage, the lifelong union of one man and one woman
- the primary right of parents to raise and educate their children

The voice of Peter strongly insisted that the faithful speak with one voice on these issues since they directly affect the coherent link between the Faith and daily life. Conversely, the same supreme magisterium respected the freedom of lay Catholics, with rightly formed consciences, to make judgments on temporal

---

12. Gerhard Ludwig Müller, "Development or Corruption? Can There Be 'Paradigm Shifts' in the Interpretation of the Deposit of the Faith?" *First Things*, Feb. 20, 2018, https://www.firstthings.com/web-exclusives/2018/02/development-or-corruption.

13. *"Relatio post disceptationem,"* Third Extraordinary General Assembly of the Synod of Bishops (On the Family), Oct. 13, 2014, 8, http://catholic-ew.org.uk/Home/News/2014/Synod-2015/Relatio-Post-Disceptationem; See James Martin's Oct. 13, 2014, *Facebook.com* post, accessed Jul. 9, 2018, https://www.facebook.com/FrJamesMartin/posts/10152324462306496.

matters involving their specialized knowledge and technical assessments.[14]

This age-old approach no longer appears valid today. It has become a victim of this paradigm shift. One sees glaring silence, coldness, and barely veiled hostility toward those who generously dedicate themselves to defend the sacredness of innocent human life from conception to natural death. Those who publicly oppose same-sex unions experience similar rejection. Yet both these forms of public witness are the non-negotiable duty of all Catholics.

On the other hand, prestige is showered on migration activists, and a boundless openness is shown to peddlers of the global warming theory-dogma. However, Christ entrusted no specific mission to the Church on these issues. It pains me to say it, but the space denied to those who are faithful to the perennial magisterium is often given to non- and even anti-Catholic figures.

While this paradigm shift appears to be purely theoretical, it undeniably impacts the practical life of parishes. As never before, ordinary Sunday Mass-attending faithful feel disoriented. Many express growing disinterest, if not manifest malaise in the face of some Church developments today. From this comes an increasingly evident paradoxical transformation. In the past, churches were full despite the hierarchy's militancy against atheism and the spirit of the world. Today, worldlings and atheists cheer Pope Francis's innovations while the churches are emptying out.

From the viewpoint of doctrine, this pontificate's pastoral revolution is highly questionable. From the practical perspective, however, it is already proving disastrous. The mysterious process of "self-destruction" mentioned by Pope Paul VI in his famous December 7, 1968 "Address to the Pontifical Lombard Seminary" is taken to a paroxysm.[15]

* * *

This work's scope is limited. It seeks to list the positions of Pope Francis that reveal a paradigm shift from the Church's perennial teaching. However, it does this solely in matters that directly affect the laity, particularly those brave souls who labor to make the Gospel's teachings honored in their countries' public lives. Consequently, I have deliberately excluded important, albeit controversial subjects concerning the Church's structure and fundamental dogmas. These surpass the awareness and learning of the average faithful Catholic.

---

14. See Stefano Fontana, "Così si cambia la dottrina sociale della Chiesa," *La Nuova Bussola Quotidiana*, Aug. 22, 2017, http://www.lanuovabq.it/it/cosi-si-cambia-la-dottrina-sociale-della-chiesa; Congregation for the Doctrine of the Faith, "Doctrinal Note on Some Questions Regarding the Participation of Catholics in Political Life," Nov. 21, 2002, http://www.vatican.va/roman_curia/congregations/cfaith/documents/rc_con_cfaith_doc_20021124_politica_en.html.

15. Paul VI, "Discorso di Paolo VI ai membri del Pontificio Seminario Lombardo," Dec. 7, 1968, http://w2.vatican.va/content/paul-vi/it/speeches/1968/december/documents/hf_p-vi_spe_19681207_seminario-lombardo.html.

Nor is this work intended as an in-depth doctrinal analysis of each of the topics it addresses. Instead, its goal is to present a straightforward account with some commentary. It serves as an inventory as it were, of Pope Francis's statements and actions that have most seriously wounded the *sensus fidei* (sense of the Faith) of his flock.

Conversely, an in-depth analysis would require a volume for each theme, and this would render an overall view, a summary evaluation of the first five years of Pope Francis's pontificate, harder to grasp. Additionally, such an analysis would exceed my competence as an author. I have no specialized training in these matters. Nevertheless, I have monitored the debates in the Catholic Church over the last half-century attentively, doing circumstantial research about some of the topics addressed therein.

Furthermore, I am a disciple of Plinio Corrêa de Oliveira (1908–1995)[16] and from my youth have been a militant in the ranks of the movement he inspired and encouraged for the defense of the three basic values of Christian civilization—tradition, family, and property.[17] Accordingly, I adopt the words of this great master of the Counter-Revolution and ardent champion of the Chair of Peter in the face of the mysterious eclipse that had befallen the papacy already in the seventies, and which has become acuter since:

> It is not with the enthusiasm of my early youth that I stand before the Holy See today. It is with even greater, much greater enthusiasm. For the more I live, think, and gain experience, the more I understand and love the pope and the papacy. This would be true even if I found myself, I repeat, in the very circumstances that Mr. Jeroboão Cândido Guerreiro depicts.[18]
>
> I still recall the catechism lessons in which the papacy was explained to me: its divine institution, powers, and mission. My young heart (I was about nine) was filled with admiration, rapture, and enthusiasm. I had found the ideal to which I would dedicate my entire life. From then until now, my love for this ideal has only grown. And I pray to Our Lady that she increase it in me always, until my dying breath. I desire that the last

---

16. For an overview of the life, thought, and work of Plinio Corrêa de Oliveira, see Roberto de Mattei, *The Crusader of the 20th Century: Plinio Corrêa de Oliveira* (Leominster, Herefordshire, U.K.: Gracewing, Fowler Wright, 1995).

17. For a summary of the history of the Brazilian TFP and autonomous sister organizations around the world, see *Um homem, uma obra, uma gesta: Homenagem das TFPs a Plinio Corrêa de Oliveira* (São Paulo: Artpress, 1989), http://www.pliniocorreadeoliveira.info/Gesta_0000Indice.htm.

18. The article's author used a literary device and invented a letter from Jeroboão Cândido Guerreiro, a fictional person, to bitingly compare two concomitant events: Paul VI's indulgence with a handful of Catholic progressives who delivered a defiant document to the Vatican, and, on the other hand, that pope's refusal to acknowledge receipt of the TFP petition requesting the Holy See to take measures against communist infiltration in the Church. The TFP petition had garnered the signatures of 1,600,368 Catholics.

act of my intellect may be an act of faith in the papacy. I want that my final act of love may be an act of love for the papacy. Thus, in fact, I would die in the peace of the elect, well united to Mary, my Mother, and, through her, to Jesus, my God, my King, and my excellent Redeemer.

In me, Mr. Guerreiro, this love of the papacy is not an abstract love. It includes a special love for the sacrosanct person of the pope, be it the one of yesterday, today, or tomorrow. It is a love made of veneration; a love of obedience.

Yes, I insist, it is a love of obedience. I want to give every teaching of this pope, as well as those of his predecessors and successors, the full measure of adherence that Church doctrine prescribes to me, holding as infallible what She says is infallible, and as fallible what She teaches is fallible. I want to obey the orders of this or any other pope to the full extent the Church commands me to obey them. That is, by never superseding them with my personal will or the might of any earthly power; and by refusing obedience to a pope's order only, and absolutely only, when it involves sin. For in that extreme case, as the Apostle Paul and all Catholic moral theologians teach, it is necessary to obey the will of God first.

That is what I was taught in catechism classes. That is what I read in the treatises I studied. This is how I think, feel, and am, with all my heart.[19]

With similar convictions and sentiments, I invite the reader to undertake this painful way of the cross, that is, to consider the events described and documented herein. They marked the first five years of the pontificate of the present Successor of Peter since he took office on March 13, 2013.

Last, but not least, I want to thank my brothers-in-ideal, Juan Miguel Montes, Samuele Maniscalco, and Federico Catani, for their invaluable help in collecting documentation and reviewing the final text of this work.

May Our Lady—in whose Wise and Immaculate Heart, the faith of all mankind was concentrated, between her Divine Son's Death and Resurrection—strengthen the faith of readers in the Church's indefectibility and their hope in a glorious reinvigoration of the papacy. Secondly, may she show compassion for this work's shortcomings.

Saint-Sauveur-Marville, France
Holy Saturday, 2018
J.A.U.

19. Plinio Corrêa de Oliveira, "A perfeita alegria" [The perfect joy], *Folha de S. Paulo*, Jul. 12, 1970, http://www.pliniocorreadeoliveira.info/1970_236_CAT_A_perfeita_alegria.htm.

CHAPTER 1
Pastoral Retreat From "Non-negotiable Values"

From the beginning of his pontificate, Francis has strived to abandon the previous paradigm built around the defense of non-negotiable principles. He has done this by establishing other priorities. Meanwhile, his strong pronouncements on moral issues—which undoubtedly exist—are usually when the matter was not in the news. It is as if he has wanted to avoid any possible clash with the establishment. As a result, these statements seem out of context and are almost always ignored by the media.

From the last years of John Paul II's papacy[20] and throughout that of Benedict XVI,[21] the Holy See has urged Catholics to defend, first and foremost, what has been called *non-negotiable values* or *principles*.[22] In his address to the European People's Party conference, the German pope listed them as follows:

> As far as the Catholic Church is concerned, the principal focus of her interventions in the public arena is the protection and promotion

---

20. "When political activity comes up against moral principles that do not admit of exception, compromise or derogation, the Catholic commitment becomes more evident and laden with responsibility. In the face of *fundamental and inalienable ethical demands*, Christians must recognize that what is at stake is the essence of the moral law, which concerns the integral good of the human person. This is the case with laws concerning *abortion* and *euthanasia*. . . . Analogously, the *family* needs to be safeguarded and promoted, based on monogamous marriage between a man and a woman. . . . The same is true for the freedom of parents regarding the *education* of their children; it is an inalienable right recognized also by the Universal Declaration on Human Rights." Congregation for the Doctrine of the Faith, "Doctrinal Note on Catholics in Political Life," Nov. 24, 2002, no. 4. See also the letter by Cardinal Joseph Ratzinger to then-Cardinal Theodore McCarrick, archbishop of Washington, D.C. (made public in July 2004), on the obligation of denying communion to authorities and legislators who formally cooperate with the promotion of abortion or euthanasia, or vote for its legalization. The letter states: "Not all moral issues have the same moral weight as abortion and euthanasia." Congregation for the Doctrine of the Faith, "Worthiness to Receive Holy Communion: General Principles," accessed Jul. 9, 2018, http://www.ewtn.com/library/curia/cdfworthycom.htm.

21. "On the other hand, all Catholics, and indeed all men and women, are called to act with purified consciences and generous hearts in resolutely promoting those values which I have often referred to as *'non-negotiable.'*" Benedict XVI, "Address of His Holiness Benedict XVI to Participants in the General Assembly of *Caritas Internationalis*," May 27, 2011, http://w2.vatican.va/content/benedict-xvi/en/speeches/2011/may/documents/hf_ben-xvi_spe_20110527_caritas.html. (My emphasis.)

22. The expression was coined by Benedict XVI when addressing the question of "Eucharistic consistency" by the public testimony of one's own faith. He says that "it is especially incumbent upon those who, by virtue of their social or political position, must make decisions regarding fundamental values, such as respect for human life, its defense from conception to natural death, the family built upon marriage between a man and a woman, the freedom to educate one's children and the promotion of the common good in all its forms. *These values are not negotiable*." Benedict XVI, Post-Synodal Apostolic Exhortation *Sacramentum Caritatis*, Feb. 22, 2007, no. 83, http://w2.vatican.va/content/benedict-xvi/en/apost_exhortations/documents/hf_ben-xvi_exh_20070222_sacramentum-caritatis.html. (My emphasis.)

of the dignity of the person, and she is thereby consciously drawing particular attention to principles which are not negotiable. Among these, the following emerge clearly today:

- protection of life in all its stages, from the first moment of conception until natural death;
- recognition and promotion of the natural structure of the family—as a union between a man and a woman based on marriage—and its defense from attempts to make it juridically equivalent to radically different forms of union which in reality harm it and contribute to its destabilization, obscuring its particular character and its irreplaceable social role;
- the protection of the right of parents to educate their children.[23]

Pope Francis: "I Have Never Understood the Expression 'Non-negotiable Values'"

Pope Francis explicitly abandoned the priority of defending these fundamental and irrevocable moral principles. Months after his election, he gave an interview to Fr. Antonio Spadaro, SJ, *La Civiltà Cattolica*'s editor-in-chief, outlining what could be considered his papacy's platform or manifesto. It was later reproduced by Jesuit magazines around the world in their respective languages. Pope Francis stated:

> We cannot insist only on issues related to abortion, gay marriage and the use of contraceptive methods. This is not possible. I have not spoken much about these things, and I was reprimanded for that. But when we speak about these issues, we have to talk about them in a context. . . .
> The Church's pastoral ministry cannot be obsessed with the transmission of a disjointed multitude of doctrines to be imposed insistently. . . . We have to find a new balance.[24]

On the first anniversary of his accession to the papal throne, Pope Francis reaffirmed this thesis in an interview with the director of *Corriere della Sera*: "I have never understood the expression 'non-negotiable values.' Values are values, and that is enough, I cannot say that one of the fingers of a hand is less

23. Benedict XVI, "Address of His Holiness Benedict XVI to the Members of the European People's Party on the Occasion of the Study Days on Europe," Mar. 30, 2006, http://w2.vatican.va/content/benedict-xvi/en/speeches/2006/march/documents/hf_ben-xvi_spe_20060330_eu-parliamentarians.html.
24. Antonio Spadaro, SJ, "A Big Heart Open to God: An Interview With Pope Francis," *America*, Sept. 30, 2013, https://www.americamagazine.org/faith/2013/09/30/big-heart-open-god-interview-pope-francis.

useful than another."[25]

His first encyclical, *Evangelii Gaudium*, gives an overview of contemporary life and the challenges facing the evangelizing action of the Church. Pope Francis put the "new balance" into practice by speaking extensively and emotionally of exclusion economy, the idolatry of money, social inequality, secularism, and urbanization. He mentions abortion and the family only in passing, and in a subdued fashion.[26]

The Argentine pope has undeniably made occasional pronouncements in defense of the right to life, marriage as the union of a man and a woman, and parental rights. Their frequency and efficacy though, seem to be measured with an eyedropper. Moreover, they are countered by actions that erase much of their pastoral effectiveness.

Some examples follow.

Closeness With Those Who Demolish Non-negotiable Christian Values

On many occasions, Pope Francis has shown that he is close to, and even displayed

---

25. Ferruccio de Bortoli, "Benedetto XVI non è una statua: Partecipa alla vita della Chiesa," *Corriere della Sera*, Mar. 5, 2014, http://www.corriere.it/cronache/14_marzo_04/vi-racconto-mio-primo-anno-papa -90f8a1c4-a3eb-11e3-b352-9ec6f8a34ecc.shtml. Even the analogy in this quote is incorrect as physiotherapists claim there is indeed a hierarchy in the usefulness of the hand's fingers. "Hierarchy of the fingers - Thumb: It has always been considered as the hand's most important finger. It intervenes in both force pressures and precision tweezers. . . . Index: It is a primordial element in fine, multiple-fingered pressures. . . . Middle: It is of little importance from a functional point of view when it is distal, except for writing and applying spherical pressure. . . . Pinky: It is essential in applying all pressures. . . . Ring finger: It is the least disturbing in amputations." Jean Delprat, Solange Ehrler, Michel Romain, Jacques Xenard, "Estudio de la prensión," *Encyclopédie Médico-Chirurgicale*, https://fr.scribd.com/document/106460939 /05-Estudio-de-La-Prension, first published as "Bilan de la préhension," Encycl. Méd. Chir. (Paris: Editions Scientifiques et Médicales Elsevier), Kinésithérapie-Médecine physique-Réadaptation, 26-008-D-20, 2002, 16 p.

26. The same idea was taken up in the Apostolic Exhortation *Gaudete et Exsultate*, published on the fifth anniversary of the inauguration of his Petrine ministry. In paragraph 101, Pope Francis writes, "The other harmful ideological error is found in those who find suspect the social engagement of others, seeing it as superficial, worldly, secular, materialist, communist or populist. Or they relativize it, as if there are other more important matters, or the only thing that counts is one particular ethical issue or cause that they themselves defend. Our defense of the innocent unborn, for example, needs to be clear, firm and passionate. . . . Equally sacred, however, are the lives of the poor, those already born, the destitute, the abandoned and the underprivileged, the vulnerable infirm and elderly exposed to covert euthanasia, the victims of human trafficking, new forms of slavery, and every form of rejection." In paragraph 102, he reiterates, "We often hear it said that, with respect to relativism and the flaws of our present world, the situation of migrants, for example, is a lesser issue. *Some Catholics consider it a secondary issue compared to the 'grave' bioethical questions.* That a politician looking for votes might say such a thing is understandable, but not a Christian, for whom the only proper attitude is to stand in the shoes of those brothers and sisters of ours who risk their lives to offer a future to their children." Francis, Apostolic Exhortation *Gaudete et Exsultate*, Mar. 19, 2018, nos. 101–2, https://w2.vatican.va /content/francesco/en/apost_exhortations/documents/papa-francesco_esortazione-ap_20180319 _gaudete-et-exsultate.html. (My emphasis.)

camaraderie with, Marco Pannella[27] and Emma Bonino.[28] Both leaders of Italy's Radical Party championed the fight to legalize divorce, contraception, *in vitro* fertilization, abortion, euthanasia, and same-sex civil unions approved in that country.

The pope phoned Pannella at the hospital shortly after he underwent surgery. He also supported the radical leader's campaign criticizing the prison system.[29]

Archbishop Vincenzo Paglia, president of the Pontifical Academy for Life (PAV), is well known for being part of the papal inner circle. Commenting on Pannella's death, he stated that it was "a great loss for our country" since he was "the inspirer of a more beautiful life not only for Italy but for our world, which needs more than ever men who can speak like him."[30]

Pope Francis also called Emma Bonino. She was notorious in the seventies for performing clandestine abortions. She once published a photo of one of these crimes to help promote procured abortion's legalization. The pope spoke to her about poverty, migrants, and Mediterranean shipwrecks of migrant boats.[31]

Later, in an interview with *Corriere della Sera*'s Massimo Franco, Pope Francis included Bonino along with former communist leader and erstwhile president Giorgio Napolitano "among the great [people] in Italy today" for being "the person who knows Africa better." "They tell me," he added, "these are people who think differently from us. It's true, but be patient! Look at people and what they do."[32]

---

27. "Among the longest-lived actors in the Italian political scene over the last five decades, he embraced and lived as a protagonist in virtually all civil battles fought in our country: from those for divorce and abortion in the '60s and '70s to more recent ones for the decriminalization of drugs, against therapeutic obstinacy, for the right to euthanasia, and in defense of prisoners' rights." Sandro Iannaccone, "Addio a Marco Pannella: Ecco la sua storia," *Wired.it*, May 19, 2016, https://www.wired.it/attualita/politica/2016/05/19/chi-era-marco-pannella/.

28. "Bonino began her political career during the 1970s as a militant feminist, vocal and active in the campaign for the legalization of abortion. She was jailed for her pro-abortion activities in 1975, but in 1976 was elected to Parliament as a deputy for the Radical Party." Gino Moliterno, *Encyclopedia of Contemporary Italian Culture* s.v. "Bonino, Emma" (London: Routledge, 2000). "Our Lady of Battles [Emma Bonino]. . . . The positions expressed by Emma Bonino are rarely conciliatory . . . for example, she recently stood up to the Vatican because of the Catholic Church's decision to oppose experiments with so-called stem cells (which would give hope of healing to people affected by various pathologies). She demonstrated before St. Peter's basilica with posters that some consider blasphemous, such as 'No Taliban. No Vatican.'" Redattori di Biografieonline.it, "Emma Bonino, biografia," last updated Apr. 28, 2013, https://biografieonline.it/biografia-emma-bonino.

29. See "Papa Francesco telefona a Pannella: E lui interrompe lo sciopero della sete," *La Repubblica*, Apr. 25, 2014, http://www.repubblica.it/politica/2014/04/25/news/papa_pannella_sciopero_sete-84450161/.

30. "L'incredibile intervento di Paglia (Pontificia Accademia Della Vita!) in memoria di Marco Pannella," *Il Timone*, Feb. 23, 2017, http://www.iltimone.org/35739,News.html.

31. See "Bonino: 'Papa Francesco mi ha telefonato per chiedermi come sto,'" *La Repubblica*, May 2, 2015, http://www.repubblica.it/politica/2015/05/02/news/bonino_papa_francesco_mi_ha_telefonato_per_chiedermi_come_sto_-113373754/.

32. Massimo Franco, "Francesco: 'Il mio abbraccioai fratelli ortodossi,'" *Corriere Della Sera*, Feb. 8, 2016, http://www.corriere.it/cronache/16_febbraio_08/francesco-il-mio-abbraccio-fratelli-ortodossi-739bf6ee-cdf6-11e5-9bb8-c57cba20e8ac.shtml.

He later granted Bonino a private audience focused mainly "on the themes of migratory flows, welcoming, and integrating immigrants."[33]

Inspired by Pope Francis's friendliness, the archbishop of Naples, Cardinal Crescenzio Sepe, opened the doors of the historic Sanctuary of Capodimonte to Emma Bonino so that she could hold a pre-election political rally there.[34] Inspired by the archbishop's actions, other Italian parishes allowed similar events in their churches.

The Catholic world also erupted in commotion when the Holy See granted the cross of the Order of Saint Gregory the Great to former Dutch minister Lilianne Ploumen. She is known for her support of abortion and the homosexual lobby's agenda.[35]

Equally shocking was the publicity the Italian bishops' daily *Avvenire* gave Beppe Grillo, founder of the 5-Star Movement and well-known proponent of abortion and euthanasia. This support was given precisely when his movement's congressional representatives in the House supported a bill that was a stepping-stone toward euthanasia. In fact, *Avvenire* published a long interview with Mr. Grillo the same day that its director, Marco Tarquinio, gave an interview to *Corriere della Sera* praising the politician's positions. TV2000 (owned by the Italian Bishops' Conference) called that simultaneous interview "a rapprochement between the 5-Star Movement and the Catholic world."[36]

Promoters of Compulsory Contraception and Abortion Are Invited to the Vatican

A day before the launch of the Encyclical *Laudato Sì*, the Pontifical Academies of Sciences and Social Sciences promoted a colloquium on climate change. The main speaker was Ban Ki-Moon, secretary general of the United Nations. Another was economist Jeffrey Sachs, a U.N. advisor on so-called sustainable

33. "Udienza. il papa riceve Emma Bonino: Al centro l'accoglienza dei migranti," *Avvenire*, Nov. 8, 2016, https://www.avvenire.it/papa/pagine/papa-riceve-in-udienza-emma-bonino.

34. A group of faithful from the archdiocese's pro-life committee wrote to the cardinal, "that the crypt of the Basilica of the Crowned Mother of Good Counsel in Capodimonte . . . was lent for political ends to Mrs. Emma Bonino, precisely the one who proudly brags about her decades of battles, unfortunately victorious, in favor of divorce, abortion, artificial fertilization, and the tenacious defender of the liberalization of so-called light drugs and the legalization of euthanasia, all of which are contrary to the magisterium and the *Catechism of the Catholic Church*." Pasquale Napolitano, "Dall'aborto all'altare: La radicale Bonino fa il comizio in Chiesa," *Il Giornale*, Feb. 19, 2018, http://www.ilgiornale.it/news/politica/dallaborto-allaltare-radicale-bonino-fa-comizio-chiesa-1495773.html.

35. See Michael Hichborn, "Pope Francis Awards Architect of Safe-Abortion Fund With Pontifical Honor," *Lepanto Institute*, Jan. 12, 2018, http://www.lepantoinstitute.org/pope-francis/pope-francis-awards-architect-safe-abortion-fund-pontifical-honor/.

36. Maria Antonietta Calabrò, "Beppe Grillo avvenire, San Pietro apre la porta ai 'barbari,'" *Huffingtonpost.it*, Apr. 20, 2017, http://www.huffingtonpost.it/2017/04/19/beppe-grillo-avvenire-san-pietro-apre-la-porta-ai-barbari_a_22046504/.

development—a low-consumption economic model that supposedly would neither deplete natural resources nor compromise the ability of future generations to meet their needs. Sachs is a leading global advocate of abortion as a means to reduce fertility and exercise population control. He argues that abortion is a "lower risk and cost option" than bringing a new human life into the world, and that "legalizing abortion significantly reduces a country's total fertility rate."[37]

In July 2015, the Pontifical Academy of Sciences organized a joint symposium with the U.N. represented by the Sustainable Development Solutions Network. The conference focused on sustainability and modern slavery.[38] Mayors from major cities around the world came to attend. Jeffrey Sachs gave the opening and closing addresses.

Bishop Marcelo Sánchez Sorondo, the Academy chancellor, justified the event saying that "to cooperate with or to cite internationally recognized institutions and authors does not mean to endorse everything they say or do." He added that the issue under discussion was not abortion, and besides, the U.N. does not promote abortion but only "reproductive health."[39] At a pre-event press conference, he stated that "To see the devil in the United Nations, which some on the right tend to do, is not the position of the Holy See."[40]

In October 2016, there was another joint conference on sustainable development and youth. Again, Jeffrey Sachs delivered its opening speech.

At the end of February 2017, the two Pontifical Academies hosted an international conference on the environment. Among the speakers were Paul Ehrlich, author of *The Population Bomb*, and John Bongaarts, vice president of the Population Council, an American non-governmental organization (NGO) that has promoted artificial contraception since the fifties. Ehrlich had previously criticized *Laudato Sì* for failing to recognize the importance of contraception and abortion in fighting climate change. Bongaarts has long proposed sterilization of women and procured abortion as methods of birth control. Catholic University of America professor Michael Pakaluk wrote:

---

37. Stefano Gennarini, "Who Is Jeffrey Sachs and Why Was He at the Vatican?" *C-Fam*, May 14, 2015, https://c-fam.org/friday_fax/who-is-jeffrey-sachs-and-why-was-he-at-the-vatican/.

38. See "SDSN and Pontifical Academy of Sciences Assembles Top Mayors to Discuss U.N. Sustainable Development Goals," *United Nations Sustainable Development Solutions Network*, Jul. 17, 2015, http://unsdsn.org/news/2015/07/17/sdsn-and-pontifical-academy-of-sciences-assembles-top-mayors-to-discuss-un-sustainable-development-goals/.

39. Marcelo Sánchez Sorondo, "A Response From the Pontifical Academy of Sciences," *First Things*, Jun. 25, 2015, https://www.firstthings.com/web-exclusives/2015/06/a-response-from-the-pas.

40. Carol Glatz, "Bishop: Vatican Is Free to Work With Everyone, U.N. Is Not the 'Devil,'" *Catholic News Service*, Jul. 15, 2015, http://www.catholicnews.com/services/englishnews/2015/bishop-says-vatican-free-to-work-with-everyone-un-is-not-devil.cfm.

Moral theologians would speak in this context of "formal cooperation with evil". . . .

The evil is compounded by the fact that an invitation to address any Pontifical Academy is a great honor. This honor can and will be used by these men in promoting their message.[41]

Changing the Nature of Leading Vatican Institutions That Defended Non-negotiable Values

The John Paul II Institute for Studies on Marriage and Family was utterly left out of the 2014 Synod on the Family. Because of the uproar over this ostracism, Fr. Jose Granados, the Institute's deputy director, was admitted to the 2015 Synod as a "consultant to the Secretariat of the Synod." He participated in the assembly as a "Collaborator with the Special Secretary," a secondary position.[42]

Founded by the Polish Pope and Fr. Carlo Caffarra, the Institute was seen as a remnant and solid reference point of the Church's traditional teaching. At least that was the reason Pope Francis gave for dissolving it and reestablishing it with a new name, the "Pontifical John Paul II Theological Institute for the Sciences of Marriage and Family." He did so with the Motu Proprio *Summa Familiae Cura* in September 2017. He also gave it a new mission and policy:

> Anthropological-cultural change that today influences all aspects of life and requires an analytic and diversified approach does not permit us to limit ourselves to practices in pastoral ministry and mission that reflect forms and models of the past. We must be informed and impassioned interpreters of the wisdom of faith in a context in which individuals are less well supported than in the past by social structures, and in their emotional and family life. With the clear purpose of remaining faithful to the teaching of Christ, we must therefore look, with the intellect of love and with wise realism, at the reality of the family today in all its complexity, with its lights and its shadows.[43]

According to Archbishop Vincenzo Paglia—an admirer of Marco Pannella appointed as the new Institute's Grand Chancellor—the pope broadened the

---

41. Michael Pakaluk, "By Inviting Enemies of the Church, Papal Academies Risk Perfect Storm," *Crux*, Feb. 8, 2017, https://cruxnow.com/commentary/2017/02/08/inviting-enemies-church-papal-academies -risk-perfect-storm/.

42. "XIV Ordinary General Assembly of the Synod of Bishops—List of Participants," *Holy See Press Office*, updated Oct. 5, 2015, sect. B, no. I., http://press.vatican.va/content/salastampa/it/bollettino /pubblico/2015/09/15/0676/01469.html.

43. Francis, Motu Proprio *Summa Familiae Cura*, Sept. 8, 2017, http://w2.vatican.va/content/francesco/en/motu_proprio/documents/papa-francesco-motu-proprio _20170908_summa-familiae-cura.html.

Institute's vision with his decision to change it. From its former perspective, "focused only on moral and sacramental theology," the Institute changed to one that "takes contemporary challenges into account."[44]

Thomas Jansen, director of the German Bishops' Conference official website, commented on the refounding: "The John Paul II Institute for Studies on Marriage and Family was known as a bastion of resistance against Francis's mercy program. Now the pope has dissolved it and founded a new one."[45]

The old Institute's rector, Msgr. Livio Melina, a well-known defender of traditional teaching and pastoral practice, was replaced by Msgr. Pierangelo Sequeri, a member of the select group that penned *Amoris Laetitia*.[46] The group also prefaced the Italian edition of the work titled, *Amoris Laetitia: An Inflection Point in Moral Theology*, in which several scholars argue that the Apostolic Exhortation "represents a paradigm shift for all moral theology and especially in interpreting *Humanae Vitae*."[47]

For its part, the Pontifical Academy for Life was also restructured. It was placed under the direction of a new president, Archbishop Vincenzo Paglia, already the Grand Chancellor of the abovementioned new family institute. The pope gave Archbishop Paglia detailed instructions to ensure that this Vatican office's activities are

- ever more clearly inscribed within the horizon of mercy. . . . [by focusing on]
- "Reciprocal respect between the sexes and among the generations."
- "Defense of the dignity of every single human being."
- "Promotion of the quality of human life. . . ."
- An "authentic human ecology. . . ."
- That will be a Church, he added, "capable of facing places of tension and conflict like a 'field hospital.'"[48]

---

44. "O Papa reforma o instituto sobre o matrimônio e a família fundado por Wojtyla," *Instituto Humanitas Unisinos*, Sept. 20, 2017, http://www.ihu.unisinos.br/78-noticias/571873-o-papa-reforma-o-instituto-sobre -o-matrimonio-e-a-familia-fundado-por-wojtyla.

45. Ricardo Cascioli, "La guerra a Giovanni Paolo II dei vescovi tedeschi," *La Nuova Bussola Quotidiana*, Sept. 22, 2017, http://www.lanuovabq.it/it/la-guerra-a-giovanni-paolo-ii-dei-vescovi-tedeschi. See Thomas Jensen, "Ein Thinktank für 'Amoris laetitia,'" *katholisch.de*, Sept. 20, 2017, http://www.katholisch.de/aktuelles/aktuelle-artikel/ein-thinktank-fur-amoris-laetitia.

46. See Lorenzo Bertocchi, "Dicastro per Laici, Famiglia e Vita: Ecco le nomine," *La Nuova Bussola Quotidiana*, Aug. 18, 2016, http://www.lanuovabq.it/it/dicastero-per-laici-famiglia-e-vita-ecco-le-nomine.

47. Dorothy Cummings McLean, "Vatican Appoints Opponents of Church Teaching on Birth Control to Pro-Life Academy," *LifeSiteNews*, Aug. 28, 2017, https://www.lifesitenews.com/news/humanae-vitae-critics -appointed-to-pontifical-academy-for-life.

48. Crux Staff, "Pope Francis Issues Marching Orders for New Pro-Life Leader," *Crux*, Aug. 18, 2016, https://cruxnow.com/vatican/2016/08/18/pope-issues-marching-orders-new-pro-life-leader/.

To expedite this radical change in direction, Archbishop Paglia quickly provided the Academy for Life with new bylaws, limiting its membership to five-year terms, and canceling the old appointments effective December 31, 2017. The new bylaws stipulate that members be chosen "without regard for their religion."[49] Further, the old requirement of a pledge to defend magisterium teaching on the inviolability of innocent human life was removed.[50]

The new membership appointments excluded some excellent scholars, such as Luke Gormally, Josef Seifert, John Finnis, Mercedes Wilson, and Christine Vollmer, all great defenders of the sacredness of innocent human life in their respective spheres. Thomas William Hilgers, a staunch opponent of artificial contraception and in vitro fertilization, was also left out. Jaroslav Sturma, a psychologist and psychotherapist who views homosexuality as a psycho-affective disorder, was similarly excluded.

By contrast, Nigel Biggar is among the forty-five new members appointed by the pope. He is an Oxford professor and Anglican pastor. For him, abortion should be legal until "18 weeks after conception." He also claims that "it's not clear that a human fetus is the same kind of thing as an adult or a mature human being, and therefore deserves quite the same treatment."[51]

Another of the Institute's new members is Rabbi Avraham Steinberg. He claims that

> An embryo has "no human status" before 40 days. After 40 days it has "a certain status of a human being, not a full status".…
>
> "So case by case, occasionally abortion might be permissible, something which is probably unheard-of in the Catholic point of view."[52]

Katarina Leblanc is another new member. She is a professor at the Karolinska Institute where she does stem cell research using *in vitro*-fertilized, supernumerary embryonic stem cells.[53] Angelo Vescovi is another new member.

49. "Statutes of the Pontifical Academy for Life," art. 5, §5 (a), *Pontifical Academy for Life*, Oct. 18, 2016, http://www.academyforlife.va/content/dam/pav/documents/academy_statute.pdf.

50. See "Bolletino radiogiornale," *Radio Vaticana*, Nov. 5, 2016, http://www.radiovaticana.va/proxy/radiogiornale/ore14/2016/novembre/16_11_05.htm .

51. Nigel Biggar and Peter Singer, "Putting a Value on Human and Animal Life," *Standpoint Magazine*, Jul./Aug. 2011, http://standpointmag.co.uk/node/3990/full.

52. Staff Reporter, "New Members of Vatican Pro-Life Academy Have Defended Abortion and Contraception," *Catholic Herald*, Jun. 16, 2017, http://catholicherald.co.uk/news/2017/06/16/new-members-of-vatican-pro-life-academy-have-defended-abortion-and-contraception/.

53. See Renzo Puccetti, "Lo scandalo della Pontificia Accademia per la Vita," *La Nuova Bussola Quotidiana*, Jun. 19, 2017, http://www.lanuovabq.it/it/articoli-lo-scandalo-della-pontificia-accademia-per-la-vitapaglia-copre-i-nuovi-membri-ecco-le-prove-20202.htm.

Although he uses adult stem cells in his work, he is not opposed to the use of embryonic stem cells in research.[54] Fr. Humberto Miguel Yáñez, of the Gregorian University, another new member, believes that artificial contraception is sometimes licit.[55] New member Fr. Maurizio Chiodi has openly criticized some of the teachings in *Humanae Vitae* and *Donum Vitae*.[56] His study group campaigned in favor of the bill that legalized the interruption of nutrition and hydration for terminal patients. This support was justified with claims in favor of proportionality and respect for different religions and ethical positions.[57] Another new member is German theologian Gerhard Höver, author of an article posted on the Academy's Vatican website which claims that the term "intrinsically evil" is too restrictive and unable to recognize the share of "regularity" existing in "irregular" situations.[58]

Austen Ivereigh, the author of a Pope Francis biography, justified these nominations saying:

> The idea that the PAV [Pontifical Academy for Life]—created in 1994 by St. John Paul II—had to be an enclave for the ideologically pure was an aberration that led, in practice, to endless problems. . . .
>
> When Pope Francis re-wrote the PAV's statutes and appointed Paglia to head the Academy, he wanted to avoid precisely the kind of situation where people of deeply conservative views could create a kind of counter-magisterium, sowing confusion about what the Church teaches.[59]

In fact, the reality is precisely the opposite: Former members defend what the Church has always taught, while current magisterium—as has repeatedly

---

54. See Eric E. Bouhassira, ed., *The SAGE Encyclopedia of Stem Cell Research*, s.v. "Vescovi, Angelo" (Singapore: SAGE, 2015), https://books.google.fr/books?id=NIqECgAAQBAJ.

55. See Luciano Moia, "Verso il sinodo: Matrimonio e sessualità, il primato della coscienza," *Avvenire*, Jul. 29, 2015, https://www.avvenire.it/chiesa/pagine/matrimonio-e-sessualit-il-primato-della-coscienza-.

56. See Lorenzo Bertocchi, "Accademia Della Vita: Lo spoil system vaticano," *La Nuova Bussola Quotidiana*, Jun. 14, 2017, http://www.lanuovabq.it/mobile/articoli-accademia-dellavita-lo-spoilsystem-vaticano-20149.htm.

57. See Andrew Guernsey, "New Pontifical Academy of Life Appointee Supports Euthanasia by Starvation," *Rorate Cæli*, Jun. 20, 2017, https://rorate-caeli.blogspot.com/2017/06/new-pontifical-academy-of-life.html.

58. Gerhard Höver, "'Time Is Greater Than Space': Moral-Theological Reflections on the Post-Synodal Apostolic Exhortation *Amoris Laetitia*," trans. Brian McNeil, http://www.academyforlife.va /content/dam/pav/documenti%20pdf/2018/01_Hoever_pdf.pdf, first published as "'Die Zeit ist mehr wert als der Raum' Moraltheologische Überlegungen zum Nachsynodalen Apostolischen Schreiben Amoris Laetitia," in *Marriage, Families and Spirituality*, vol. 23, no. 1 (2017): 3–18.

59. Austen Ivereigh, "Academy for Life No Longer an 'Enclave of the Ideologically Pure,'" *Crux*, Jun. 20, 2017, https://cruxnow.com/commentary/2017/06/20/academy-life-no-longer-enclave-ideologically-pure/.

been pointed out—spreads confusion concerning Church teaching.

This paradoxical situation led a group of Catholic intellectuals to establish the John Paul II Academy for Human Life and Family in October 2017. The Academy provides continuity to the original Institute's mission, as created by the Polish Pope. Accordingly, it exists to "reject the horrible evils and errors which shape modern society and have even entered the doors of the sanctuary of the Church by the clear exposition of, and by living, the truth about human life and the family."[60]

New Vatican Position Clears the Way for Euthanasia

Pope Francis's stances on end-of-life issues are also at variance with those of his immediate predecessors. For example, many were perplexed at the Holy See's silence and passivity between February and July 2017 while Charlie Gard's parents fought health authorities in U.K. courts.

Charlie suffered from a rare and deadly disease. Against the will of British authorities, his parents wanted to prevent his life support from being disconnected. They also wanted to move him to the U.S. for medical treatment.

Concerning this, Cardinal Carlo Caffarra stated, "We have reached the terminal station in the culture of death. Public institutions and courts now decide, even against his parents' will, whether a child has or does not have the right to live. We are at the pit of barbarity."[61]

In contrast to this judgment, the Pontifical Academy for Life claimed that any U.S. medical treatment for the eleven-month-old boy was futile. Supporting this claim, Academy president, Archbishop Vincenzo Paglia, openly sided with the English hospital, saying: "All therapeutic obstinacy should be avoided."[62] However, this was clearly a case of court-ordered euthanasia, not one of discontinuation of disproportionate therapy.

Equally surprising was the message Pope Francis sent the participants of the European Regional Meeting of the World Medical Association. The meeting was organized in the Vatican in conjunction with the Pontifical Academy for Life. Several speakers who opposed the Church's end-of-life teaching participated.[63]

---

60. Peter Baklinski, "Catholic Laity Launch New Academy for Life After Francis Gutted the Original," *Life-SiteNews*, Oct. 28, 2017, https://www.lifesitenews.com/news/breaking-catholic-laity-launch-new-academy-for-life-after-pope-francis-gutt.

61. Francesco Boezi, "L'arcivescovo di Bologna, Caffarra, su Charlie Gard: 'Fermatevi in nome di Dio!'" *Il Giornale*, Jun. 30, 2017, http://www.ilgiornale.it/news/cronache/caffarra-su-charlie-gard-fermatevi-nome-dio-1415087.html.

62. Tommaso Scandroglio, "Il pavido assenso di vescovi e alti prelati," *La Nuova Bussola Quotidiana*, Jun. 30, 2017, http://www.lanuovabq.it/it/il-pavido-assenso-di-vescovi-e-alti-prelati.

63. See Benedetta Frigerio, "Vaticano: si apre dolcemente la porta all'eutanasia," *La Nuova Bussola Quotidiana*, Nov. 13, 2017, http://www.lanuovabq.it/it/vaticano-si-apre-dolcemente-la-porta-alleutanasia.

The pope stated, "Medical interventions have become ever more effective, but they are not always beneficial: they can sustain, or even replace, failing vital functions, but that is not the same as promoting health. Greater wisdom is called for today, because of the temptation to insist on treatments that have powerful effects on the body, yet at times do not serve the integral good of the person."[64]

Bioethics professor Tommaso Scandroglio said that prolonging life with proportionate means even with an inferior quality of life is not "therapeutic obstinacy" but a moral obligation for both patient and doctor. This is because proportion is not measured in relation to the well-being effect, but to the positive life effect.

Moreover, if medical intervention is effective, as the pope acknowledges, it cannot be labeled "therapeutic obstinacy" even when it does not lead to solutions. Wearing glasses does not fix eye defects but improves vision. Equally disconcerting is the passage where the pontiff affirms that the patient has the right "in dialogue with medical professionals, to evaluate a proposed treatment and judge its actual proportionality in his or her concrete case."[65] By contrast, the *Catechism of the Catholic Church* specifies that, if reasonable, the patient's expressed will must be respected, for otherwise, one opens the door to euthanasia. Finally, given cases like Charlie Gard,[66] and more recent ones like Alfie Evans, the insinuation that "therapeutic obstinacy" is a real danger in hospitals, not euthanasia, is deceitful.

Researcher Federico Catani highlights another concern. "The biggest concern about the message is where Pope Francis calls for an agreement between the different struggling factions and even for an eventual approval of end-of-life legislation: 'Within democratic societies, these sensitive issues must be addressed calmly, seriously, and thoughtfully, in a way open to find, to the extent possible, agreed solutions, also on the legal level. On the one hand, there is a need to take into account differing world views, ethical convictions, and religious affiliations, in a climate of openness and dialogue.'"[67]

Incredible as it may seem, an English judge used the papal message as an argument to authorize passive euthanasia for Alfie Evans, who suffered from a brain disease. After months of dispute over a Liverpool hospital policy,

---

64. Francis, "Message of His Holiness Pope Francis to the Participants in the European Regional Meeting of the World Medical Association," Nov. 7, 2017, https://w2.vatican.va/content/francesco/en/messages/pont-messages/2017/documents/papa-francesco_20171107_messaggio-monspaglia.html.

65. Ibid.

66. See Tommaso Scandroglio, "Papa ed eutanasia, un intervento problematico," *La Nuova Bussola Quotidiana*, Nov. 17, 2017, http://lanuovabq.it/it/papa-ed-eutanasia-un-intervento-problematico.

67. Federico Catani, "Notas de perplexidade acerca da mensagem do Papa Francisco sobre o final da vida," trans. Hélio Dias Viana, *Fratres in Unum*, Nov. 23, 2017, https://fratresinunum.com/2017/11/23/notas-de-perplexidade-acerca-da-mensagem-do-papa-Francis-sobre-o-final-da-vida/.

basing itself on the words of Pope Francis, a court order dated February 20, 2018 authorized doctors to suspend the child's ventilator and nutrition against the will of his parents. After the European Court of Human Rights threw out the parents' appeal, Alfie's father, a Catholic like his son, said, "We have no more legal ways to defend our son, who wants to live, as doctors and judges cannot wait to see him dead. We beg Pope Francis to intervene. He is the only one who can defend us."[68]

According to Archbishop Vincenzo Paglia, however, "[the judge's] decision was not intended to shorten life but to suspend a situation of therapeutic obstinacy." Prof. Tommaso Scandroglio commented, "For the president of the Pontifical Academy for Life, to allow a patient to continue to live in a condition of disability is therapeutic obstinacy" and not "an unpostponable act of healing," since "the ventilator keeping Alfie alive is a treatment disproportionate to the ends envisaged but absolutely proportionate to its proper purpose, that is, to oxygenate him and thus keep him alive." The doctors' decision, the expert concludes, "is based on the principle of quality of life and not on respect for the dignity of the person, including the disabled."[69]

On the pretext that "the diversity of opinions in the Church is wealth," the PAV president asserted that "the laws of a State represent mediation between different positions,"[70] as if such mediation were acceptable when it violates non-negotiable values.

Papal Silence on Crucial Ballot Measures
The silence of the Holy See had already caused perplexity during the final debates leading up to legislative approval for same-sex "marriage" in the French National Assembly on May 18, 2013. Catholics were further puzzled at the

68. Benedetta Frigerio, "La cedu nega il ricorso: 'Papa Francesco aiuti Alfie!'" *La Nuova Bussola Quotidiana*, Mar. 29, 2018, http://lanuovabq.it/it/la-cedu-nega-il-ricorso-papa-francesco-aiuti-alfie. On April 4, 2018, Pope Francis broke the silence on the Alfie Evans case with a tweet. On April 13, he spoke of him during the Sunday recitation of the *Regina Coeli*, and on the 18th of the same month, he met the boy's father, Tom Evans. In parallel with the pope's interventions, Archbishop Paglia also spoke out in defense of Alfie's life. Not so the English bishops, for whom criticism of the doctors at the Liverpool hospital where the boy was being treated was unfounded. It should be noted, however, that the pronouncements by the pope and Archbishop Paglia came only after they had received stringent pressures from the boy's advocates and from public opinion. Nor did they ever deny their previous statements on euthanasia. In fact, they did not help to save the boy's life. See Sandro Magister, "Alfie Evans's Easter: Day by Day, a Chronology," trans. Matthew Sherry, *L'Espresso–Settimo Cielo*, Apr. 23, 2018, http://magister.blogautore.espresso.repubblica.it/2018/04/23/alfie-evanss-easter-day-by-day-a-chronology/.

69. Tommaso Scandroglio, "Via libera di monsignor Paglia all'uccisione di Alfie," *La Nuova Bussola Quotidiana*, Mar. 10, 2018, http://lanuovabq.it/it/via-libera-di-monsignor-paglia-alluccisione-di-alfie.

70. Valerio Pece, "Alfie Evans: Per monsignor Paglia potrebbe trattarsi di 'sospendere una situazione di accanimento terapeutico,'" *Tempi*, Mar. 9, 2018, https://www.tempi.it/alfie-evans-per-monsignor-paglia-si-tratta-di-sospendere-una-situazione-di-accanimento-terapeutico.

Vatican silence over the referendum to change the Irish Constitution to legalize same-sex "marriage" in that country as well.

The Holy See was silent even when bishops of these respective countries made declarations that were ambiguous or favorable to same-sex "marriage." In the case of Ireland, Vatican Secretary of State Cardinal Pietro Parolin limited himself to making an after-the-fact statement that the ballot box results had been "a defeat for humanity."[71]

When the Italian Parliament was debating a bill proposed by pro-homosexual Senator Monica Cirinnà, to legalize same-sex civil unions, Pope Francis was asked during a media interview about the adoption of children by homosexual couples. He declined to comment, stating:

> First of all, I do not know what's happening in the Italian Parliament. The pope does not interfere with Italian politics. In the first meeting that I had with [Italian] bishops in May 2013, one of the three things I said, "With the Italian government: sort it out for yourselves." Because the pope is for everyone, and he cannot engage in the practical, domestic politics of one country. This is not the pope's role. What I think is what the Church thinks and I have said this on many occasions. This is not the first country to have this experience: there are many[72]

Even worse was the position taken by Mexico's new apostolic nuncio. Amidst a national debate on so-called marriage equality, he publicly rebuked Mexico's bishops during a press conference at the Basilica of Guadalupe for their crusade against same-sex "marriage." He said, "Rather than confront one another, make proclamations, or marches, Mexicans must sit at a table and talk." He added, "One of the things Pope Francis recommends is to be on the alert for clericalism, in other words, priests who want to do everything."[73]

The Church Acts as If "It Does Not Take Its Teachings Seriously"
All these pronouncements, administrative measures, and symbolic acts express a radical change of attitude or paradigm on the part of Holy See agencies

71. "Vatican Calls Irish Referendum a 'Defeat for Humanity,'" *Irish Times,* last updated May 26, 2015, http://www.irishtimes.com/news/social-affairs/religion-and-beliefs/vatican-calls-irish-referendum-a-defeat-for-humanity-1.2226957.

72. Francis, "In-Flight Press Conference of His Holiness Pope Francis From Mexico to Rome," Feb. 17, 2016, http://w2.vatican.va/content/francesco/en/speeches/2016/february/documents/papa-francesco_20160217_messico-conferenza-stampa.html .

73. Astrid Rivera, "Rechaza nuncio apostólico mediar debate de matrimonio igualitario," *El Universal,* Nov. 7, 2016, http://www.eluniversal.com.mx/articulo/nacion/sociedad/2016/11/7/rechaza-nuncio-apostolico-mediar-debate-de-matrimonio-igualitario.

regarding the "non-negotiable values" of previous pontificates. The Catholic Church increasingly appears to have stopped its war against immorality and accepted the Sexual Revolution as a side effect of so-called anthropological change. This has produced disastrous results in Catholic ranks, particularly those of pro-life and pro-family activists.

Fr. Shenan Boquet underscored how the Academy for Life nominations had a demoralizing effect on pro-lifers: "Whatever the admirable intentions of the leadership of the PAV, the real-world effect of appointing an abortion supporter is the same as if they had appointed a pro-slavery advocate: The appearance in the public eye that the Church does not take its teaching against abortion as seriously as it once did. This has a direct impact upon pro-life advocates on the ground, who stand exposed to the accusation of being 'more Catholic' than the Vatican."[74]

The Human Life International chairman's assessment applies to all of the other initiatives mentioned above.

74. Shenan J. Boquet, "Why the Pontifical Academy for Life Must Be Unapologetically Pro-Life," *Crux*, Jun. 26, 2017, https://cruxnow.com/commentary/2017/06/26/pontifical-academy-life-must-unapologetically-pro-life/.

CHAPTER 2

Promoting the Neo-Marxist and Alter-Globalization Agenda of Popular Movements

Catholic doctrine teaches that communism is "intrinsically wrong."[75] However, Marxist movements and leftist regimes around the world see Pope Francis as a point of reference. Indeed, the current pontiff has shown himself very close to the claims of these groups and governments. Despite the disastrous results of real socialism—for example, the martyrdom of many Christians and the spread of misery—and its unnatural character, Francis has repeatedly stated that communism has stolen Christianity's banner in the struggle for the poor. He thus gives the impression that this ideology is well-intentioned. Vatican geopolitics now also seem to cultivate a privileged relationship with its regimes, from Venezuela to China. These regimes are more or less directly inspired by real socialism, dubbed "this shame of our time" by Cardinal Joseph Ratzinger in the celebrated document Libertatis Nuntius,[76] *which condemned liberation theology during the pontificate of John Paul II.*

In a press conference shortly after his visit to the Vatican, Cuban dictator Raul Castro said, "I told [Pope Francis] that in Cuba, the leadership group and I, read all his speeches every day. If you [Pope Francis] continue speaking like this, sooner or later, I will return to prayer and I will return to the Catholic Church. . . . I may convert again to Catholicism, even though I am a Communist."[77] Was this pure political manipulation,[78] or are the pope's positions really that close to communism? That is the question.

Pope Francis has repeatedly denied being a Communist claiming that he is

---

75. "Communism is intrinsically wrong, and no one who would save Christian civilization may collaborate with it in any undertaking whatsoever. Those who permit themselves to be deceived into lending their aid toward the triumph of Communism in their own country will be the first to fall victims of their error." Pius XI, Encyclical *Divini Redemptoris*, Mar. 19, 1937, no. 58, https://w2.vatican.va/content/pius-xi/en/encyclicals/documents/hf_p-xi_enc_19370319_divini-redemptoris.html.

76. Congregation for the Doctrine of the Faith, "Instruction on Certain Aspects of the 'Theology of Liberation,'" Aug. 6, 1984, sec. 11, no. 10, http://www.vatican.va/roman_curia/congregations/cfaith/documents/rc_con_cfaith_doc_19840806_theology-liberation_en.html.

77. Gerard O'Connell, "Cuba's Raul Castro Tells Pope Francis: 'I Could Become a Catholic Again,'" *America*, May 10, 2015, https://www.americamagazine.org/content/dispatches/cubas-raul-castro-tells-pope-francis-i-could-become-catholic-again.

78. For details on the meaning of the encounter between Pope Francis and Raul Castro, see Armando Valladares, "Francis, el nuncio y el tirano," *CubDest*, May 12, 2015, http://www.cubdest.org/1506/c1505castrorom.htm.

merely defending the poor. However, on several occasions, he has expressed friendship for communist personalities and seems to believe that the only mistake of Marxism is to seek to turn the struggle of the poor into an ideology.

Propensity to Sympathize With Communism
Eugenio Scalfari, an avowed atheist and founder of the secularist Italian newspaper *La Repubblica*, held one-on-one meetings with the pope. He later wrote about them in sensation-causing articles. Scalfari claimed not to have recorded the conversations but only taken notes on them.[79] After an October 7, 2016 meeting, he claimed to have had this dialogue with the pope:

> [ES:] So you yearn for a society where equality dominates. This, as you know, is the program of Marxist socialism and then of communism. Are you therefore thinking of a Marxist type of society?
> [Pope:] It has been said many times and my response has always been that, if anything, it is the communists who think like Christians. Christ spoke of a society where the poor, the weak and the marginalized have the right to decide. Not demagogues, not Barabbas, but the people, the poor, whether they have faith in a transcendent God or not. It is they who must help to achieve equality and freedom.[80]

A journalist from *Il Messaggero* asks him:

> — Q: You were regarded as a communist, pauperist, populist pope. *The Economist*, which has dedicated a cover to you, stated that you speak like Lenin. Do you identify yourself in this depiction?
> — Pope Francis: I say only that the communists have stolen the flag. The flag of the poor is Christian. Poverty is at the center of the

---

79. After Pope Francis's first interview with Eugenio Scalfari, Vatican spokesman Fr. Lombardi said that the words that appeared between quotation marks in the daily *La Repubblica* were a reconstitution from memory so that not all of the aforementioned expressions could be safely attributed to the pope. It so happens that at an international meeting for journalists, Scalfari said that before publishing the interview he sent it to the pope and obtained approval for the publication from his secretary. This fact was never denied. Moreover, the controversial phrases were all published *verbatim* in *L'Osservatore Romano*, in the book *Interviews and Conversations with Journalists*, published by Libreria Editrice Vaticana, and on the Vatican website, where they were online for several months. Therefore, official and semi-official (in the case of *L'Osservatore Romano*) organs of the Holy See have given credence to its veracity. It is noteworthy that Pope Francis never formally denied the words attributed to him by Eugenio Scalfari despite the perplexity expressed by many faithful, who legitimately interpret his silence as an approval: *Qui tacet consentire videtur* (silence gives consent).

80. Eugenio Scalfari, "Pope Francis: 'Trump? I Do Not Judge. I Care Only If He Makes the Poor Suffer,'" *La Repubblica*, Nov. 11, 2016, http://www.repubblica.it/vaticano/2016/11/11/news/pope_francis _trump-151810120/. See also "Abbattere i muri: Intervista del papa alla Repubblica," *L'Osservatore Romano*, Nov. 11, 2016, http://www.osservatoreromano.va/it/news/abbattere-i-muri.

Gospel. The poor are at the center of the Gospel. Take Matthew 25. . . .
Or, let us look at the Beatitudes, another flag. The communists say
that all this is communist. Yes, right, twenty centuries later. Now when
they speak one could say to them: but you are Christians (laughs).[81]

In an interview with five young Belgians, reaffirming his love for the poor,
he said, "That's precisely why, two months ago, a person said, 'This pope is a
Communist!' No! This is a flag of the Gospel, not of communism. It is poverty
without ideology. . . . Just read the Gospel. The problem is that throughout history sometimes this attitude toward the poor has been turned into ideology."[82]

In a book-interview with French intellectual Dominique Wolton, he repeated: "I was once told: 'But you are a communist!' No. Communists are Christians. It was the others who stole our flag!"[83] What flag is this that Communists
would have stolen from Christians? It clearly is not just the defense of the poor,
which the Church has always done, but the demand for full socioeconomic
equality and moral license, which Catholic social doctrine has always rejected.

During an interview published in the Turin daily *La Stampa*, Vatican correspondent Andrea Tornielli asked, "What does it feel like to be called a 'Marxist'?" The pope replied: "The Marxist ideology is wrong. But I have met many
Marxists in my life who are good people, so I don't feel offended."[84]

In fact, while speaking with Marcelo López Cambronero and Feliciana
Merino Escalera, authors of *Francisco: El Papa Manso*, he praised Esther
Ballestrino de Careaga, a communist Paraguayan exile who was his boss in a
laboratory and who introduced him to political thought, helping him acquire
a clear awareness that capitalism is essentially unjust.[85]

Similarly, in Francesca Ambrogetti and Sergio Rubin's book, *Pope Francis:
His Life in His Own Words*, the pope commented about his youth, saying: "My

---

81. "Full English Text of Pope Francis' Interview With 'Il Messaggero'—Pope Francis: Communism Stole
Our Flag," *Zenit*, Jul. 2, 2014, https://zenit.org/articles/full-english-text-of-pope-francis-interview-with
-il-messaggero/; see "Papa Francesco: 'Il comunismo ci ha rubato la bandiera.'" *Il Messaggero*, Jun. 29, 2014,
https://www.ilmessaggero.it/PRIMOPIANO/VATICANO/papa_francesco_serve_argine_deriva_morale
/notizie/770510.shtml.

82. Juan Vicente Boo, "Papa Francisco: 'Dicen que este Papa es comunista, pero el amor a los pobres es
la bandera del Evangelio,'" *ABC*, last updated Apr. 7, 2014, https://www.abc.es/sociedad/20140404
/abci-papa-francisco-comunismo-201404041917.html.

83. Dominique Wolton, *Politique et société: Pape François, rencontres avec Dominique Wolton* (Paris: Observatoire, 2017), 227.

84. Andrea Tornielli, "Never Be Afraid of Tenderness," *La Stampa–Vatican Insider*, Dec. 15, 2013,
http://www.lastampa.it/2013/12/16/vaticaninsider/eng/the-vatican/never-be-afraid-of-tenderness
-3sMZy95oJWmaNvfq4m1sTN/pagina.html.

85. See Iván de Vargas, "Entrevista a los autores de libro documento 'Francisco, el Papa manso,'" *Zenit*, Nov. 29,
2013, https://es.zenit.org/articles/entrevista-a-los-autores-de-libro-documento-francisco-el-papa-manso/.

mind was not made solely for religious questions. . . . I read *Our word and pro-posals*, a publication by the Communist Party, and I loved every article ever written by Leónidas Barletta, one of their best-known members."[86]

In the book-interview with Dominique Wolton, the author asked if after childhood and adolescence any women had left a mark on him. The pope re-sponded that Esther Ballestrino had been one such woman, affirming:

> Yes. There is one that taught me to think about political reality. She was a communist. . . .
> She gave me books, all communist, but taught me to think politics. I owe so much to this woman. I owe this woman a lot because she is the woman who taught me to think. . . .
> This woman really taught me to think.[87]

These words imply that the Marxist theory of class struggle as the founda-tion of society is the reading of political reality that Pope Francis learned from Esther Ballestrino. However, class struggle directly contradicts Catholic teach-ing, which sees both society and the State stemming from the family's harmo-nious relationships.

"Inequality Is the Root of Social Ills"

For Pope Francis, the Christian ideal is a society without social classes. Speak-ing to a boy from The Peace Factory NGO who asked him: "But according to you, pope, one day we will all be equal?" the pontiff responded: "This question can be answered in two ways: we are all equal—all!—but this truth is not rec-ognized, this equality is not recognized, and therefore some are—let's say the word, but between quotation marks—happier than others. But this isn't a right! We all have the same rights! When this is not acknowledged, that society is unjust [*sic*]. It isn't according to justice."[88]

In his Apostolic Exhortation *Evangelii Gaudium*, in the section titled, "No to the inequality which spawns violence," Pope Francis stated: "Until exclusion and inequality in society and between peoples are reversed, it will be impossible to eliminate violence." He then added, "This is not the case simply because inequality provokes a violent reaction from those excluded from the system, but because the socioeconomic system is unjust at its root." Furthermore, he said: "Inequality

---

86. Francesca Ambrogetti and Sergio Rubin, *Pope Francis: His Life in His Own Words—Conversations With Jorge Bergoglio* (New York: G. P. Putnam's Sons, 2010, 2013), 39.

87. Wolton, *Politique et société*, 376–7, 379.

88. "Pope's Audience With Children of 'The Peace Factory,'" *Zenit*, May 12, 2015, https://zenit.org/articles /pope-s-audience-with-children-of-the-peace-factory/.

eventually engenders a violence which recourse to arms cannot and never will be able to resolve."[89] In short, according to Pope Francis, "Inequality is the root of social ills."[90] This is at variance with Catholic social doctrine, which teaches that sin is the root of all evil (including social evils), and the essential equality of all the baptized as children of God and heirs of Heaven does not contradict accidental inequality resulting from varied talents, diligence, education, and condition.[91]

Promoting Theology of the People and Liberation Theology
By favoring a classless society, it is no wonder that Pope Francis sympathizes with liberation theology and especially its Argentine version, known as "Theology of the People."[92] The latter was conceptualized by Fr. Lucio Gera[93] and Fr. Juan Carlos Scannone.[94] The difference between this and other strains of this erroneous theology is that the driving force building the *Kingdom* is not left-wing political groups or unions—generally secularists. Instead, the Argentine form of liberation theology has a Gramscian matrix and a third world, Peronist bias. It attributes the role of fomenting revolution to the Latin Americans in their struggle against Anglo-Saxon[95] imperialism and considers the dynamism

---

89. Francis, Apostolic Exhortation *Evangelii Gaudium*, Nov. 24, 2013, nos. 59, 60, http://w2.vatican.va /content/francesco/en/apost_exhortations/documents/papa-francesco_esortazione-ap_20131124 _evangelii-gaudium.html.

90. Ibid., no. 202.

91. Leo XIII teaches: "No one doubts that all men are equal one to another, so far as regards their common origin and nature, or the last end which each one has to attain, or the rights and duties which are thence derived. But, as the abilities of all are not equal, as one differs from another in the powers of mind or body, and as there are very many dissimilarities of manner, disposition, and character, it is most repugnant to reason to endeavor to confine all within the same measure, and to extend complete equality to the institutions of civic life." Leo XIII, Encyclical *Humanum Genus*, Apr. 20, 1884, no. 26, http://w2.vatican.va /content/leo-xiii/en/encyclicals/documents/hf_l-xiii_enc_18840420_humanum-genus.html.

92. For a summary view of the origin and proposals of the Theology of the People, see João Vitor Santos, "O Papa Francisco e a teologia do povo: entrevista especial com Juan Carlos Scannone," trans. André Langer, *Revista IHU Online*, no. 465 (May 18, 2015), http://www.ihuonline.unisinos.br/index.php?option =com_content&view=article&id=5919&secao=465.

93. In recognition of Fr. Lucio Gera's work, Cardinal Jorge Mario Bergoglio, archbishop of Buenos Aires, had him interred in the crypt of that city's cathedral.

94. "Juan Carlos Scannone, a Jesuit, was a professor at several Latin-American and European universities, including the Pontifical Gregorian University. He is a former dean of the San Miguel College of Philosophy and Theology of the University of Salvador. He is considered the greatest living theologian. A disciple of Karl Rahner, he actively participated in the development of the intense post-conciliar debate in Latin America." "Prof. Dr. Juan Carlos Scannone–Argentina," *Instituto Humanitas Unisinos*, Dec. 15, 2017, http://www.ihu.unisinos.br/184-conferencistas/574652-prof-dr-juan-carlos-scannone-argentina.

95. In the above-cited interview, Juan Carlos Scannone states: "Although he does not consider class struggle as a 'determining hermeneutic principle' to understand society and history [the Theology of the People] attributes an historical role to conflict—even class [struggle]—by conceiving it from the previous unity of the people. Accordingly, institutional and structural injustice is understood as betrayal of the people by a part of it which thus becomes anti-people." Santos, "O Papa Francisco e a teologia do povo."

of their religious beliefs as the greatest potential element for advancing the revolution.[96]

His fervor for the Argentine Theology of the People led Pope Francis to rehabilitate liberation theology's founder. Accordingly, he received Fr. Gustavo Gutierrez in a private audience at the Vatican only six months after being elected pope.[97] He also submitted a preface in his own handwriting for the book *Poor for the Poor: The Mission of the Church*, by Cardinal Gerhard Müller, a disciple of Father Gutierrez, who contributed two chapters to the book. At its February 25, 2014 launching, spokesman for the Holy See Fr. Federico Lombardi declared that liberation theology, "has now definitively entered into the normal life of the Church."[98] Earlier, in September of 2013, *L'Osservatore Romano* had already begun to devote ample space to Fr. Gustavo Gutierrez's writings.[99]

Alliance With Marxist-Inspired Popular Movements
Putting into practice the postulates of liberation theology, Pope Francis has placed the prestige of the papacy at the service of so-called popular movements

---

96. In his interview with Dominique Wolton, Francis explains the difference: "In the 1980s there was a tendency toward a Marxist analysis of reality, but later it was renamed 'theology of the people.' I do not really like the name, but that is how I got to know it. To go with the people of God and do the theology of culture. There is a thinker you should read: Rodolfo Kusch, a German who lived in northeastern Argentina, a very good philosopher and anthropologist. He made me understand one thing: The word 'people' is not a logical word. It is a mythical word. One cannot speak of people logically because it would only be a description. To understand a people, to understand the values of this people one must enter into the spirit, the heart, the work, the history and myth of their tradition. This point is truly at the basis of the theology called 'of the people.' That is to say, to go along with the people, to see how they express themselves." Wolton, *Politique et société*, 47–8. Commenting on this passage, Vatican analyst Sandro Magister adds an interesting point: "Kusch took his inspiration from Heidegger's philosophy to distinguish between 'being' and 'dwelling,' describing with the first category the rationalistic and domineering vision of Western man and with the second the vision of the indigenous Latin American peoples, in peace with nature and animated by none other than a 'myth.'" Sandro Magister, "The Myth of the 'Pueblo': Francis Reveals Who Told It to Him," trans. Matthew Sherry, *L'Espresso–Settimo Cielo*, Sept. 18, 2017, http://magister.blogautore.espresso.repubblica.it/2017/09/18/the-myth-of-the-pueblo-francis-reveals-who-told-it-to-him/.

97. In August 2014, Pope Francis lifted the suspension *a divinis* that Pope John Paul II had imposed on the priests Ernesto Cardenal, Fernando Cardenal, Miguel d'Escoto, and Edgard Parrales in 1984. All of them had been "liberationist" cabinet ministers of Nicaragua's Sandinista government. See Saturnino Rodriguez, "La teología de la liberación (III)—En la actualidad: futuro esperanzado," *Religión Digital*, Jun. 27, 2017, http://www.periodistadigital.com/religion/opinion/2017/06/27/religion-iglesia-opinion-saturnino-rodriguez-la-teologia-de-la-liberacion-iii-teologia-de-la-liberacion-en-la-actualidad-futuro-esperanzado-papa-francisco.shtml.

98. "Maradiaga, Mueller e Guttierez: Chiesa povera per i poveri," *Rossoporpora*, Feb. 26, 2014, http://www.rossoporpora.org/rubriche/interviste-a-cardinali/346-maradiaga-mueller-e-gutierrez-chiesa-povera-per-i-poveri.html.

99. See "L'Osservatore Romano riabilita la teologia della liberazione" *La Stampa*, Sept. 3, 2013, http://www.lastampa.it/2013/09/03/vaticaninsider/ita/vaticano/losservatore-romano-riabilita-la-teologia-della-liberazione-HgyXjIIAMrXsKYBYxupTAJ/pagina.html.

that do not hide their clearly Marxist orientation. This support goes notably to the World Meeting of Popular Movements, "a platform built by various popular movements around Francis's call for the poor and organized peoples not to resign themselves but to be protagonists of change."[100]

In fact, this platform was formed by a seminar on "The Emergence of the Excluded" that the Pontifical Academy of Sciences, headed by Bishop Marcelo Sánchez Sorondo, organized in Rome on December 5, 2013.[101] This seminar will be discussed later. Event organizers invited avowedly Marxist leaders of Brazil's Landless Workers Movement-MST (João Pedro Stédile), the Movement of Excluded Workers of Argentina (Juan Grabois), and the international organization Via Campesina to attend. They came with all travel expenses paid by the Vatican.

These movements claim that "the road to change through institutional channels seems decisively blocked." Thus, they do not hesitate to resort to "the practice of mass occupations"—that is, to the systematic invasion of properties—to open "another space" of confrontation and cause "the class struggle" to become global and enter a new "ascension phase" that makes the earth tremble.[102] For such movements, only when the economy is "socialized and planned"[103] can a "society without exploiters or exploited"[104] be realized, which entails "powerful State intervention."[105] In 2003, the MST leader's son went so far as to state: "We want the socialization of the means of production. We will adapt the Cuban and Soviet experiments to Brazil."[106]

Marxist Preaching at the World Meetings of Popular Movements

So far, there have been three World Meetings of Popular Movements.

The First World Meeting was held in the Vatican on October 27–29, 2014.

---

100. "Quienes somos," *Encuentro Mundial de Movimientos Populares*, accessed Jul. 13, 2018, http://movimientospopulares.org/es/emmp-2/.

101. "Latin American People's Movements With Pope Francis," *Alainet.org*, Dec. 18, 2013, https://www.alainet.org/de/node/81811.

102. João Pedro Stédile, "E la terra tremerà," *Adista News*, Jan. 3, 2014, http://www.adista.it/articolo/53494.

103. Juan Grabois, "Capitalismo popular: Una variante salvaje del modelo. Nota en agenda oculta," *La Alameda*, Sept. 10, 2012, https://laalameda.wordpress.com/2012/09/10/capitalismo-popular-una -variante-salvaje-del-modelo/.

104. Juan Grabois, "Capitalismo popular: La respuesta liberal a la crisis de la sociedad salarial," *Blog de Juan Grabois*, Sept. 1, 2012, http://juangrabois.blogspot.com/.

105. "La economía popular 'Surge de la exclusión. No es una expresión de la solidaridad humana,'" *Prudentia Politica*, Oct. 24, 2014, https://prudentiapolitica.blogspot.com/2014/10/la-economia-popular -no-va-ser-nunca.html.

106. Alexandre Mansur and Gerson Camarotti, "MST–Os filhos querem revolução; guerra no campo," *Época*, Jul. 7, 2003, http://revistaepoca.globo.com/Epoca/0,6993,EPT564366-1653-5,00.html.

Its undisputed attraction was Evo Morales, the president of Bolivia, an icon of the social and indigenist movements. He declared the meeting would give rise to "a great alliance of the excluded" in the struggle against capitalism "that buys and sells everything."[107]

The Second World Meeting took place in Santa Cruz de la Sierra, Bolivia, on July 7–9, 2015 during Pope Francis's apostolic visit to that country. Its climax was a long speech by the pontiff.

The Third World Meeting was again held at the Vatican on November 3–5, 2016. Its star was Uruguay's former president José Mujica (aka "comrade Pepe"). Journalist Ignacio Ramonet, director of the ultra-leftist *Le Monde Diplomatique*, introduced him to the participants. "Speaking from the heart," he stated, "Pepe is also an example of coherence of life. He is a man who fought when his country had a horrible military dictatorship, one of the worst in the Southern Cone, and he chose the path of arms because the way of politics was not possible."[108]

The World Meetings provide an overview of the global situation as seen by the popular movements, from a Marxist perspective naturally.

In his summary of the inaugural day of the First World Meeting, the Brazilian MST leader João Pedro Stédile stated that the international effort was informed by the Marxist intellectual Antonio Gramsci. He went on to conclude:

> There is a growing concentration of land ownership, wealth . . . by a minority of capitalists. . . .
> [That] the United States' empire controls the world economy. . . .
> That in most countries [the judiciary branch] acts as an instrument to defend the interests of capital. . . .
> [That] social struggles are still in the phase of "protests" and not in that of building a project of society that involves workers and is

---

107. Ignacio Ramonet, "Impressiones de una jornada histórica," *Movimientos Populares*, Oct. 27–29, 2014, http://movimientospopulares.org/wp-content/uploads/2014/10/EMMP-Una-jornada-historica-IR.pdf.

108. http://www.movimientospopulares.org/wp-content/uploads/2016/11/pepemujica4.mp3, at 5:58, 8:08–8:28. This was not the only time the guerrillas were praised. On the second day of the First World Meeting, Víctor Hugo López Rodríguez, director of the Chiapas-based Frei Bartolomé de Las Casas Human Rights Center **made an apology of the Zapatista National Liberation Army** (of Comandante Marcos), who "rebelled [against] memory to break into history and begin to build a world with justice and dignity." Victor Hugo López Rodríguez, "El Evangelio del Papa Francisco en la alegría de los pueblos originarios," Oct. 28, 2014, https://redtdt.org.mx/wp-content/uploads/2014/11/Ponencia-Frayba-en-Vaticano.pdf. During one of the sessions of the Third Meeting, Argentine activist Alejandra Díaz, representing the magazine *La Garganta Poderosa*, stated, "*We have come with the thought and utopia of Che Guevara*, wishing we have a better world for everyone, not only for us or for a few, a world that is truly egalitarian for all." http://movimientospopulares.org/wp-content/uploads/2016/10/Alejandra_Diaz._Argentina2 -online-audio-converter.com_.mp3, 1:10-1:23.

based on solidarity, equality, and especially justice.[109]

In turn, the Second World Meeting's discussion workshops concluded, among other things, that:

> The labor world's problems are structural, [for] the capitalist economic model seeks very high profitability at low cost.
>
> [And should, therefore, be replaced by] a popular and social community economy that safeguards the life of communities . . . in which comradeship prevails.
>
> [It was also stated that] the city belongs to the workers; it was the workers who built the cities. They are currently occupied by those with large capitals and spurious interests.
>
> [Which requires] expropriation, urbanization, and regularization of informal settlements and emergency villages.
>
> [Hence] the urgent need to organize an urban reform and an agrarian reform.[110]

Moderate Final Statements Allow Radical Message to Get Through

A slightly more moderate statement is always adopted at the end of these meetings. Here are some examples.

The First World Meeting stated that "the structural causes of inequality and exclusion have been analyzed," and concluded that "the roots of social and environmental ills must be sought in the inequitable and predatory nature of the capitalist system that places profit above the human being."[111]

The Second World Meeting's "Santa Cruz Charter" declared:

> We must overcome a social, political, economic and cultural model where the market and money have become the regulators of human relations at all levels. . . .
>
> We do not want to exploit or be exploited; we do not want to exclude or be excluded. . . .
>
> We reaffirm our commitment to the processes of transformation

---

109. João Pedro Stédile, "El mundo en crisis: Síntesis del primer día de trabajo del Encuentro Mundial de Movimentos Populares, Roma, 27 de Octubre, de 2014," *Movimientos Populares*, accessed Jul. 14, 2018, http://movimientospopulares.org/wp-content/uploads/2014/10/El-Mundo-en-Crisis-EMMP-Joa -Pedro-Stedile.pdf.

110. "La tierra y la producción campesina," *Movimientos Populares*, accessed Jul. 14, 2018, http://movimientospopulares.org/wp-content/uploads/2015/06/conclusiones-de-los-talleres-EMMP.pdf.

111. "Declaración final Encuentro Mundial Movimientos Populares," no. 3, *Movimientos Populares*, Oct. 29, 2014, http://movimientospopulares.org/wp-content/uploads/2014/10/DECLARACION-FINAL -EMMP-rivista-da-Czerney.pdf.

and liberation . . . to give life to the hopes and utopias that call us to
revolutionize the deeper structures of oppression, domination, col-
onization, and exploitation. . . .[112]

> We will foster alternative forms of economy. . . . We want a commu-
> nity and social economy. . . in which solidarity prevails over profit. . . .
> [Therefore, w]e foster an integral agrarian reform to distribute the
> land in a fair and equitable manner.[113]

The Third World Meeting issued "Proposals for Transformative Action That
We, the World's Popular Movements Have Assumed in Dialogue With Pope
Francis." These proposals summarized a critique of Western democracies and
a call for "participatory democracy" in the Chavista mold:[114]

> The so-called representative democracies increasingly represent
> corporate elites, capital, banks. . . .
> [And therefore one needs to foster] legislative initiatives that pro-
> mote a participatory democracy in which protagonism belongs to
> the people. . . .
> [About migration, one must] demand the existence of universal
> citizenship that cuts across borders and establishes an inclusive mi-
> gration policy. . . .
> [by creating] international opinion courts with the capacity to im-
> pose ethical and symbolic sanctions to raise awareness at the inter-
> national level.[115]

Their communist goal shows through more clearly on the socio-economic
level, as they aim at,

> The democratization of the soil and the restructuring of land

---

112. "Carta de Santa Cruz," Jul. 9, 2015, *Movimientos Populares,* http://movimientospopulares.org/wp-content
/uploads/2015/07/Carta-di-Santa-Cruz-Portoghese.pdf.

113. Nelson Vilca, "Documento final del II Encuentro Mundial de Movimientos Populares en Santa Cruz
de la Sierra, Bolivia" Jul. 10, 2015, https://agenciadenoticiaspueblosoriginarios.wordpress.com
/2015/07/10/documento-final-del-ii-encuentro-mundial-de-movimientos-populares-en-santa-cruz
-de-la-sierra-bolivia/.

114. "Propuestas de acción transformadora que asumimos los movimientos populares del mundo en diálogo con el Papa Francisco," *Movimientos Populares*, accessed Jul. 14, 2018, http://movimientospopulares.org
/es/propuestas-de-accion-transformadora-que-asumimos-los-movimientos-populares-del-mundo-en
-dialogo-con-el-papa-Francis/.

115. "Síntese de los movimientos populares en los tres dias del EMMP," *Movimientos Populares*, accessed
Jul. 15, 2018, http://movimientospopulares.org/espanol/.

ownership so it can be distributed among those who work it.

[For which it is necessary] to move toward the existence of forms of collective ownership that avoid commercialization and for-profit use. . . .

Land must be collectively owned and ensure the fulfillment of its social function, which is to feed and give life to the people.[116]

On February 16–19, 2017, "the first U.S. regional World Meeting of Popular Movements" was held in Modesto, California. Its message stated, "Racism and White Supremacy are America's original sins. They continue to justify a system of unregulated capitalism that idolizes wealth accumulation over human needs."[117]

The Church Officially Assumes the Agenda of the "Popular Movements"
The World Meetings were sponsored by the now dissolved Pontifical Council for Justice and Peace, as well as by the enormous Dicastery for Promoting Integral Human Development, both presided over by Cardinal Peter Turkson. In a July 6, 2015 Santa Cruz, Bolivia press conference, he stated that the Second World Meeting "promised to be a great dialogue that will perpetuate in time the communication, cooperation, and coordination between the grassroots movements and the Church at all levels"; that the marginalized "must be the protagonists of the indispensable economic, social, political, and cultural changes"; and, therefore, that "the Church intends to take the needs and aspirations of the popular movements as its own."[118]

On the following day, the Ghanaian cardinal explained that such popular movements "promote an alternative lifestyle. . . . They reject consumerism, waste, and the technocratic paradigm. They seek community forms of organization of work, land [ownership] and housing." Using rhetoric palatable to any Marxist, he concluded: "They want neither to exploit nor be exploited, to exclude or be excluded."[119]

Pope Francis embraced the same type of rhetoric in his addresses to participants in each of these World Meetings. He renewed his calls to radically change the current socioeconomic structures based on private property and free enterprise even though only their excesses are condemnable.

At the First World Meeting, he said:

116. EMMP, "Síntese de los movimientos populares en los tres dias del EMMP," *America Latina en Movimiento*, Nov. 7, 2016, https://www.alainet.org/es/articulo/181509.

117. "Message from Modesto," World Meeting of Popular Movements, Feb. 19, 2017, http://popularmovements.org/news/message-from-modesto/.

118. Peter Turkson, "Conferencia de prensa," *Movimientos Populares*, Jul. 6, 2015, http://movimientospopulares.org/wp-content/uploads/2015/06/press-conference-ESP.pdf.

119. Peter Turkson, "Conferencia," *Movimientos Populares*, Jul. 7, 2015, http://movimientospopulares.org/wp-content/uploads/2015/06/2015.07.07-pkat-intro.pdf.

It [solidarity] means thinking and acting in terms of community. It means that the lives of all take priority over the appropriation of goods by a few. It also means fighting against the structural causes of poverty and inequality; of the lack of work, land and housing; and of the denial of social and labor rights. . . .

Today I want to join my voice to yours and support you in your struggle. . . .

We Christians have . . . a program we could call revolutionary.[120]

According to Ignacio Ramonet, this speech confirms "Pope Francis's new historical role as a flag-bearer in solidarity with the struggle of the poor of Latin America and the marginalized of the world."[121]

Speaking in Santa Cruz de la Sierra, Bolivia, during the Second World Meeting, Pope Francis stated:

You have mentioned the many forms of exclusion and injustice. . . . Can we recognize that invisible thread which links them? I wonder whether we can see that those destructive realities are part of a system which has become global. Do we realize that that system has imposed the mentality of profit at any price, with no concern for social exclusion or the destruction of nature?

Let us not be afraid to say it: We want change, real change, structural change. . . .

Positive change, a change which is good for us, a change—we can say—which is redemptive. . . .

Once capital becomes an idol and guides people's decisions, once greed for money presides over the entire socioeconomic system, it ruins society, it condemns and enslaves men and women. . . .

The universal destination of goods. . . . [i]s a reality prior to private property. Property, especially when it affects natural resources, must always serve the needs of peoples.[122]

In his address to the participants of the Third World Meeting, after the Paris,

120. Francis, "Address of Pope Francis to the Participants in the World Meeting of Popular Movements," Oct. 28, 2014, http://w2.vatican.va/content/francesco/en/speeches/2014/october/documents /papa-francesco_20141028_incontro-mondiale-movimenti-popolari.html.

121. Ramonet, "Impressiones de una jornada histórica."

122. Francis, "Address of the Holy Father—Participation at the Second World Meeting of Popular Movements," Jul. 9, 2015, http://w2.vatican.va/content/francesco/en/speeches/2015/july/documents /papa-francesco_20150709_bolivia-movimenti-popolari.html.

Brussels, and Nice bloody attacks by ISIS, the pope condemned,

> That unjust structure linking all the forms of exclusion that you
> experience . . . [which] enslaves and robs of freedom. Some it lashes
> mercilessly, while constantly threatening others, in order to herd
> everyone, like cattle, to wherever the god of money chooses.
>   There is . . . a basic terrorism that is born of the overall control of
> money worldwide.[123]

In a letter to participants in the Regional World Meeting in the United
States, after thanking Cardinal Turkson for his "continued support of popular
movements" from his new dicastery, Pope Francis wrote: "For some time, the
crisis of the prevailing paradigm has confronted us. I am speaking of a system
that causes enormous suffering to the human family, simultaneously assaulting
people's dignity and our Common Home in order to sustain the invisible
tyranny of money that only guarantees the privileges of a few."[124]

Lifesaver for a Foundering Marxist Left
What is the practical effect of Pope Francis's revolutionary preaching and Vatican cooperation with popular movements to advance Marxist and post-Marx-
ist left-wing trends?

While in Rome for the December 5, 2013 "Emergence of the Excluded" symposium, activist João Pedro Stédile stated at a parallel meeting of the alter-
globalization movement, that "in the current historical context, the balance
of forces at the class struggle level is very unfavorable to the working classes"
and that "the world is experiencing a period of reflux in the mass movement."
However, drawing on the "school of British historical Marxists," the MST leader
hoped that the current period of reflux would also be a "period of resistance
as a prelude to a process of recovery" which would require "the working class
to unite on an international level."[125]

After the three World Meetings were held, Stédile could well say: "Mission
accomplished!"

That was the enthusiastic exclamation of Marxist lawyer Juan Grabois who

---

123. Francis, "Address of His Holiness Pope Francis to Participants in the 3rd World Meeting of Popular
Movements," Nov. 5, 2016, http://w2.vatican.va/content/francesco/en/speeches/2016/november
/documents/papa-francesco_20161105_movimenti-popolari.html.

124. Francis, "Message of His Holiness Pope Francis on the Occasion of the World Meetings of Popular
Movements in Modesto (California) [16-18 February 2017]," Feb. 10, 2017, http://movimientospopulares.org
/es/carta-del-papa-Francis-a-los-movimientos-populares-modesto-california-16-19-feb-2017/.

125. "Movimenti di tutto il mondo, unitevi! La lotta di classe secondo i senza terra brasiliani," *Amig@s MST
– Italia*, accessed Jul. 15, 2018, http://www.comitatomst.it/node/1058.

is a consultant to the Dicastery for Promoting Integral Human Development, coordinator of Buenos Aires's *cartoneros* (scrap cardboard collectors) and of the World Meeting of Popular Movements. In his lecture presenting the principal documents published by the latter, he stated:

> Francis has updated the sense of the preferential option for the poor by clarifying that it implies not only solidarity with them but also recognizing them as a social and political subject, promoting their protagonism in all fields, always accompanying them in their own reality and never from abstract ideological schemes. In other words, it is not merely a question of working for the poor but of struggling with the poor against the structural causes of inequality and injustice. In this sense, Francis's contributions to popular thought—including the two speeches to popular movements offered in this edition—have not only renewed Church social doctrine but are now a priceless tool for the theoretical and doctrinal updating of those who aspire for the structural transformation of society and the overcoming of capitalism.[126]

In preparation for the Bolshevik Revolution's centennial, Rome's well-known virtual newspaper *Il Manifesto*, the only one in Italy to call itself a "Communist daily," featured a book containing Pope Francis's three speeches to popular movements in its October 4, 2017 edition. The director explained the reason to the bishops' newspaper *Avvenire*: "Because we hold these messages from the pope as our own and want to bring the radicalism and simplicity of these words to our readers."[127] In the book edited by *Il Manifesto*, Juan Grabois and Alessandro Santagata do not hide the fact that many popular movements oppose the Church on issues such as abortion and homosexual rights.[128]

These facts suggest reasons why Francis X. Rocca titled his December 22, 2016 article in *The Wall Street Journal*, "How Pope Francis Became the Leader of the Global Left."[129]

---

126. Juan Grabois, "Documentos: Encuentro Mundial de Movimientos Populares," intro., accessed Jul. 14, 2018, http://movimientospopulares.org/wp-content/uploads/2016/10/Documents_castellano_web.pdf.

127. "'Publicamos as palavras do papa. Com convicção.' Entrevista com Norma Rangeri, redatora-chefe do jornal italiano *Il Manifesto*," *Instituto Humanitas Unisinos*, Oct. 6, 2017, http://www.ihu.unisinos.br/572416 -publicamos-as-palavras-do-papa-com-conviccao-entrevista-com-norma-ranger-redatora-chefe-do -jornal-italiano-il-manifesto.

128. See Sandro Magister, "The Communists the Pope Likes. And Vice Versa," trans. Matthew Sherry, *L'E-spresso–Settimo Cielo*, Oct. 11, 2017, http://magister.blogautore.espresso.repubblica.it/2017/10/11 /i-comunisti-che-piacciono-al-papa-e-viceversa/.

129. Francis X. Rocca, "How Pope Francis Became the Leader of the Global Left," *The Wall Street Journal*, Dec. 22, 2016, http://www.wsj.com/articles/how-pope-francis-became-the-leader-of-the-global-left-1482431940.

Sympathy for the Castro Brothers' Cuban Dictatorship

Support for popular movements has not been the only way for the pope to express his preference for left-wing politics. It has been apparent also during his visits to left-leaning countries in Latin America, through his attitude toward their respective rulers.

In Cuba, Pope Francis avoided criticizing the regime that rules that island prison. This spurred an *Agence France Presse* reporter on the papal flight out of Havana to contrast this omission with his attacks on capitalism during an earlier trip to Latin America. When she asked the pope why he had treated the two so differently, he justified himself by saying, "In my speeches in Cuba, I always mentioned the Church's social teaching. I spoke clearly, not gingerly or gently, about the things that need to be corrected. . . . But here in Cuba—and this perhaps will help to answer your question—the visit was a very pastoral visit with the Catholic community, with Christians, but also with people of goodwill, and for this reason my interventions were homilies. . . . It was a more pastoral language."[130]

His benevolence for the Cuban regime was so blatant that in the same press conference, the pope tried to deny that the regime's police had arrested fifty dissidents for attempting to meet him:

> First, I didn't hear that this happened. I didn't hear any news. . . . Yes, I would like to meet with them. . . . First of all, the Nunciature made it very clear that I was not going to grant audiences because audiences were being sought not only by dissidents but also by other groups. . . . Secondly, phone calls were made from the Nunciature to certain people belonging to this group of dissidents . . . to tell them that, when I arrived at the Cathedral for the meeting with the consecrated persons I would be happy to greet those who were there. . . . But since no one spoke up in the greeting, I don't know if they were there or not.[131]

From the public's perspective, however, the visit's highlight was Pope Francis's meeting with Fidel Castro; a meeting which the pontiff, himself, requested. According to former Cuban political prisoner, well-known writer, and former U. S. Ambassador to the United Nations Commission on Human Rights, Armando Valladares, Pope Francis's attitude, which was recorded in photographs that went around the world, "was that of someone who was visiting a venerable

130. "In-Flight Press Conference of His Holiness Pope Francis From Santiago de Cuba to Washington, D.C.," Sept. 22, 2015, http://w2.vatican.va/content/francesco/en/speeches/2015/september/documents/papa-francesco_20150922_intervista-santiago-washington.html.

131. Ibid.

prophet rather than a bloodthirsty dictator."[132]

A report from the Inter American Press Association published less than two weeks after the visit, confirmed the gravity of the situation in Cuba, denouncing the ongoing repression and lack of freedom which continued during the pope's visit.

Venezuela: Pope Francis Saves the Regime and Turns His Back on the Bishops

Equally surprising has been his attitude toward Venezuela. Hugo Chavez, the sponsor of what he called twenty-first century socialism, passed away the same week as Pope Francis's election. Until then, the diplomatic position of the Holy See was one of unequivocal support for the bishops of Venezuela, defending the Church against the hostility of the *Chavista* regime. That position has changed, however, despite the worsening economic and social situation under the new president Nicolás Maduro and even as misery and protests spread throughout the nation's territory.

Since February 2014, massive street protests have been almost continuous resulting in hundreds of deaths, especially of young demonstrators killed by the Chavez militias. As Cardinal Jorge Urosa, archbishop of Caracas, explained during a visit to Rome in February 2015, "that the main cause for Venezuela's scarcity and crisis is that the government wants to establish 'a totalitarian, Marxist-Communist political system.'"[133]

Nevertheless, the Vatican came to its aid on two occasions when the government was particularly fragile, calling on the parties to dialogue. In April 2014, the Vatican sent Archbishop Aldo Giordano, apostolic nuncio in Caracas, to participate as an observer at the talks between Maduro and the opposition, fulfilling a naïve request by a sector of the latter. Then, in October 2016, the pope received Maduro at the Vatican. He was seeking Francis's mediation while mass demonstrations were taking place in Venezuela. At the same time, the National Assembly declared that Maduro's actions could be called a coup d'état. That mediation occurred, chaired by Archbishop Emil Paul Tscherrig, a special envoy of the pope.

However, less than three months later, Andrés Oppenheimer, a well-known Argentine analyst of Latin American affairs wrote in his column in Miami's *El Nuevo Herald*:

---

132. Armando F. Valladares, "Cuba: Francisco abraza a los lobos y apuntala el 'muro' comunista," *CubDest*, Oct. 3, 2015, http://www.cubdest.org/1506/c1510pastorlobosav.htm.

133. Marta Jiménez, "Cardenal Urosa: Totalitarismo marxista-comunista trajo la crisis a Venezuela," *ACI Prensa*, Feb. 16, 2015, https://www.aciprensa.com/noticias/cardenal-urosa-totalitarismo-marxista -comunista-trajo-la-crisis-a-venezuela-83288/.

The Vatican's mediation effort was a disaster. It legitimized that country's authoritarian ruler, Nicolás Maduro, throwing him a life-saver, as millions of street protesters demanded his resignation in October 2016. It allowed Maduro to gain time, strengthen himself and repress the opposition even more....

[He concluded:] It is time to end this drama. And Pope Francis should take the first step by ceasing to be an obstacle to collective pressure for the restoration of democracy in Venezuela.[134]

The Vatican's patient benevolence toward Maduro's totalitarian regime reached a climax during Holy Week of 2017. On Holy Thursday, *Chavista* thugs interrupted the Mass of Chrism celebrated by Cardinal Urosa in the Caracas cathedral, shouting threats and physically attacking the celebrant. At the time, Pope Francis and the Secretariat of State did not publish any official statement repudiating the sacrilegious aggression or manifesting solidarity with the victim. In his *Urbi et Orbi* message a few days later, the pontiff did not even mention the suffering Venezuelan people.[135]

Worse, in the regular press conference during his return flight from Egypt, the pope attributed significant blame for the failure of peace efforts to the opposition:

There was the intervention of the Holy See . . . and . . . it did not succeed. It was left there. It did not succeed because the proposals were not acceptable, or were diluted, or it was a "yes, yes" but then a "no, no".... I believe . . . they are insisting to renew this work of facil-itating.... I think that this must be with conditions now. Very clear conditions. Part of the opposition does not want this. Interesting, the opposition itself is divided.[136]

This is how Alberto Ruiz-Gallardón, Spain's former Minister of Justice, re-acted to this balancing act between government and opposition:

With immense pain, I include the Vatican in my complaint about

134. Andrés Oppenheimer, "Papa Francisco, ¡Dé un paso atrás en Venezuela!" *El Nuevo Herald*, Feb. 8, 2017, last updated Feb. 10, 2017, http://www.elnuevoherald.com/opinion-es/opin-col-blogs/andres -oppenheimer-es/article131574119.html.

135. See Raymond J. de Souza, "It's Time for Francis and the Vatican to Get Tough on Venezuela," *Crux*, Apr. 24, 2017, https://cruxnow.com/global-church/2017/04/24/time-francis-vatican-get -tough-venezuela/.

136. Francis, "Return Flight Press Conference of His Holiness Pope Francis From Egypt to Rome," Apr. 29, 2017, http://w2.vatican.va/content/francesco/en/speeches/2017/april/documents/papa-francesco _20170429_egitto-volo.html.

equal consideration for victims and executioners. . . . The Venezuelan bishops . . . have been heroes before the tyrant. But Rome has addressed the issue as if it were a dispute over territorial boundaries.[137]

On May 5, 2017, the bishops of Venezuela issued a public note stating: "We reject the convocation for the Constitutional Assembly and urge the population in general not to resign themselves, to raise their voice of protest but do so without falling into the game of those who, by generating violence, seek to lead the country to scenarios of greater confrontation in order to aggravate the situation."[138] That same day, the pope sent them a letter saying he was convinced that "the serious problems of Venezuela can be solved if there is the will to build bridges and if one wishes to seriously dialogue."[139]

When the Holy See finally decided to ask the Maduro government to suspend the convocation of the National Constitutional Assembly, the *Clarín* newspaper of Buenos Aires commented:

> Jorge Bergoglio chose to break the silence and oppose the Venezuelan constitutional convention when it was too late.
> The Argentine pope has made the worst diplomatic blunder of his over four-year long pontificate, a gaffe evidenced by the rush to try and break the silence on the Venezuelan regime when time had practically run out.[140]

The disagreement between the pope and the Venezuelan bishops on the Church's attitude toward the *Chavista* regime was such that the six bishops of the Bishops' Conference leadership took the initiative to fly to Rome and report on the country's dramatic situation. They held an unscheduled meeting with the pope, explaining to him that the upheaval in Venezuela was "a fight between a government which has turned into a dictatorship . . . and an entire people which is crying out for freedom and desperately seeking, at the risk of its youngest lives,

137. Alberto Ruiz-Gallardón, "Venezuela, una nación secuestrada," *El Mundo,* Aug. 2, 2017, http://www.elmundo.es/opinion/2017/08/02/5980d07246163f58278b4643.html.

138. Venezuelan Bishops Conference, "Comunicado de la presidencia de la CEV: 'No reformar la constitución sino cumplirla,'" *Il Sismografo,* May 5, 2017, http://ilsismografo.blogspot.fr/2017/05/venezuela -comunicado-de-la-presidencia.html.

139. "Papa Francisco envía carta a los obispos de Venezuela," *Conferencia Episcopal Venezolana,* May 5, 2017, http://www.cev.org.ve/index.php/noticias/224-papa-francisco-envia-carta-a-los-obispos -de-venezuela.

140. Julio Algañaraz, "El comunicado vaticano: El peor papelón diplomático del pontificado del Papa Francisco," *Clarín,* Aug. 4, 2017, https://www.clarin.com/mundo/comunicado-vaticano-peor -papelon-diplomatico-pontificado-papa-Francis_0_SysX14zv-.html.

bread, medicine, security, work and fair elections,"[141] as *The Economist* reported.

Later, after a meeting with the pope during his visit to Colombia, Cardinal Jorge Urosa, archbishop of Caracas, told the press:

> The dialogue and culture of encounter that Pope Francis wants in Venezuela is not possible because the government does not listen.... The government is committed to implementing a totalitarian, statist, and communist system and does not listen to what we say, that this way is a wrong way.[142]

The Wall Street Journal thought it appropriate to publish an article by William McGurn titled, "Speak for Venezuela, Pope Francis," in which he states that,

> When Pope Francis wants to make the objects of his disfavor feel his sting, he's never lacked for words—especially when it involves the U.S.
> But when it comes to the brutality of Venezuela's government against its own people, Pope Francis and the Vatican have mostly avoided calling out Nicolás Maduro by name.[143]

The Buenos Aires daily *Clarín* published an article titled, "When will the pope speak about Venezuela? Francis's silence is shuddering: A silence that afflicts."[144] However, during his return flight from Colombia, when asked if he could speak out stronger and more clearly regarding President Maduro, who claims to be in union with him, the pontiff replied: "I believe that the Holy See has spoken out forcefully and clearly. What President Maduro says, it is up to him to explain; I don't know what his thoughts are."[145]

The conflict between the first Latin American pope and his continent's people was also evident at the October 2, 2016 referendum on the Colombia Peace

---

141. Erasmus [pseud.], "Stop Being Soft on Our Despot, Venezuela's Bishops Tell Francis: A Plea to the Pope," *The Economist*, Jun. 11, 2017, http://www.economist.com/blogs/erasmus/2017/06/plea-pope.

142. "Obispos venezolanos se reunieron con el Papa: 'El diálogo no es posible con un gobierno totalitario,'" *NTN24*, Sept. 7, 2017, http://archivo.ntn24america.com/noticia/Obispos-venezolanos-se-reunieron-con-el-papa%3A-%22El-di%C3%A1logo-no-es-posible-con-un-gobierno-totalitario%22-151775.

143. William McGurn, "Speak for Venezuela, Pope Francis: The First Latin American Pontiff Is Harder on Trump Than on Caracas's Despot," *The Wall Street Journal*, Aug. 7, 2017, https://www.wsj.com/articles/speak-for-venezuela-pope-francis-1502144547.

144. Ricardo Roa, "Cuándo el Papa va a hablar de Venezuela: El silencio de Francisco es estruendoso: Un silencio que lastima," *Clarín*, Aug. 1, 2017, https://www.clarin.com/opinion/papa-va-hablar-venezuela_0_Sy-1zYa8W.html.

145. "Press Conference of His Holiness Pope Francis on the Return Flight From Colombia to Rome," Sept. 10, 2017, http://w2.vatican.va/content/francesco/en/speeches/2017/september/documents/papa-francesco_20170910_viaggioapostolico-colombia-voloritorno.html.

Deal which President Juan Manuel Santos and the narco-Marxist FARC guerrillas negotiated in Cuba. Despite the intense moral pressure exerted on them, a majority of the Colombian people voted against it. On the eve of the vote, the main television stations broadcast a video message over and over again, in which the pope promised to go to Colombia if the Peace Accord was approved.

Still, the population voted against it, judging correctly that it clearly favored the guerrillas. The same people, who welcomed the Vicar of Christ with devotion, did not hesitate to reject the FARC in the subsequent parliamentary elections; and they did so even more categorically then at the time of the referendum.

Extending a Hand to China's Communist Dictatorship at the Expense of Underground Catholics

The Holy See has adopted the same conciliatory attitude toward China, a regime for which it manifests sympathy.

The chancellor of the Pontifical Academy of Sciences, Bishop Marcelo Sánchez Sorondo, an Argentine who is close to the pope, surprised Catholics by declaring, after a trip to Mao's country:

> Right now, those who are best implementing the social doctrine of the Church are the Chinese.
>
> They hold the common good above all else, everything else comes second to the common good.
>
> I met an extraordinary China: What people don't realize is that the central value in China is work, work, work.
>
> You do not have shantytowns, you do not have drugs, young people do not take drugs.
>
> [Beijing] is defending the dignity of the person.[146]

On an earlier trip to a conference on organ transplants (China is one of the largest organ traffickers on earth), he told the Chinese Communist Party-controlled *Global Times* newspaper: "The real thing is that at this moment China and pope have a very good relation."[147]

---

146. "Msgr. Sanchez Sorondo: China, the Best Implementer of the Social Doctrine of the Church," *AsiaNews.it*, Feb. 7, 2018, http://www.asianews.it/news-en/Msgr.-Sanchez-Sorondo:-China,-the-best-implementer-of-the-social-doctrine-of-the-Church-43033.html; see also "Vatican Official Praises China for Witness to Catholic Social Teaching," *National Catholic Register*, Feb. 7, 2018, http://www.ncregister.com/daily-news/vatican-official-praises-china-for-witness-to-catholic-social-teaching; Bernardo Cervellera, "Msgr. Sanchez Sorondo in Wonderland," *AsiaNews.it*, Feb. 7, 2018, http://www.asianews.it/news-en/Msgr.-Sanchez-Sorondo-in-Wonderland-43037.html.

147. Li Ruohan, "Pope, China 'Have a Very Good Relation': Vatican Bishop," *Global Times*, Aug. 5, 2017, http://www.globaltimes.cn/content/1059768.shtml.

This sympathy leads the Vatican to seek the establishment of relations with the Chinese communist regime. This same regime, however, has doggedly hounded the underground Catholic Church while extending its hand to the Vatican. It proposes a working agreement whereby the atheistic rulers would control bishops' appointments and the whole life of the Church in the country.[148]

Cardinal Joseph Zen, bishop emeritus of Hong Kong, firmly opposes any agreement which would be contrary to Catholic doctrine and the rights of the papacy. This is because it implies recognizing the so-called Patriotic Church, whose bylaws are formally schismatic. He calls for resistance, preferring to remain underground to apostasy through the acceptance of a national church.

In an interview with *LifeSiteNews* in February 2017, Cardinal Zen said, "I can understand that the pope is really naïve. . . . He doesn't know the Chinese communists. But unfortunately the people around him are not good at all. They have very wrong ideas. And I'm afraid that they may sell out our underground Church. That would be very sad." The cardinal said that he has written the pope several times, "but then he doesn't answer my letters."[149]

Referring to the bad influence of the secretary of state, on another occasion the cardinal said,

> Pope Francis does not know the real Communist Party in China, but [Cardinal Pietro] Parolin should know. . . . Pope Francis needs someone to calm him down from his enthusiasm. . . .
>
> "I told the pope that he [Parolin] has a poisoned mind. He is very sweet, but I have no trust in this person. He believes in diplomacy, not in our faith."[150]

In an interview with *Corriere della Sera*, the Chinese cardinal said,

> In Beijing, they know very well that irregular bishops are not well

---

148. In an editorial in *La Civiltà Cattolica*, Chinese Jesuit Fr. Joseph You Guo Jiang wrote: "As long as the Chinese Communist Party is the only leading party in the government, Marxism will continue to [be] the ideological guideline for society. Thus, the Chinese Catholic Church will have to redefine its role and relationship with the Party and its ideological theories. This does not necessarily mean that the Church has to agree completely with Party politics and values, but it must find flexible and effective way[s] to continue its mission and ministry in China." Joseph You Guo Jiang, SJ, "Catholicism in 21st Century China," *La Civiltà Cattolica*, Jun. 1, 2017, https://laciviltacattolica.com/catholicism-in-21st-century-china/.

149. Claire Chretien, "Exclusive: Cardinal Zen Says 'Naïve' Pope and Bad Advisors Are Betraying Underground Church in China," *LifeSiteNews*, Feb. 21, 2017, https://www.lifesitenews.com/news/interview-cardinal-zen-begs-vatican-not-to-sell-out-to-chinese-govt.

150. Christopher White, "Cardinal Says Pope's Top Diplomat Has 'Poisoned Mind' on China," *Crux*, Oct. 16, 2017, https://cruxnow.com/global-church/2017/10/16/cardinal-says-popes-top-diplomat-poisoned-mind-china/.

regarded by the people. Therefore, a known schismatic church is a lesser evil than an objectively schismatic church actually blessed by the pope with an agreement. . . .

Inviting members of our faithful clergy to the Holy See to come out into the open through a bad agreement, would mean imposing upon them the acceptance of government control. They would feel betrayed after years of suffering.[151]

Also, Cardinal Zen spoke regarding the bishops of the Patriotic Church in a video released on the 14th of that same month on the website of the magazine *Polonia Christiana*. He said, "I really cannot believe that the Holy See doesn't know that there is no bishops' conference! There is only a name. They never really have a discussion, meetings. They meet when they are called by the government. The government gives instructions. They obey. It's fake."[152]

"Now We Must Die at the Hand of Our Father!"
Turning a deaf ear to these reflections, the Vatican continued negotiations undaunted and removed the Chinese Archbishop Savio Hon Tai-Fai, then the secretary of the Congregation for the Evangelization of Peoples, to be Nuncio in Greece. He also opposed the proposed agreement.[153]

Shortly before Christmas 2017, Archbishop Claudio Maria Celli traveled to Beijing as Vatican envoy to meet with communist rulers and two underground bishops who were faithful to the Holy See. He asked them, on the pope's behalf, to renounce their dioceses so that he could replace them with excommunicated prelates of the Patriotic Church. One of these bishops then asked Cardinal Zen to deliver a personal letter to Pope Francis. The pope received this letter in Rome after the weekly general audience of January 10. Two days later the cardinal had a private meeting with the pontiff, and on January 29, 2018, he revealed in his blog hitherto confidential aspects of his meetings with Pope Francis.

In fact, he disclosed that at the time of Archbishop Savio Hon's farewell he and the Archbishop had spoken to the pope about these two dioceses. Pope Francis was surprised and told them he would look into the matter. In their

---

151. Guido Santevecchi, "Il cardinale di Hong Kong in piazza: Ho scritto al papa, non ceda a Pechino," *Corriere della Sera*, Jul. 1, 2017, http://www.corriere.it/esteri/17_luglio_01/joseph-zen-ze-kiun-cardinale-85-anni-marcia-ragazzi-ho-scritto-papa-non-ceda-pechino-9b9d0e9e-5e91-11e7-a166-a251b30d0494.shtml.

152. John Horvat II, "Cardinal Zen: Situation of Church in China Worse Than Before," *TFP.org*, Jul. 31, 2017, http://www.tfp.org/cardinal-zen-situation-church-china-worse/. See also, https://www.youtube.com/watch?v=zKHtiRmIicM.

153. See Andrea Tornielli, "Savio Hon nunzio in Grecia," *La Stampa–Vatican Insider*, Sept. 28, 2017, http://www.lastampa.it/2017/09/28/vaticaninsider/ita/vaticano/savio-hon-nunzio-in-grecia-1ZYVPLLJqZuu32MhiFLPLI/pagina.html.

last conversation, they asked him if he had investigated the situation. "Yes," he replied, "I told them [his collaborators in the Holy See] not to create a new Mindszenty case!" In this same post, Cardinal Zen clarified his views on Vatican intervention in China, saying:

> So, do I think that the Vatican is selling out the Catholic Church in China? Yes, definitely, if they go in the direction which is obvious from all what they are doing in recent years and months. . . .
>
> Am I the major obstacle in the process of reaching a deal between the Vatican and China? If that is a bad deal, I would be more than happy to be the obstacle.[154]

In response, the Vatican spokesman, Mr. Greg Burke, stated that there is consonance between the secretary of state and the pope "on the steps in the dialogue in progress . . . which he [the pope] follows with special attention. It is therefore surprising and regrettable that the contrary is affirmed by people in the Church, thus fostering confusion and controversy."[155]

Moreover, the secretary of state himself gave an interview to journalist Gianni Valente to defend these initiatives. He stated that the Vatican's principal goal in the dialogue with the Chinese government is preparing for unity between the two Catholic communities, the underground and the patriotic, so

> that we won't have to speak of "legitimate" and "illegitimate," "underground" and "official" bishops in the Church in China.
>
> [In a direct reference to Cardinal Zen, the secretary of state added that] criticism should be directed at building communion and not at stirring up divisions. . . .
>
> [so] expressions such as power, betrayal, resistance, surrender, confrontation, failure, compromise should make room for others, such as service, dialogue, mercy, forgiveness, reconciliation, collaboration, communion.[156]

The secretary of state's harshness toward Cardinal Zen and underground Catholics is in stark contrast with his openness to Chinese communist rulers.

---

154. "Dear Friends in the Media," Jan. 29, 2018, http://oldyosef.hkdavc.com/?p=967.

155. Greg Burke, dir., "Dichiarazione del direttore della Sala Stampa, Greg Burke," *Holy See Press Office*, Jan. 30, 2018, https://press.vatican.va/content/salastampa/it/bollettino/pubblico/2018/01/30/0089 /00168.html#ing.

156. Gianni Valente, "Parolin: 'Ecco perché dialoghiamo con la Cina,'" *La Stampa–Vatican Insider*, Feb. 3, 2018, http://www.lastampa.it/2018/01/31/vaticaninsider/parolin-why-we-are-in-dialogue-with -china-C8mlJsD0PDNsmsx7db6ZIJ/pagina.html.

Indeed, he later stated that "the mission proper to the Church is not to change the structures or administration of the State," because it "does not want to replace the State but wants to make a positive and serene contribution for the good of all."[157]

The Chinese cardinal soon responded in his blog, saying that Cardinal Parolin "loves the *Ostpolitik* diplomacy of his master [Cardinal] Casaroli and despises the genuine faith of those who firmly defend the Church." Regarding the calls for reconciliation, the prelate wrote, "It is not a question of personal offenses to forgive, but of slavery from which to be freed." And he asks: "Mercy for the persecutors? For their accomplices? Rewarding traitors? Punishing the faithful? Forcing a legitimate bishop to hand over his post to an excommunicate one? Is this not what rather puts salt in the wounds?"

In addition, the Vatican cannot ignore the existence of two structures in China: "One structure is based on the principle of the Primacy of Peter upon which Jesus established his Church; the other structure is imposed by an atheistic government that intends to create a schismatic church subject to its power," thus forcing underground Catholics "into [a] cage." The cardinal concludes by saying that "if by chance a bad agreement is signed with China someday, obviously with the pope's approval, [I will] withdraw in silence to 'monastic life.'"[158]

In a "Painful Appeal" posted on his blog in August 2016, just before the section titled, "Agreement acceptance and conscientious objection. Fidelity to the pope despite the pope," the veteran cardinal wrote, "I remember an expression that appeared long ago on the Internet, on a Catholic site in China: 'After so many years, our enemies have not yet been able to make us die. Now we must die at the hand of our Father. All right then, let's die!'"[159]

That is what he sought to avoid with his Painful Appeal, and it is also what Catholics around the world must avoid even if doing so means they must exercise conscientious objection and maintain "fidelity to the pope despite the pope."

157. Ibid.

158. "Non sono ancora riuscito a capire per che cosa dialogano con la Cina," Feb. 13, 2018, http://oldyosef.hkdavc.com/?p=987.

159. Joseph Zen Ze-kiun, "Card. Zen: Le mie perplessità sul dialogo Cina-Santa Sede e le ricadute sulla Chiesa cinese," *AsiaNews.it*, http://www.asianews.it/notizie-it/Card.-Zen:-Le-mie-perplessitC3A0
-sul-dialogo-Cina-Santa-Sede-e-le-ricadute-sulla-Chiesa-cinese-38222.html.

CHAPTER 3

Promoting the Green Agenda, World Governance, and an Ambiguous "Mother Earth" Mysticism

According to oft-reiterated Church social doctrine, there are issues such as abortion, divorce, and the natural structure of marriage, about which Catholics are bound to have a unanimous position. Conversely, other topics are left to the judgment of the rightly formed consciences of the faithful. However, by embracing environmentalist ideology, Pope Francis establishes a new paradigm.

Although unsupported by any definitive scientific data, the Encyclical *Laudato Sì* presupposes catastrophic ecological theories are true. It invites the faithful to focus primarily on environmental issues rather than those like the right to life where they are obliged to speak with one voice. In recent years, the Holy See has been organizing international congresses, providing platforms to speakers who have always promoted global population reduction (through contraception and abortion) supposedly to save the planet. Moreover, as one senior Vatican official put it, for the first time in history, the Holy See's agenda coincides with that of the United Nations, which opposes Catholic truth on many points.

In July 2014, Pope Francis called concern for the environment "one of the greatest challenges of our time." Giving a theological tone to his comments, he said the world needs to "chang[e] to a form of development which seeks to respect creation. . . . This is our sin: exploiting the land and not allowing it to give us what it has within it."[160]

Launching an Ecological Encyclical Hand in Hand With the U.N.

Pope Francis published the Encyclical *Laudato Sì*[161] a few months before three crucial U.N. meetings on Sustainable Development Goals. In so doing, he ignored the recommendations of a coalition of solid theologians, scientists, and

---

160. Francis, "Meeting With the World of Labor and Industry: Address of Pope Francis," Jul. 5, 2014, https://w2.vatican.va/content/francesco/en/speeches/2014/july/documents/papa-francesco _20140705_molise-mondo-del-lavoro.html.

161. At a Vatican-organized colloquy, Ban Ki-Moon, U.N. secretary general, linked the encyclical with U.N. initiatives: "This year, with the upcoming encyclical, the Sustainable Development Goals Summit in September, and a global climate agreement, we have an unprecedented opportunity to articulate—and create—a more sustainable future and a life of dignity for all." Ban Ki-Moon, "Secretary-General's Remarks at Workshop on the Moral Dimensions of Climate Change and Sustainable Development 'Protect the Earth, Dignify Humanity' [As Delivered]," Apr. 28, 2015, https://www.un.org/sg/en/content/sg/statement /2015-04-28/secretary-generals-remarks-workshop-moral-dimensions-climate-change.

economists[162] while, on the other hand, he requested the collaboration of controversial intellectuals such as ex-friar Leonardo Boff,[163] a follower of liberation theology. He also consulted Hans Schellnhuber,[164] a member of the failed Club of Rome. The 1972 *Limits to Growth* study published by this group posited that the world's 1970-known oil reserves would be exhausted by 1990.[165] Also, Schellnhuber is sympathetic to the "Gaia theory."[166] He promotes the Earth Charter, a Global Council to be elected by the world's population, and a Planetary Court with universal jurisdiction.[167] He also peddles the idea that the human population of the earth should not surpass one billion. His proposals are so radical that even *The New York Times* described him as "a scientist known for his aggressive stance on climate policy."[168]

In preparation for the encyclical's publication, the Vatican hosted a day dedicated to climate change. It had the following objectives:

> To help strengthen the global consensus on the importance of climate change in the context of sustainable development. . . .
> The desired outcome is a joint statement on the moral and religious imperative of dealing with climate change in the context of sustainable development."[169]

162. For the Sept. 17, 2014 and April 27, 2015 letters sent by the Cornwall Alliance to Pope Francis, see http://cornwallalliance.org/landmark-documents/protect-the-poor-ten-reasons-to-oppose-harmful-climate-change-policies/; http://cornwallalliance.org/anopenlettertopopefrancisonclimatechange/.

163. "—Did the pope read your books? —More than that. He asked me for material for *Laudato Sì*. I gave him advice and sent him things I wrote. . . . The pope told me directly: 'Boff, do not send me your letters directly.' —Why not? —He said to me, 'Otherwise under-secretaries will intercept them and I will not receive them. It is better to send things to the Argentine ambassador to the Holy See, with whom I have a good relationship. . . . The day before the publication of the encyclical the pope sent for me to thank me for the help." Joachim Frank, "Leonardo Boff im interview: "Papst Franziskus ist einer von uns," *Kölner Stadt-Anzeiger*, Dec. 16, 2015, https://www.ksta.de/kultur/leonardo-boff-im-interview—papst-franziskus-ist-einer-von-uns—25372660.

164. For details on his positions and contribution in writing *Laudato Sì*, see Voice of the Family, "Professor Schellnhuber: Climate Science and the 'Population Problem,'" *Voice of the Family*, Jun. 26, 2015, http://voiceofthefamily.com/professor-schellnhuber-climate-science-and-the-population-problem/.

165. See Donella H. Meadows, Dennis L. Meadows, Jørgen Randers, and William W. Behrens III, *The Limits to Growth* (New York: Universe, 1972), 58, http://www.donellameadows.org/wp-content/userfiles/Limits-to-Growth-digital-scan-version.pdf ; Bjørn Lomborg, "The Limits to Panic," *Project Syndicate*, Jun. 17, 2013, https://www.project-syndicate.org/commentary/economic-growth-and-its-critics-by-bj-rn-lomborg.

166. See Voice of the Family, "Schellnhuber: Climate Science and the 'Population Problem.'"

167. See Hans Joachim (John) Schellnhuber, "Expanding the Democracy Universe," *Center for Humans & Nature*, accessed Jul. 16, 2018, http://www.humansandnature.org/democracy-hans-joachim-schellnhuber.

168. James Kanter, "Scientist: Warming Could Cut Population to 1 Billion," *The New York Times*, Mar. 13, 2009, https://dotearth.blogs.nytimes.com/2009/03/13/scientist-warming-could-cut-population-to-1-billion/.

169. "Protect the Earth, Dignify Humanity. The Moral Dimensions of Climate Change and Sustainable Humanity," *Pontifical Academy of Sciences*, Apr. 28, 2015, http://www.casinapioiv.va/content/accademia/en/events/2015/protectearth.html.

Speakers included U.N. Secretary-General Ban Ki-Moon; Ecuador's leftist ex-president, Rafael Correa; and Jeffrey Sachs, an economist who favors population control through abortion.

Hans Schellnhuber participated in the press conference following the publication of *Laudato Sì*. He was later made a member of the Pontifical Academy of Sciences.

Apocalyptic Vision Founded on Dogmas With No Scientific Basis
Departing from his role as guardian of the Faith and Christian morals, Pope Francis intervened in a highly technical debate in his encyclical. He proposed solutions that broad sectors of the scientific, economic, and political worlds consider harmful to humanity, and particularly the globe's more impoverished regions and peoples. He did this despite having written in the Apostolic Exhortation *Evangelii Gaudium* that "neither can believers claim that a scientific opinion which is attractive but not sufficiently verified has the same weight as a dogma of faith."[170] Moreover, in *Laudato Sì*, he recognized that there are discussions about environmental problems in which it is difficult to reach a consensus, and, therefore, he "encourage[d] an honest and open debate."[171]

Nevertheless, he stated, "A very solid scientific consensus indicates that we are presently witnessing a disturbing warming of the climatic system." Furthermore, he affirmed that "a number of scientific studies indicate that most global warming in recent decades is due to the great concentration of greenhouse gases . . . released mainly as a result of human activity" and "the problem is aggravated by a model of development based on the intensive use of fossil fuels."[172]

Pope Francis did not even support these assertions with footnotes.[173] Nevertheless, the encyclical uses them to give an apocalyptic view of environmental threats:[174] "The pace of consumption, waste and environmental change has

---

170. Francis, *Evangelii Gaudium*, no. 243.

171. Francis, Encyclical *Laudato Sì*, May 24, 2015, no. 188, http://w2.vatican.va/content/francesco/en/encyclicals/documents/papa-francesco_20150524_enciclica-laudato-si.html.

172. Ibid., no. 23.

173. On this subject, Cardinal George Pell stated, "The Church has got no mandate from the Lord to pronounce on scientific matters." Rosie Scammell, "Cardinal George Pell Takes a Swing at Pope Francis' Environmental Encyclical," *The Washington Post*, Jul. 17, 2015, https://www.washingtonpost.com/national/religion/cardinal-george-pell-takes-a-swing-at-pope-francis-environmental-encyclical/2015/07/17/ecc04ef8-2cbb-11e5-960f-22c4ba982ed4_story.html?utm_term=.59375c01abea.

174. For example, although CO^2 is a natural part of the atmosphere necessary for the growth of any plant, including marine phytoplankton, and for the release of oxygen into the atmosphere, the pope says that "Carbon dioxide pollution [*sic*] increases the acidification of the oceans and compromises the marine food chain." Francis, *Laudato Sì*, no. 24.

so stretched the planet's capacity that our contemporary lifestyle, unsustainable as it is, can only precipitate catastrophes, such as those which even now periodically occur in different areas of the world."[175]

Promoting a Miserabilist[176] Lifestyle That Will Mostly Burden the Poor

According to Pope Francis, "the deepest roots of our present failures . . . have to do with the direction, goals, meaning and social implications of technological and economic growth,"[177] which seeks an indefinite increase in wealth. Conversely, he calls for "a new synthesis,"[178] a "radical change"[179] and "a bold cultural revolution."[180] Although not suggesting "a return to the Stone Age,"[181] he argues that "humanity is called to recognize the need for changes of lifestyle, production and consumption, in order to combat this warming or at least the human causes which produce or aggravate it."[182]

This new ecological culture, he argues, "needs to be a distinctive way of looking at things, a way of thinking, policies, an educational program, a lifestyle and a spirituality which together generate resistance to the assault of the technocratic paradigm."[183] As an example of "harmful habits of consumption" for the environment, the pope quotes "the increasing use and power of air-conditioning."[184] In this, he forgets that air-conditioning is not a frivolous luxury, but a necessity for the living and working conditions of millions of people in warmer climates. Had they had air-conditioning, 14,000 elderly people probably would not have died in the 2003 heat wave that afflicted southern France.[185]

Pope Francis also seems to forget that around 1820 there were some 1 billion people on Earth (Hans Schellnhuber's ideal population figure). Since then, industrial improvements have helped boost worldwide life expectancy

---

175. Ibid., no. 161.

176. [Publisher's Note: By *miserabilism*, the author means a leftist mindset of growing, *quasi* mystical disgust with dignity, progress, and, ultimately, Christian culture and civilization.]

177. Ibid., no. 109.

178. Ibid., no. 112.

179. Ibid., no. 171.

180. Ibid., no. 114.

181. Ibid., no. 114.

182. Ibid., no. 23.

183. Ibid., no. 111.

184. Ibid., no. 55.

185. "Air conditioning is not systematically used in France, even in retirement homes or hospitals. . . . the overall excess mortality rate in France between August 1 and August 20 was estimated at 14,800 deaths." Stéphanie Vandentorren, MD, et al., "Mortality in 13 French Cities During the August 2003 Heat Wave," *American Journal of Public Health* 94, no. 9 (Sept. 2004): 1518–20, https://www.ncbi.nlm.nih.gov/pmc/articles/PMC1448485/.

at birth by 30 years.[186] In addition, Angus Maddison, a pioneer in quantitative macroeconomic history, estimates that global per capita income increased more than tenfold, from $667 in 1820 to $7,285 in 2006. He expects this to increase to $11,814 by 2030 (amounts are in 1990 international Geary-Khamis dollars).[187]

According to Pope Francis, "they [the excluded] are the majority of the planet's population, billions of people." They are the main victims of development. Thus, an "ecological approach" becomes indispensable to "hear both the cry of the earth and the cry of the poor."[188]

On the one hand, the encyclical also seems to overlook that the world has succeeded in diminishing extreme poverty. From 1990 to 2010, it was halved. This information comes from a U.N. 2014 report on Millennium Development Goals, a presumably unbiased source. On the other hand, if the encyclical's proposals were implemented, the greatest victims would be the poor on the peripheries. The encyclical would ensure that those residing in the world's less developed regions would remain in their underdeveloped state.

As for the "cry of the earth," it is demagogic to claim that humanity today leaves only "debris, desolation and filth" to future generations.[189] As columnist George Will pointed out, to disprove this assertion, it suffices to compare London's pollution levels in Charles Dickens's novels to what anyone can see there today.[190] Nor is the reality of trash as bad as it sounds. Much of the waste is recycled, which is an additional source of jobs and wealth.[191]

Indigenous Peoples, a Model of Ecological Respect for Nature

Pope Francis's romantic vision of indigenous peoples stands in stark contrast to his criticism of progress and development. As he sees it, the Indians of the Americas are models of wisdom in their relationship with nature: "For them, land is not a commodity but rather a gift from God and from their ancestors who rest there, a sacred space with which they need to interact if they are to

---

186. See *How Was Life? Global Wellbeing Since 1820*, ed. Jan Luiten van Zanden, et al. (Paris: OECD, 2014), 106, http://www.oecd.org/statistics/how-was-life-9789264214262-en.htm.

187. See Angus Maddison, "The West and the Rest in the World Economy: 1000–2030 Maddisonian and Malthusian Interpretations," *World Economics* 9, no. 4 (Oct.–Dec. 2008), 76, https://www.researchgate.net/publication/237678324.

188. Francis, *Laudato Sì*, no. 49.

189. Ibid., no. 161.

190. See George F. Will, "Pope Francis's Fact-Free Flamboyance," *The Washington Post*, Sept. 18, 2015, https://www.washingtonpost.com/opinions/pope-franciss-fact-free-flamboyance/2015/09/18/7d711750-5d6a-11e5-8e9e-dce8a2a2a679_story.html?utm_term=.3063b1df62ac.

191. See James V. Schall, SJ, "Concerning the 'Ecological' Path to Salvation," *Catholic World Report*, Jun. 21, 2015, https://www.catholicworldreport.com/2015/06/21/concerning-the-ecological-path-to-salvation/.

maintain their identity and values. When they remain on their land, they themselves care for it best."[192]

In another passage, speaking of cooperatives and self-sufficiency, Francis affirms: "They are able to instill a greater sense of responsibility, a strong sense of community, a readiness to protect others, a spirit of creativity and a deep love for the land." He adds, "these values are deeply rooted in indigenous peoples."[193]

During the pope's trip to Mexico, he preached a sermon to the Chiapas Indians. After stating that humanity is in "one of the greatest environmental crises in world history," he affirmed, "In this regard, you have much to teach us, much to teach humanity. Your peoples, as the bishops of Latin America have recognized, know how to interact harmoniously with nature, which they respect as a 'source of food, a common home and an altar of human sharing.'"[194]

Evidently, such praise is related to the conflicts in various parts of the world between these communities and national governments regarding hydroelectric dams or mining projects on indigenous lands.

Furthermore, Pope Francis acknowledged in the encyclical that "the principle of the subordination of private property to the universal destination of goods, and thus the right of everyone to their use, is a golden rule of social conduct and 'the first principle of the whole ethical and social order.'"[195] Contradictorily, however, this principle of subordination of private property to the common good loses all validity when it comes to indigenous populations. For them, the right to ancestral lands is absolute, even if this sanctuary-making is detrimental to the common good of the nation and of the indigenous peoples themselves.

Thus, during a meeting with participants at the Third Indigenous Peoples' Forum, organized by the International Fund for Agricultural Development, Pope Francis affirmed that in "reconcil[ing] the right to development . . . with the protection of the particular characteristics of indigenous peoples and their territories," something which is "especially clear when planning economic activities which may interfere with indigenous cultures and their ancestral relationship to the earth. . . . the right to prior and informed consent should always prevail."[196]

---

192. Francis, *Laudato Sì*, no. 146.

193. Ibid., no. 179.

194. Francis, "Homily of His Holiness Pope Francis: Holy Mass With Representatives of the Indigenous Communities of Chiapas," Feb. 15, 2016, http://w2.vatican.va/content/francesco/en/homilies/2016/documents/papa-francesco_20160215_omelia-messico-chiapas.html.

195. Francis, *Laudato Sì*, no. 93.

196. Francis, "Address of His Holiness Pope Francis to Participants of the III Global Meeting of the Indigenous Peoples' Forum of the International Fund for Agricultural Development," Feb. 15, 2017, https://w2.vatican.va/content/francesco/en/speeches/2017/february/documents/papa-francesco_20170215_popoli-indigeni.html.

Pope Francis held other meetings with indigenous peoples during his January 2018 trip to Chile and Peru, where he visited the Amazon region.

Speaking to natives of that vast region, the pope used strong rhetoric: "Those of us who do not live in these lands need your wisdom and knowledge to enable us to enter into, without destroying, the treasures that this region holds. And to hear an echo of the words that the Lord spoke to Moses: 'Remove the sandals from your feet, for the place on which you are standing is holy ground' (Exod. 3:5)." The pontiff went on to reiterate his preference for the indigenous lifestyle over that of the developed West, which he deems reprehensible: "The fact is your lives cry out against a style of life that is oblivious to its own real cost. You are a living memory of the mission that God has entrusted to us all: the protection of our common home."[197]

This begs the question: Is this continuous rebuke of the West's cultural and economic model and unending praise for the supposed wisdom of the indigenous lifestyles a key to understanding the guidelines to be issued at the upcoming 2019 Special Synod on the Amazon? The answer should be categorically affirmative, considering the liberation theology leanings of some of the Pre-Synodal Council's eighteen members, for example, Cardinal Claudio Hummes, and Most Rev. Erwin Kräutler, bishop emeritus of Xingu, Brazil.[198]

These two Brazilian prelates have raised concern because of their support for the priestly ordination of married men (*viri probati*). This could encourage the revision of the Latin Church's policy on priestly celibacy—a practice that might spread from the Amazon to the rest of the Church. Additionally, it will be necessary to keep a close watch on the Amazon Synod to see if it will try to impose on all Catholics the indigenist ideology promoted by a pro-liberation theology sector of the Brazilian bishops. This ideology was denounced forty years ago by Plinio Corrêa de Oliveira in his well-documented book, *Indigenous Tribalism: A Communist-Missionary Ideal for Brazil in the Twenty-First Century*.[199]

Global Governance to Promote a Teilhardian "Universal Communion"
Also disturbing is that *Laudato Sì* strongly endorses global control of ecological problems. In several passages, it insists "that our planet is a homeland and that

---

197. Francis, "Address of the Holy Father: Meeting With Indigenous People of Amazonia," Jan. 19, 2018, http://w2.vatican.va/content/francesco/en/speeches/2018/january/documents/papa-francesco_20180119_peru-puertomaldonado-popoliamazzonia.html.

198. The Council will work with the General Secretariat to prepare the Special Assembly.

199. See Plinio Corrêa de Oliveira, *Indian Tribalism: The Communist-Missionary Ideal for Brazil in the Twenty-First Century*, in *Crusade for a Christian Civilization* vol. 10, no. 4 (Oct.-Dec. 1980), http://www.tfp.org/indian-tribalism-the-communist-missionary-ideal-for-brazil-in-the-twenty-first-century/.

humanity is one people living in a common home."[200] "What is needed . . . is an agreement on systems of governance for the whole range of so-called 'global commons,'"[201] "a true world political authority"[202] "empowered to impose sanctions"[203] and "penalties for damage inflicted on the environment."[204]

Finally, despite claims that the ecological defense of nature does not require "a divinization of the earth,"[205] that would "put all living beings on the same level . . . depriv[ing] human beings of their unique worth,"[206] *Laudato Sì* contains passages that echo the pantheistic and evolutionist mysticism of Fr. Pierre Teilhard de Chardin. Indeed, he is even mentioned by name in footnote 83.[207]

According to the encyclical, the world is a "sacrament of communion. . . . [in which] the divine and the human meet . . . in the last speck of dust of our planet."[208] "The ultimate destiny of the universe is in the fullness of God, which has already been attained by the risen Christ, the measure of the maturity of all things."[209] From this premise, Pope Francis reasons that "ecological conversion"[210] "entails a loving awareness that we are not disconnected from the rest of creatures, but joined in a splendid universal communion."[211]

Likewise, *Laudato Sì* presents man as the product of evolutionary processes, whose qualitative novelty "presupposes a direct action by God."[212] The author never mentions the God-created, rational human soul, save covertly in footnote 141, which says, "love is always lived out in body and spirit."

---

200. Francis, *Laudato Sì*, no. 164.

201. Ibid., no. 174.

202. Ibid., no. 175, quoting Benedict XVI and John XXIII.

203. Ibid.

204. Ibid., no. 214.

205. Ibid., no. 90.

206. Ibid.

207. See Arnaldo Xavier da Silveira, "Notes on *Laudato Sì*," Aug. 3, 2015, http://www.unavox.it/ArtDiversi /DIV1294_Da-Silveira_Note_su_Laudato-si.html. On November 18, 2017, the plenary assembly of the Pontifical Council for Culture passed a motion asking Pope Francis to remove the *Monitum* issued by the Holy Office of June 30, 1962 stating that his theological and philosophical texts contained grave errors of Catholic doctrine. See Flavia Grossi, "Plenaria Pontificio Consiglio Della Cultura e Teilhard de Chardin: Approvata petizione al papa per rimuovere il monitum," *DISF.org*, Nov. 18, 2017, http://www.disf.org /teilhard-de-chardin-petizione-monitum-consiglio-cultura.

208. Francis, *Laudato Sì*, no. 9, quoting Bartholomew I, "Global Responsibility and Ecological Sustainability: Closing Remarks," Halki Summit I, Istanbul, Jun. 20, 2012.

209. Ibid., no. 83.

210. Ibid., no. 219.

211. Ibid., no. 220.

212. Ibid., no. 81.

Support for the Anti-Christian Agenda Behind Sustainable Development

Pope Francis implemented the principles of *Laudato Sì* in his address to the United Nations General Assembly on September 25, 2015. He denounced the "misuse and destruction of the environment," and the "dramatic reality of this whole situation of exclusion and inequality." He did this, "together with all those who are seeking urgently needed and effective solutions." For him, "the adoption of the 2030 Agenda for Sustainable Development at the World Summit, which opens today, is an important sign of hope."[213]

His support for the "2030 Agenda for Sustainable Development" is all the more serious and surprising given the Vatican's own reservations about it. Earlier that same month, the Permanent Observer Mission of the Holy See to the United Nations had filed at the General Assembly's September 1 session, an official statement expressing its misgivings. The statement said the agenda would only be acceptable if the concepts "'sexual and reproductive health' and 'reproductive rights'" explicitly excluded abortion or abortifacients from its definition. It further expressed its reservations with the term "contraception" and asked that "family planning" only include morally licit methods. Likewise, to be acceptable, the term "gender" should mean biological sexual identity. Finally, the statement reiterated that parents' "primary responsibility" and "prior rights" in their children's education must include their right to religious freedom.[214]

None of that prevented Bishop Marcelo Sánchez Sorondo, chancellor of the Holy See's two Academies of science, from declaring emphatically that "for the first time the pope's teaching . . . runs parallel to that of the United Nations."[215]

Moreover, the September 1, 2016 papal message celebrating the "World Day of Prayer for the Care of Creation" gave guidelines for individual behavior and approved questionable government initiatives.

To address individuals' supposed ecological responsibilities, Pope Francis quoted the schismatic Patriarch Bartholomew of Constantinople *verbatim*: "Inasmuch as we all generate small ecological damage," we are called to acknowledge "our contribution, smaller or greater, to the disfigurement and destruction of

213. Francis, "Address of the Holy Father: Meeting With the Members of the General Assembly of the United Nations Organization," Sept. 25, 2015, http://w2.vatican.va/content/francesco/en/speeches/2015/september/documents/papa-francesco_20150925_onu-visita.html.

214. "On the Outcome Document of the United Nations Summit for the Adoption of the Post-2015 Development Agenda 'Transforming Our World: The 2030 Agenda for Sustainable Development,'" Sept. 1, 2015, https://holyseemission.org/contents//statements/55e60e559a5749.94098476.php.

215. "Obispo Sánchez Sorondo: 'Por primera vez el magisterio del Papa es paralelo al de las Naciones Unidas,'" *La Gaceta*, Jul. 20, 2017, https://gaceta.es/civilizacion/pri%C2%ADme%C2%ADra-vez-ma%C2%ADgis%C2%ADte%C2%ADrio-papa-pa%C2%ADra%C2%ADle%C2%ADlo-na%C2%ADcio%C2%ADnes-uni%C2%ADdas-20170720-0725/.

creation." The Argentine pontiff then concluded, "Let us repent of the harm we are doing to our common home."[216]

Pope Francis described this supposed ecological sin, then called for a firm purpose of amendment:

> As individuals we have grown comfortable with certain lifestyles shaped by a distorted culture of prosperity and a "disordered desire to consume more than what is really necessary". . . .
>
> Examining our consciences, repentance and confession . . . lead to a firm purpose of amendment. This in turn must translate into concrete ways of thinking and acting that are more respectful of creation. For example: "avoiding the use of plastic and paper, reducing water consumption, separating refuse, cooking only what can reasonably be consumed, showing care for other living beings, using public transport or car-pooling, planting trees, turning off unnecessary lights, or any number of other practices."[217]

To make this commitment more cogent, the pope suggested as "a complement to the two traditional sets of seven [spiritual and corporal works of mercy]: may the works of mercy also include care for our common home."[218]

At the institutional level, the pope declared that "the protection of our common home requires a growing global political consensus." Accordingly, he expressed his satisfaction at the fact that "in September 2015, the nations of the world adopted the Sustainable Development Goals, and that, in December 2015, they approved the Paris Agreement on climate change, which set the demanding yet fundamental goal of halting the rise of the global temperature."[219]

The Holy See's support for the "2030 Agenda for Sustainable Development" is all the more disconcerting as it is already being implemented through the proliferation of initiatives such as the World Health Organization's Innov8 approach, which aims to impose abortion, contraception, and hedonistic sex education on children in less developed countries.

On behalf of the Society for the Protection of the Unborn Child (SPUC), British researcher Matthew McCusker stated that, "the approval of the SDGs [goals of the Sustainable Development agenda] by Pope Francis and other organs of the

---

216. Francis, "Show Mercy to Our Common Home: Message of His Holiness Pope Francis for the Celebration of the World Day of Prayer for the Care of Creation," Sept. 1, 2016, no. 3, http://w2.vatican.va/content /francesco/en/messages/pont-messages/2016/documents/papa-francesco_20160901_messaggio -giornata-cura-creato.html.

217. Ibid., nos. 3–4.

218. Ibid., no. 5.

219. Ibid., no. 4.

Holy See greatly increases the threat to the most innocent and vulnerable amongst us." Hence, "it is absolutely necessary for all Catholics to resist, in the manner most appropriate to their position with[in] the Church, this alignment between ecclesiastical authorities and an international agenda that pursues the destruction of innocent life and of the very structure of the family."[220]

"Gnostic and Pagan Melodrama" on the Facade of Saint Peter's Basilica
Pope Francis's convergence with the most radical and pagan green agenda promoted by the U.N. and international organizations was evident on December 8, 2015, when the show "Fiat Lux: Illuminating Our Common Home" was projected on the facade of Saint Peter's Basilica. It was a true "ecological manifesto." Financed by the World Bank Group, it aimed at translating the Encyclical *Laudato Sì* into images. It showed lions, tigers, and leopards where the early Christians were martyred and a huge owl hovering above, as marching Buddhist monks seemed to point to a way of salvation other than Christianity.[221]

Journalist Antonio Socci noted that "at St. Peter's, on the feast of the Immaculate Conception, instead of celebrating the Mother of God they preferred to celebrate Mother Earth to propagandize the dominant ideology, this neo-pagan and neo-Malthusian 'climate and ecology religion' held by the great world powers." He called the show "a Gnostic and neopagan melodrama that had a very precise anti-Christian ideological message."[222]

220. Matthew McCusker, "The Impact of the United Nations' Sustainable Development Goals on Children and the Family, and Their Endorsement by the Holy See," *Voice of the Family*, Feb. 3, 2017, http://voiceofthefamily.com/wp-content/uploads/2017/02/Impact-of-the-United-Nations-Sustainable-Development-Goals22-2-17.pdf.

221. See Roberto de Mattei, "San Pietro: Una basilica oltraggiata," *Corrispondenza Romana*, Dec. 11, 2015, https://www.corrispondenzaromana.it/san-pietro-una-basilica-oltraggiata/.

222. Antonio Socci, "I retroscena della profanazione di San Pietro," *AntonioSocci.com*, Dec. 10, 2015, http://www.antoniosocci.com/i-retroscena-della-profanazione-di-san-pietro-2/.

CHAPTER 4

Favorable to Islam and Migration, but Reluctant to Speak Out for Persecuted Middle Eastern Christians

In Pope Francis's speeches, migration and welcoming are recurrent topics. The intensity of his pronouncements far surpasses those of previous pontiffs. In fact, according to Francis, opening the West to migrants seems to be a non-negotiable principle. Added to this is a policy of dialogue with Islam, whatever the cost. The pope pursues this goal by minimizing Islam's terrorism matrix while showing extreme caution in denouncing the religious nature of the persecution of Christians in Muslim-majority countries.

Unfortunately, the Holy See's slide toward unbridled migration is not new. Laurent Dandrieu documented it abundantly in his book *Église et immigration: Le grand malaise.*[223]

This policy's starting point can be roughly traced back to John XXIII's encyclical *Pacem in Terris*. It stated, "Every human being has the right to freedom of movement and of residence within the confines of his own State. When there are just reasons in favor of it, he must be permitted to emigrate to other countries and take up residence there."[224]

Two essential conditions established by Pius XII, John XXIII's predecessor, are missing in this text. The first was the migrant's extreme need. The second was the host nation's right to restrict access for the sake of the common good.

According to John XXIII, everyone has the right to migrate to "a country in which he hopes to be able to provide more fittingly for himself and his dependents. It is therefore the duty of State officials to accept such immigrants."[225]

Half a century later, that first imbalanced favoring of migrants has grown into an exaltation of immigration as such. For Benedict XVI, "multiethnic and intercultural" societies[226] are signs of the times to express the unity of the human family. More than this, they would be "to some degree an anticipation

---

223. Laurent Dandrieu, *Église et immigration: Le grand malaise—Le pape et le suicide de la civilisation européenne* (Paris: Renaissance, 2017).

224. John XXIII, Encyclical *Pacem in Terris*, Apr. 11, 1963, no. 25, http://w2.vatican.va/content/john-xxiii/en/encyclicals/documents/hf_j-xxiii_enc_11041963_pacem.html.

225. Ibid., no. 106.

226. Benedict XVI, "Message of His Holiness Benedict XVI for the 97th World Day of Migrants and Refugees (2011): 'One Human Family,'" Sept. 27, 2010, http://w2.vatican.va/content/benedict-xvi/en/messages/migration/documents/hf_ben-xvi_mes_20100927_world-migrants-day.html.

and a prefiguration of the undivided city of God."[227] Local populations are criticized for a "nationalist attitude"[228] and the "xenophobia, at times racism, fear and intolerance"[229] they supposedly show.

The Supposed Theological and Redemptive Character of Welcoming Migrants

Under Pope Francis, the imbalance has been exacerbated. He has made his visits to the Mediterranean islands of Lampedusa and Lesbos, and his harsh rebukes on behalf of migrants, one of his pontificate's central planks.

"Between these two islands . . ." says Laurent Dandrieu, "Francis has issued an ocean of statements about migrants in his typically spontaneous, disjointed, and often approximate style." According to the *Valeurs Actuelles* editor, his "speeches are mixed with spectacular and symbolic gestures that eventually form a kind of obsessive hype."[230] For example, in Lampedusa, Pope Francis celebrated Mass on a boat-shaped altar. He brought three Syrian Muslim migrant families back with him on the plane from Lesbos. The pope celebrated Holy Thursday in a migrant center. He washed the feet of twelve migrants, three of which were Muslim. During a general audience, he walked into the throng of pilgrims to greet a dozen young migrants. He brought them onto the dais, and, surrounded by them, stated, "A Christian excludes no one, gives a place to everyone, allows everyone to come!"[231]

In his first message for Migrants Day, Pope Francis said that migration can "open vistas for the growth of a new humanity foreshadowed in the paschal mystery: a humanity for which every foreign country is a homeland and every homeland is a foreign country."[232] His statement misapplied a second-century text which aimed instead to show that, for a Catholic, Heaven is his true home. The early Church never alluded to a Universal Republic as an ideal for mankind.

---

227. Benedict XVI, Encyclical *Caritas in Veritate*, Jun. 29, 2009, no. 7, http://w2.vatican.va/content /benedict-xvi/en/encyclicals/documents/hf_ben-xvi_enc_20090629_caritas-in-veritate.html.

228. Paul VI, Apostolic Letter *Octogesima Adveniens*, May 14, 1971, no. 17, http://w2.vatican.va/content/paul-vi/en/apost_letters/documents/hf_p-vi_apl_19710514_octogesima -adveniens.html. The Vatican site's version mistranslated the French original "*étroitement nationaliste*" as "strictly nationalist."

229. Pontifical Council for the Pastoral Care of Migrants and Itinerant People and Pontifical Council *Cor Unum*, "Welcoming Christ in Refugees and Forcibly Displaced Persons," Jun. 6, 2013, no. 42, http://www.pcmigrants.org/documento%20rifugiati%202013/927-INGL.pdf.

230. Dandrieu, *Église et immigration*, 72.

231. Francis, "General Audience," Jun. 22, 2016, http://w2.vatican.va/content/francesco/en/audiences/2016 /documents/papa-francesco_20160622_udienza-generale.html.

232. Francis, "Message of His Holiness Pope Francis for the World Day of Migrants and Refugees (2014)," Aug. 5, 2013, http://w2.vatican.va/content/francesco/en/messages/migration/documents /papa-francesco_20130805_world-migrants-day.html.

In his book-interview with Dominique Wolton, the pope gave the migration phenomenon a theological dimension: "Our theology is a theology of migrants. Because we all are migrants since the call of Abraham, with all the migrations of the people of Israel, and then Jesus himself was a refugee, an immigrant. Moreover, existentially, because of our faith, we are migrants."[233]

In this commentary, the pontiff again confuses humanity's pilgrimage toward Heaven with the sporadic migrations of individuals, families, or peoples in dire need. Moreover, he fails to state that the Holy Family returned to Nazareth as soon as political conditions allowed it with Herod's death and that the Chosen People saw their successive migrations as a punishment or trial which increased their longings for the Promised Land and their desire to return. Therefore, migration was considered something anomalous and contrary to God's designs.

During the 2017 Christmas Mass, Pope Francis's homily again applied a religious connotation to the welcoming of migrants:

> Mary and Joseph, for whom there was no room, are the first to embrace the One who comes to give all of us our document of citizenship. . . .
> Little Child of Bethlehem, we ask that. . . . your tenderness awaken our sensitivity and recognize our call to see you in all those who arrive in our cities.[234]

Does the Right to Migrate Trump National Security?

On the eve of Hamburg's G20 meeting in July 2017, Pope Francis invited Eugenio Scalfari to Casa Santa Marta for a conversation. Scalfari later said that the pope expressed concern about alliances among the great powers. According to the journalist, when asked to elaborate on this threat, the pontiff responded, "The danger is related to immigration. We, you know, have as the main problem, unfortunately growing in the world today, the poor, the weak, the excluded, of which immigrants are a part. . . . Other [countries] have few local poor, but they fear the invasion of immigrants. That's why the G20 worries me: It strikes a blow at migrants in countries in half of the world, and it hurts them even more as time goes by."[235]

According to Francis, neither fear of invasion nor security concerns should restrict immigration. In his Message for the 104th World Day of Migrants and Refugees, published on January 14, 2018, Francis affirmed: "The principle of

233. Wolton, *Politique et société*, 26–7.

234. Francis, "Homily of His Holiness Pope Francis," Dec. 24, 2017, http://w2.vatican.va/content/francesco/en/homilies/2017/documents/papa-francesco_20171224_omelia-natale.html.

235. Eugenio Scalfari, "Scalfari intervista Francesco: 'Il mio grido al G20 sui migranti,'" *La Repubblica*, Jul. 8, 2017, http://www.repubblica.it/vaticano/2017/07/08/news/scalfari_intervista_francesco_il_mio_grido_al_g20_sui_migranti_-170253225/.

the centrality of the human person . . . obliges us to always prioritize personal safety over national security."[236]

His statement caused consternation. It contradicts the Aristotelian principle embodied in Catholic social doctrine, according to which the common good of society (*koinion sumpheron*) prevails over the private good of individuals.[237] Moreover, the pope's statement is contradictory in itself because, as the *Catechism of the Catholic Church* says, the common good presupposes that "authority should ensure by morally acceptable means the security of society and its members," so that the common good "is the basis of the right to legitimate personal and collective defense."[238]

The few words Pope Francis has uttered recognizing the right of states to regulate migration, seem to echo voters' sentiments in several countries, for example, his January 8, 2018 address to the members of the Diplomatic Corps. However, in themselves, these milder statements are insufficient to counterbalance his strong, relentless hype in favor of widespread migrant acceptance during these past five years.[239]

Moreover, such caution did not prevent the pope from clearly intruding into Italy's immigration policy in his message for the 104th World Day of Migrants and Refugees 2018. Issued amid the discussion of a legislative bill that would grant citizenship to the children of immigrants born in Italy, based on *jus soli*, it stated, "The universal right to a nationality should be recognized and duly certified for all children at birth."[240] According to Most Rev. Ignazio Zambito, bishop emeritus of Patti, the pope-endorsed bill is "inopportune" and "unfortunate." The prelate continued: "We cannot give citizenship, which instead is earned, deserved, obtained with fatigue, by fully and truly embracing the principles, rules, and laws of the host country."[241] Similarly, philosopher Stefano Fontana posited that the papal

---

236. Francis, "Message of His Holiness Pope Francis for the 104th World Day of Migrants and Refugees 2018," Jan. 14, 2018, http://w2.vatican.va/content/francesco/en/messages/migration/documents/papa-francesco_20170815_world-migrants-day-2018.html.

237. "The common good of society is superior to any other interest because it is the creative principle, the conservative element of human society; it follows that every true citizen must desire it and seek it at all cost." Leo XIII, Letter to French Bishops *Notre Consolation,* May 3, 1892, https://w2.vatican.va/content/leo-xiii/fr/letters/documents/hf_l-xiii_let_18920503_notre-consolation.html.

238. *Catechism of the Catholic Church,* no. 1909, http://www.vatican.va/archive/ccc_css/archive/catechism/p3s1c2a2.htm.

239. See Francis, "Address of His Holiness Pope Francis to the Members of the Diplomatic Corps Accredited to the Holy See for the Traditional Exchange of New Year Greetings," Jan. 8, 2018, http://w2.vatican.va/content/francesco/en/speeches/2018/january/documents/papa-francesco_20180108_corpo-diplomatico.html.

240. Francis, "104th World Day of Migrants."

241. Rachele Nenzi, "Il vescovo critica Bergoglio: 'Lo ius soli è sciagurata follia,'" *Il Giornale,* Oct. 19, 2017, http://www.ilgiornale.it/news/cronache/vescovo-critica-bergoglio-ius-soli-sciagurata-follia-1454344.html.

intrusion violated the State's legitimate autonomy in the temporal sphere.[242]

Disregarding Europe's Christian Roots for the Sake of Multiculturalism

In July 2017, responding to the pope's remarks to Eugenio Scalfari, philosopher Marcello Pera, former president of the Italian Senate, stated, "I do not understand this pope. What he says is beyond any rational understanding. . . . Why does he insist on total acceptance? The pope does this because he detests the West. He aspires to destroy it. He does everything to achieve that end."[243]

Indeed, the flip side of the pope's pro-migration stance seems to be a distaste for Europe's Christian identity. In a *La Croix* interview, journalists pointed out that he spoke much of Europe's roots but avoided calling them *Christian*.[244] He replied, "We need to speak of roots in the plural. There are many. In this sense, when I hear about the Christian roots of Europe, I am sometimes afraid of the tone, which can be triumphalist or avenging. That becomes colonialism."[245]

In a similar vein, Francis commented on European culture in his book-interview with Dominique Wolton, saying:

> It has important Christian roots, that is true. But that is not enough to define it.
>
> There are all our capabilities. These abilities to integrate, to receive others. There is also language, within the culture. In our Spanish language, 40% of the words are Arabic [*sic*]. Why? Because they were there for seven centuries. And they left their mark.[246]

In these statements, the pontiff's wishful thinking reaches a climax. In fact, the last edition of the Royal Spanish Academy's dictionary includes more than 93,000 entries.[247] "[Renowned Spanish linguist Rafael] Lapesa's . . . inflated but often-quoted figure of four thousand Arabisms includes formal variants, derivatives

---

242. See Fontana, "Così si cambia."

243. Niccolò Magnani, "Marcello Pera vs papa Francesco/'Bergoglio fa politica, è in atto uno scisma nella Chiesa,'" *Il Sussidiario*, Jul. 10, 2017, http://www.ilsussidiario.net/News/Cronaca/2017/7/10/Marcello-Pera-vs-Papa-Francesco-Bergoglio-fa-politica-e-in-atto-uno-scisma-nella-Chiesa-/773071/.

244. In his November 25, 2014 address to the Council of Europe, Francis mentioned Europe's roots twelve times but never called them Christian. See Francis, "Address of Pope Francis to the Council of Europe," Nov. 25, 2014, http://w2.vatican.va/content/francesco/en/speeches/2014/november/documents/papa-francesco_20141125_strasburgo-consiglio-europa.html.

245. Guillaume Goubert and Sébastien Maillard, "Le pape François à *La Croix*: 'Il faut intégrer les migrants,'" *La Croix*, May 16, 2016, http://www.la-croix.com/Religion/Pape/Pape-Francois-Il-faut-integrer-migrants-2016-05-16-1200760525.

246. Wolton, *Politique et société*, 135.

247. See http://www.rae.es/diccionario-de-la-lengua-espanola/presentacion.

coined within Spanish . . . and the numerous Arabic place names found in Spain."[248] Even that inflated figure represents only 4.3% of the Spanish dictionary, ten times less than the number claimed by Francis.

When receiving the Charlemagne Prize, the pope stated, "The roots of our peoples, the roots of Europe, were consolidated down [through] the centuries by the constant need to integrate in new syntheses the most varied and discrete cultures. The identity of Europe is, and always has been, a dynamic and multicultural identity."[249]

According to the pontiff, European invasions were good for the formation of its identity. Speaking to the director of the progressive Catholic weekly *La Vie*, Francis acknowledged that "today one can speak of Arab invasion. It is a social fact." Then he added optimistically, "How many invasions Europe has known throughout her history! She always knew how to rise again, to go forward and find herself as if magnified by the exchange between cultures."[250] He returned to the subject during his return flight from Lesbos: "Today, Europe must resume this capacity that it has always had, of integrating. Because the nomads, the Normans and many peoples came to Europe and Europe has integrated them and enriched its culture."[251]

Favoring *Jus Soli* to the Detriment of the Civil Authority's Autonomy

The illusory character of Europe's supposedly unlimited capacity to absorb an uninterrupted and massive immigrant flow without detriment to its traditional identity was evident in the Facebook post that Rome's mayor, Virginia Raggi, published on June 13, 2017. The Eternal City's mayor said:

> Rome is under heavy migratory pressure. We cannot continue like this. In the past days, I have sent a letter . . . asking the Interior Ministry for a moratorium on new arrivals of immigrants to the city. . . .
>
> It is time to listen to the Roman citizens: we cannot allow new social tensions. That is why I find it impossible, besides risky, to think

248. Steven N. Dworkin, *A History of the Spanish Lexicon: A Lingusitic Perspective* (New York: Oxford University Press, 2012), 83.

249. Francis, "Address of His Holiness Pope Francis: Conferral of the Charlemagne Prize," May 6, 2016, http://w2.vatican.va/content/francesco/en/speeches/2016/may/documents/papa-francesco_20160506_premio-carlo-magno.html.

250. Jean-Pierre Denis, "Conversation politique avec le pape François," *La Vie*, Mar. 2, 2016, http://www.lavie.fr/religion/catholicisme/conversation-politique-avec-le-pape-francois-02-03-2016-71086_16.php.

251. Francis, "In-Flight Press Conference of His Holiness Pope Francis From Lesbos to Rome," Apr. 16, 2016, http://w2.vatican.va/content/francesco/en/speeches/2016/april/documents/papa-francesco_20160416_lesvos-volo-ritorno.html.

about creating new reception structures.[252]

Despite her moratorium request, at his June 21, 2017 general audience eight days later, the pope expressed his "sincere appreciation" for the "I was a foreigner" campaign, a Radical Party initiative that collected signatures demanding a more liberal immigration law.[253] Unrelenting, at his September 27, 2017 general audience, he welcomed "the representatives of many organizations from civil society engaged in assistance to migrants and refugees who, together with Caritas, have given their support to the petition for a new law on migration better adapted to the current context."[254] He did this despite saying on his return flight from Mexico: "The pope does not interfere with Italian politics. . . . Because the pope is for everyone, and he cannot engage in the practical, domestic politics of one country."[255] He said this in response to a reporter's question about a pending bill to legalize same-sex civil unions.

However, Rome is not an isolated case. Its experiences mirror what is happening in every major European city. Because of this relentless hype to open borders indiscriminately, Catholic bishops everywhere are in solidarity with secular trends wishing to turn Europe into an open space, a land of freedom and human rights. These liberals want the Old Continent to renounce its Catholic past and Christian identity. They want it to become a Euro-Babel, a multi-ethnic and multicultural melting pot, the model for a globalized world.[256]

A Misunderstood Charity Prepares for a Future Submission to Islam
In concrete terms, this means passively accepting the irresponsible mass immigration policies promoted by important European leaders. It entails allowing mostly Islamic immigrant ghettos to form inside European nations. In these enclaves, Muslims refuse to assimilate into the culture of their host countries. They are filled with men who dream of extending the Islamic

252. Virginia Raggi, *Facebook.com*, Jun. 13, 2017, https://www.facebook.com/virginia.raggi.m5sroma/posts/795231333992651:0.

253. Francis, "General Audience," Jun. 21, 2017, http://w2.vatican.va/content/francesco/en/audiences/2017/documents/papa-francesco_20170621_udienza-generale.html.

254. Francis, "General Audience," Sept. 27, 2017, https://w2.vatican.va/content/francesco/en/audiences/2017/documents/papa-francesco_20170927_udienza-generale.html.

255. Francis, "From Mexico to Rome."

256. Throughout history, many utopianists dreamed of abolishing states and building a Universal Republic, from Jan Amos Komensky (17th century) to socialist European M.P. Antonio Giolitti, for whom the United Nations "has finally become an embryo, a first cell of the world government," [Pier Giorgio Betti, "L'utopia del governo mondiale," *L'Unità*, Sept. 4, 1990, pg. 5, col. 4], all the way to baron Jean-Baptiste du Val-des-Grâces, Giuseppe Mazzini, Victor Hugo, Henri de Saint-Simon, Alexandre Saint-Yves d'Alveydre, and Jean-Jacques Servan-Schreiber.

umma to all of Europe. "Who has the right to say that France will not be Muslim in thirty or forty years?" Marwan Muhammad, the spokesman of the Collective against Islamophobia, asked in the Grand Mosque of Orly. "No one in this country has the right to define for us what constitutes the French identity."[257]

Imbibed with this hegemonic pretension, immigrant communities that dominate the urban outskirts of large cities (*banlieues*) have become Salafist hotbeds. In them, young Muslims are radicalized and recruited into the Islamic holy war. These no-go zones pose a permanent threat to the national security of Europe. Consider, for example, the ISIS and al-Qaeda terrorist attacks in France, Belgium, Germany, Spain, and England.

In short, Pope Francis's rhetoric and symbolic gestures continuously encourage Europeans to let their guard down in the face of the threat posed by ongoing, massive invasions by populations who refuse to assimilate. The pope's message is a prelude to chaos if not outright submission to Islam, as Michel Houellebecq's novel of the same name suggests.[258]

"The Church's drama today," Laurent Dandrieu concludes, "is that she often gives Europeans the feeling that the Old Continent is already lost. By reducing Europe's identity to a 'culture of encounter,' the Church seeks to open the continent's gates to forces that threaten to destroy its real identity."[259]

An Idyllic View of Islam That Ignores Its Violent Nature

The promotion of a "culture of encounter"[260] has led Pope Francis to idealize Muhammad's religion. Thus, the pontiff has seemingly tried to exonerate him from responsibility for the violence perpetrated on his behalf.

Pope Francis's rosy vision of Islam was displayed in his first official document, the Apostolic Exhortation *Evangelii Gaudium*. He stated, "We Christians should embrace with affection and respect Muslim immigrants to our countries. . . . Faced with disconcerting episodes of violent fundamentalism, our respect for true followers of Islam should lead us to avoid hateful generalizations, for authentic Islam and the proper reading of the Koran are opposed to every

---

257. Fabien Roland-Lévy, "Islam français, le livre que va scandaliser: Choc. Elisabeth Schemla dénonce la montée de l'islam radical. A tort?" *Le Point*, Apr. 25, 2013, http://www.lepoint.fr/societe/islam-francais -le-livre-qui-va-scandaliser-25-04-2013-1690484_23.php.

258. See Michel Houellebecq, *Submission: A Novel*, trans. Lorin Stein (New York: Farrar, Straus & Giroux, 2015).

259. Dandrieu, *Église et immigration*, 285.

260. Francis, "For a Culture of Encounter: Morning Meditation in the Chapel of the Domus Sanctae Marthae," Sept. 13, 2016, https://w2.vatican.va/content/francesco/en/cotidie/2016/documents/papa -francesco-cotidie_20160913_for-a-culture-of-encounter.html.

form of violence."[261]

Fr. Guy Pagès is a very active evangelizer of Muslims and Internet apologist. In an open letter to Pope Francis, he noted that this pontifical statement contained

> a terrifying inaccuracy. . . .
> [because, according to Muslims,] Allah alone knows the interpre-
> tation of the Koran (Koran 3:7). . . .

This is so because Islam has no magisterial authority. Likewise, the Koran's tolerant verses were abrogated by the "sword verse (Koran 9:5, 29),"[262] and "over half of the Koran's 6,235 verses scorn non-Muslims and manifest the ominous intention of killing or subjecting them."[263] Finally, history and current events flatly belie the pope's claim of Islam's supposedly peaceful nature.

Nevertheless, in a December 21, 2014 letter to Christians in the Middle East, Pope Francis wrote: "The majority of you live in environments which are pre-dominantly Muslim. You can help your Muslim fellow citizens to present with discernment a more authentic image of Islam, as so many of them desire, reit-erating that Islam is a religion of peace."[264]

Moreover, in July 2016, while returning by plane from Krakow's World Youth Day, the pope responded to a question about Fr. Jacques Hamel's "barbaric murder" just days before, while celebrating Mass outside Rouen, saying:

> I don't like to speak of Islamic violence because every day when I open the newspapers I see acts of violence, here in Italy: Someone kills his girlfriend, someone else his mother-in-law. . . . And these vi-olent people are baptized Catholics! They are violent Catholics. . . . If I spoke about Islamic violence, I would also have to speak about Catholic violence. Not all Muslims are violent; not all Catholics are violent. It's like a fruitcake, there's a little bit of everything, there are

261. Francis, *Evangelii Gaudium*, no. 253. It is significant that the pope's claim to Islam's peaceful character was made five months after the diplomatic adviser of the al-Azhar mosque's Grand Imam demanded "a statement [by Pope Francis] affirming that Islam is a peaceful religion," as a condition for resuming diplo-matic relations, which had been interrupted after Benedict XVI's Regensburg address. Benjamin Roger, "Al-Azhar tente de renouer le dialogue avec le Vatican," *Jeune Afrique*, Jun. 7, 2013, http://www.jeuneafrique.com/170368/societe/al-azhar-tente-de-renouer-le-dialogue-avec-le-vatican/.

262. Guy Pagès, "Deuxième lettre ouverte au pape François," *Islam & Verité*, Nov. 27, 2015, http://www.islam-et-verite.com/deuxieme-lettre-ouverte-au-pape-francois/.

263. Ibid. See *Center for the Study of Political Islam*, "Statistical Islam," accessed Aug. 21, 2018, http://www.cspipublishing.com/statistical/pdf/Statistical_Islam.pdf.

264. Francis, "Letter of His Holiness Pope Francis to the Christians in the Middle East," Dec. 21, 2014, http://w2.vatican.va/content/francesco/en/letters/2014/documents/papa-francesco_20141221 _lettera-cristiani-medio-oriente.html.

violent people in these religions. One thing is true: I believe that in almost all religions there is always a small fundamentalist group. Fundamentalist. We have some ourselves. And when fundamentalism gets to the point of killing—and one can kill with the tongue (these are words of the Apostle James, not mine) as well as with a knife . . . I believe that it is not right to identify Islam with violence. It is not right and it is not true. I had a long talk with the Grand Imam at the University of al-Azhar, and I know what they are thinking: they are looking for peace, for encounter.[265]

As Laurent Dandrieu rightly points out:

> Here the will to exempt Islam as such from any complacency toward violence borders on the most complete absurdity through the path of sophistry: For what relationship can there be between private violence . . . led by the passion of jealousy or anger . . . [and] in opposition to the more explicit precepts of one's own religion[266] and a series of systematic, organized attacks done not in spite of Islam but in its name and justified by Koran texts that are not disputed by anyone? . . . Here the pope gives way to a particularly harmful form of cultural relativism by implying that all religions are equated in terms of violence, each harboring in its bosom—as collateral damage— "small fundamentalist groups."[267]

Is Islam a Means of Salvation?

There is worse. For Pope Francis, Islam is not only peaceful but a means of salvation for Muslims. Addressing immigrants at the end of his January 19, 2014 visit to the Roman parish of Sacro Cuore di Gesù a Castro Pretorio, the pontiff said, "It is important that you share . . . the Bible with those who are Christian; the Koran with those who are Muslim. Share with them the faith they have received from their parents. Go forward always. Share your own faith too. God is only one. He is the same. Some [worship Him] in one way, some in another."[268]

---

265. Francis, "In-Flight Press Conference of His Holiness Pope Francis From Poland to Rome," Jul. 31, 2016, https://w2.vatican.va/content/francesco/en/speeches/2016/july/documents/papa-francesco_20160731 _polonia-conferenza-stampa.html.

266. With a bit of irony, Riccardo Cascioli observed: "Perhaps we are distracted, but we never read in any paper's crime section of a man attacking his ex-wife to the cry of 'Long live Christ the King.' Riccardo Cascioli, "Ma chi vuole una guerra di religione?" *La Nuova Bussola Quotidiana*, Aug. 1, 2016, http://www.lanuovabq.it/it/ma-chi-vuole-una-guerra-di-religione.

267. Dandrieu, *L'Église et immigration*, 134–5.

268. Francis, "Bergoglio ai presunti rifugiati: Bibbia e Corano lo stesso Dio, condividere la propria fede," *YouTube*, uploaded Aug. 10, 2015, https://youtu.be/BXaqlOj4qlg.

Pope Francis's repeated expressions idealizing Islam led a large group of former Muslims who converted to Catholicism to write an open letter to the pope on Christmas Day, 2017. Together with friends who signed on, they express their perplexity:

> If Islam is a good religion in itself, as you seem to teach, why did we become Catholic? Do not your words question the soundness of the choice we made at the risk of our lives? . . .
> That the pope seems to propose the Quran as a way of salvation, is that not cause for worry? Should we return to Islam?
> We beg you not to seek in Islam an ally in your fight against the powers that want to dominate and enslave the world, since they share the same totalitarian logic based on the rejection of the kingship of Christ.[269]

Reluctance to Talk About Christian Persecution, Not to Offend Muslim Powers

It is perplexing to note how the pope's friendliness for Islam has been accompanied by an enigmatic discretion when it comes to defending persecuted Christians in Muslim lands. Marc Fromager is the director of the French affiliate of Aid to the Church in Need. He gave an interview to *Le Figaro* online titled, "Are persecuted Christians in the east the great forgotten ones in Pope Francis's discourse?" Fromager stated:

> Eastern Christians tell me they no longer understand anything. They sometimes feel they have been abandoned even by their Christian brothers in the West. . . .
> They have the impression that we do not understand what is happening to them.[270]

The height of this perceived abandonment came during the Islamic State's onslaught on Iraq's Nineveh Plains. The Islamist attack forced 200,000 Christians (and other minorities) to leave their villages. Millions around the world sympathized with the persecuted Christians by adopting the Nazarene symbol—used to identify Christians slated to be killed or expelled.[271] Meanwhile, the Vatican

269. "From Former Muslims Who Became Catholics, and Their Friends, to His Holiness Pope Francis, About His Attitude Toward Islam," Dec. 24, 2017, http://exmusulmanschretiens.fr/en/.

270. Alexis Feertchak, "Les chrétiens persécutés d'orient, grands oubliés du discours du pape François?" *Le Figaro*, Aug. 1, 2016, http://www.lefigaro.fr/vox/religion/2016/08/01/31004-20160801ARTFIG00208-les-chretiens-persecutes-d-orient-grands-oublies-du-discours-du-pape-francois.php.

271. See Heba Kanso, "Symbol of Mideast Oppression Becomes Source of Solidarity," *CBSnews*, Oct. 20, 2014, https://www.cbsnews.com/news/for-christians-symbol-of-mideast-oppression-becomes-source-of-solidarity/.

merely published a simple "note," that was dreadfully late. In it, spokesman Fr. Federico Lombardi, asked the international community, on the pope's behalf, to end the "present humanitarian drama."[272]

> Nothing is said in this cold little statement, [wrote journalist Giuliano Ferrara] about those responsible for these "harrowing events." Not a nod to the causes that forced the "troubled communities" to flee from their villages. . . .
> [It showed] disconcerting reticence in the face of bloodthirsty criminals, [added Antonio Socci] with whom, local bishops say, there is no possibility of dialogue.[273]

What is the reason for this reluctance? Pope Francis himself hinted at it in an interview with the Barcelona daily *La Vanguardia*: "Persecuted Christians are a concern that touches me closely as a pastor. I know many things about persecutions that I do not think it prudent to tell here to not offend anyone. But in some places, it is forbidden to have a Bible, or teach catechism, or carry a cross."[274] In other words, from Francis's own lips one learns that his reluctance in speaking out against the persecution of Christians is to not offend Muslim authorities.

Pope Francis's extreme caution has long been a source of bewilderment. He has avoided taking a firm stand in the case of Asia Bibi, a Catholic Pakistani mother condemned to death for an alleged blasphemy against Muhammad that she never uttered. Despite numerous and prolonged requests that he speak out in her defense, the pontiff never mentioned that heroic woman by name. At an April 2015 public audience, he limited himself to a quick handshake with the victim's husband and daughter. Many Vatican observers and commentators immediately noticed the gesture and pointed it out. Finally, in February 2018, to diminish the scandal caused by the pope's sidestepping of this crucial issue, papal advisers organized a private audience with Asia Bibi's relatives. One of the many Nigerian students kidnapped by the Islamist movement Boko Haram also attended that audience. Mrs. Bibi's tragedy had moved the world. The pope addressed it merely in one tweet.

Also, while making little reference to the repulsive terrorist attack against Christian mothers and children after an Easter 2016 celebration in Lahore,

---

272. "Dichiarazione del Direttore della Sala Stampa a nome del Santo Padre," *Holy See Press Office*, Aug. 7, 2014, https://press.vatican.va/content/salastampa/it/bollettino/pubblico/2014/08/07/0559/01234.html. (Our translation of the Italian original.)

273. Antonio Socci, "Iraq, Antonio Socci: I cristiani muoiono e papa Francesco sta in silenzio," *Libero Quotidiano*, Aug. 11, 2014, http://www.liberoquotidiano.it/news/sfoglio/11671032/Iraq—Antonio-Socci—i.html.

274. Henrique Cymerman Benarroch, "Entrevista al Papa Francisco: 'La secesión de una nación hay que tomarla con pinzas,'" *La Vanguardia*, Jun. 12, 2014, http://www.lavanguardia.com/internacional /20140612/54408951579/entrevista-papa-Francis.html.

Pakistan, Pope Francis expressed his solidarity with the victims' families. However, he carefully avoided condemning the perpetrators or denouncing their Christianophobic motives. He simply called it "an abominable attack."[275]

This was not an isolated case. The pontiff said nothing when the young Sudanese mother Meriam Yahia Ibrahim was imprisoned with her young children. She was sentenced to death for one reason alone: She was Christian. After her release, thanks solely to international pressure, the pope received her.[276] Sandro Magister's August 2014 evaluation that Pope Francis is repeating his behavior toward evangelicals in Argentina, remains valid:

> Not to fight their leaders, but to make them his friends.
> This is the same approach that he has adopted with the Muslim world: prayer, invocation of peace, general condemnations of the evil that is done, but with careful attention to keep his distance from specific cases concerning precise persons, whether victims or butchers.[277]

This consistent behavior led analyst Alexandre del Valle to comment early on in the current pontificate: "Pope Francis's silence about the new Christianophobia and his Islamically correct professions of faith will not stop death penalties for 'apostates' and other persecutions of Christians in Pakistan, Syria, North Africa, or elsewhere."[278]

"A 'Dialogue' Based on Complacency, Compromise, and Duplicity"

This very worldly prudence does not stem from ignorance. Well-known Catholic Islamicists have warned against the illusory nature of this "policy of the extended handed." For example, after Father Hamel's assassination in France and the terrorist attacks in Germany, Egyptian Jesuit Fr. Samir Khalil Samir, professor emeritus at Rome's Pontifical Oriental Institute and one of the world's leading Islamicists, stated: "We also must have the courage to say that Islam has elements of violence in the Koran and in the life of Muhammad. If we continue to say that

275. Francis, "Regina Cæli," Mar. 28, 2016, http://w2.vatican.va/content/francesco/en/angelus/2016/documents/papa-francesco_regina-coeli_20160328.html.

276. See Elise Harris, "Meriam Ibrahim Lands in Rome, Meets With Pope Francis," *Catholic News Agency*, Jul. 24, 2014, https://www.catholicnewsagency.com/news/meriam-ibrahim-lands-in-rome-meets-with-pope-francis-76068.

277. Sandro Magister, "The Strange Silences of a Very Talkative Pope," trans. Matthew Sherry, *L'Espresso–Settimo Cielo*, Aug. 1, 2014, http://chiesa.espresso.repubblica.it/articolo/1350853bdc4.html?eng=y.

278. Alexandre Del Valle, "Christianophobie: Le calvaire des chrétiens dans le monde," *Atlantico*, Apr. 1, 2013, http://www.atlantico.fr/decryptage/christianophobie-calvaire-chretiens-dans-monde-alexandre-del-vall-685762.html/page/0/1.

'Islam is a religion of peace,' we only create confusion and mystification."[279]

After the Palm Sunday 2017 slaughter in Egypt, when questioned by the *National Catholic Register*'s Edward Pentin on whether Islamism is true Islam, Father Samir replied: "ISIS ['Islamic State'] is the application of what is taught. It's not outside Islam, or something invented. No, they are applying Islam. When we hear it has nothing to do with Islam—that it means *salaam*; that it means peace—this is all false. It's not true. ISIS is not doing anything which is neither in the Quran nor in the Mohammedan tradition."[280]

The assessment of Egyptian Jesuit Henri Boulad was even more incisive. He is a former president of Caritas for North Africa and the Middle East. In an interview with *Le Figaro*, he deplored the "monumental disingenuousness" of some theologians and bishops who "ignore the systematic plan of Islam to conquer the planet." He fears that gestures such as bringing three Muslim families on the papal plane back from Lesbos "are viewed by Islam as signs of weakness." "The pope should take more into account the sensitivity of Eastern Christians. They feel marginalized and barely consulted in the dialogue with Muslims."[281]

After the Palm Sunday Islamist attack on Coptic Christians, Father Boulad said:

> **I accuse** Islam of being the cause of this barbarity and of all acts of violence committed in the name of the Muslim faith. I accuse not only terrorists or terrorism. I accuse not only the Muslim Brotherhood or the nebula of small groups that gravitate around this violent and totalitarian jihadist confraternity. I accuse not only Islamism or radical and political Islam.
>
> **I merely accuse** Islam, which is political and radical by its very nature.
>
> As I wrote more than twenty-five years ago, Islamism is Islam without disguise, in all its logic and rigor. . . .
>
> **I accuse** the Catholic Church of maintaining with Islam a 'dialogue' based on complacency, compromise, and duplicity. After more than fifty years of one-way initiatives, such monologue is today in neutral [gear].[282]

279. Samir Khalil Samir, "Fr. Samir: Islamic Terror in France and Germany a Crisis of Integration, but Above All of Politics," *AsiaNews.it*, Jul. 26, 2016, http://www.asianews.it/news-en/Fr-Samir:-Islamic-terror-in-France-and-Germany-a-crisis-of-integration,-but-above-all-of-politics-38144.html.

280. Edward Pentin, "Father Samir: Egypt's Palm Sunday Terror Reflects a Sickness Within Islam," *National Catholic Register*, Apr. 13, 2017, http://www.ncregister.com/daily-news/father-samir-egypts-palm-sunday-terror-reflects-a-sickness-within-islam.

281. Jean-Marie Guénois, "Migrants: les coulisses de l'opération controversée du Pape," *Le Figaro*, May 6, 2016, http://www.lefigaro.fr/actualite-france/2016/05/06/01016-20160506ARTFIG00277-migrants-les-coulisses-de-l-operation-controversee-du-pape.php.

282. François Sweydan, "Père Henri Boulad: 'Attentats contre les chrétiens coptes dimanche des ramaux: J'accuse l'Islam,'" *Dreuz.info*, Apr. 19, 2017, http://www.dreuz.info/2017/04/19/pere-henri-boulad-attentats-contre-les-chretiens-coptes-dimanche-des-ramaux-jaccuse-lislam/.

CHAPTER 5

Religious Indifferentism, Philosophical Relativism, Theological Evolutionism

One of the most expressive signs of a paradigm shift in Francis's pontificate has been the primacy of praxis[283] replacing the traditional primacy of doctrine. There has been talk of a "pastoral about-face" in the Church. The pope has set aside theological issues for the sake of pastoral care. He has embraced a theological evolutionism according to which nothing is certain and permanent in time. Instead, everything changes with the historical-cultural context. This was evident in the celebrations for the 500th anniversary of Luther's so-called Reformation.

We closed the previous chapter with Father Boulad's critique of the Church's pernicious and ineffective relationship with Islam. It could be applied just as well to Catholic dialogue with other Christian religions, Judaism, and Eastern pagan religions. This dialogue too is based on "complacency, compromise, and duplicity." It also instills religious indifferentism and doctrinal relativism in the minds of the Catholic faithful.

"There Is No Catholic God," "We Are All Children of God"

The most visible manifestation of this deviation was the disturbing video portraying the pope's January 2016 intentions for the Worldwide Prayer Network. This first video was a new initiative that was widely disseminated on social media. It featured a Buddhist, a Jew, a Catholic priest, and a Muslim taking turns by saying, "I confide in Buddha," "I believe in God," "I believe in Jesus Christ," and "I believe in God, Allah." They are followed by Pope Francis, who says: "Many think differently, feel differently, seeking God or meeting God in different ways. In this crowd, in this range of religions, there is only one certainty we have for all: We are all children of God."[284] Then, the pope gave the month's prayer intention, "that sincere

---

283. *Praxis*: of Latin and Greek origin, it is used in philosophy and political science to describe the process by which a theory, teaching, or aptitude can be applied or embodied. Immanentist and evolutionist schools of thought, such as Marxism, defend the primacy of praxis over theory, which is supposedly incapable of following the unceasing transformation of reality.

284. Pope's Worldwide Prayer Network, "Inter-religious Dialogue," *Holy Cross TV*, Jan. 8, 2016, https://www.youtube.com/watch?v=XODAb0ImTKg.
    In addition to the final scene's disturbing symbolism, there are three serious errors in this short text:
    (1) The statement that all men are "children of God." Fr. Ignace de la Potterie wrote: "Divine sonship is always a gratuitous gift of grace and cannot preclude grace bestowed gratuitously in baptism and recognized and embraced in the faith." Ignace de la Potterie, "Men Are Not Born Sons of God. They Become So," *30Days*, 12–2009, http://www.30giorni.it/articoli_id_22029_l3.htm.

dialogue among men and women of different faiths, may produce fruits of peace and justice." At the same time, each of the religious representatives presented a symbol of their respective creed. The final scene shows those symbols together. The arrangement places the Buddha statue in the highest position, below which is placed, the *masbaha* (Islamic prayer beads), with the Christ Child at the bottom, next to the menorah (the seven-branched candelabra of Judaism).

Pope Francis reportedly made two more disturbing statements that are consistent with the interconfessionalism promoted by this video. Both statements are found in his first celebrated interview with Eugenio Scalfari. The October 2013 conversation was transcribed by *La Reppublica* and republished in both *L'Osservatore Romano* and the Vatican's website. In it, the pope asserted problematically: "I believe in God, not in a Catholic God, there is no Catholic God, there is God."[285] The second statement is found later in the interview. Smiling at the idea of trying to convert the atheistic reporter, the pope said: "Proselytism[286] is solemn nonsense, it makes no sense. We need to get to know each other, listen to each other and improve our knowledge of the world around us."[287]

The pope developed this idea in his book-interview with Dominique Wolton:

---

(2) One can seek God in various ways. However, one cannot "find God in many ways." There is only one way to find God and that is in the one, true, and revealed religion, the Holy Roman Catholic Church, founded by Our Lord Jesus Christ.

(3) There is not just "one certainty for all." There are many other religious certainties. They are obtained both by reason and by the true faith. They start with the existence of a personal God (which Buddhists deny). Canon 2, "On Revelation," of the First Vatican Council's Dogmatic Constitution *Dei Filius*, decreed, "If anyone says that the one, true God, our creator and lord, cannot be known with certainty from the things that have been made, by the natural light of human reason: let him be anathema." Vatican Council I, Dogmatic Constitution *Dei Filius*, Apr. 24, 1870, can. 2, no. 1, in Norman P. Tanner, SJ, ed., *Decrees of the Ecumenical Councils* (Washington: Georgetown University Press, 1990), 2:810, https://www.ewtn.com /library/councils/v1.htm#4.

285. Simone Sereni, "'God Is Not Catholic': And According to Some, Neither Is the Pope," *Aleteia*, Oct. 7, 2013, https://aleteia.org/2013/10/07/god-is-not-catholic-and-according-to-some-neither-is-the-pope/.

286. From the context of this interview and other uses he makes of the word, it follows that Pope Francis condemns *proselytism* not just in the word's negative sense, namely, the use of dishonest means to attract new co-religionists, but even in the word's legitimate meaning, that is, the apostolate, missionary activity aimed at bringing a person from another religion or none to the Catholic Church, using only loyal and persuasive means. Incidentally, in this second and entirely correct meaning, proselytism was wrongly condemned in the 1993 joint Catholic-Orthodox Balamand declaration and in the "Joint Declaration of Pope Francis and Patriarch Kirill of Moscow and All Russia" in Havana in February 2016. The latter document improperly condemned *uniatism* for that very reason: "It is today clear that the past method of 'uniatism,' understood as the union of one community to the other, separating it from its church, is not the way to reestablish unity." "Joint Declaration of His Holiness Pope Francis and His Holiness Kirill, Patriarch of Moscow and All Russia," Feb. 12, 2016, no. 25, https://w2.vatican.va/content/francesco/en/speeches/2016/february/documents /papa-francesco_20160212_dichiarazione-comune-kirill.html.

287. Scalfari, "Così cambierò la Chiesa"; Jimmy Akin, "Did Pope Francis Just Say That Evangelization Is 'Nonsense'? 8 Things to Know and Share," *National Catholic Register*, Oct. 1, 2013, http://www.ncregister.com/blog/jimmy-akin/did-pope-francis-just-say-that-evangelization -is-nonsense-8-things-to-know.

> Proselytism destroys unity. And that is why interreligious dialogue does not mean that everyone agrees: No, it means walking together, each with his own identity. . . . But the master of oppositions, of bipolar tensions as we say, is [Romano] Guardini, who teaches us this path of unity in diversity. What happens with fundamentalists today? Fundamentalists close themselves up in their own identity and want to hear nothing else. . . .
>
> Go to Africa, where there are so many missionaries. They spend their entire lives there. They make true revolutions. Not to convert—that was in another time when one talked about conversion—but to serve.[288]

This last sentence proves that Pope Francis's earlier criticism of proselytism was not aimed at spurious methods of persuasion, which harm the evangelizing effort. Instead, he meant the very intent of attracting non-Catholics to the true Faith. How does he reconcile that with Our Lord's Great Commission to the Apostles, prior to his Ascension: "Go ye into the whole world, and preach the Gospel to every creature" (Mark 16:15)?

Luther a "Reformer" Who "Offered the Church a Remedy"?

The audience Pope Francis granted in the Vatican on October 13, 2016—the opening day of the Fatima centennial year—to a thousand Lutherans was another disconcerting symbolic gesture. After receiving their gift, a lavish copy of Luther's heretical 95 theses, the pope spoke to them wearing a stole with inscriptions that alluded to the quincentennial of Luther's revolt, while flanked by a statue of the heresiarch in a place of honor. Extending to adult Lutherans a status that is held only by those who are in full communion with the Catholic Church, the pope said, "The Apostle Paul tells us that, by virtue of our baptism, we all form the one Body of Christ. . . . Let us continue with confidence on our ecumenical journey, because we know that, beyond the many open questions that still separate us, we are already united."[289]

---

288. Wolton, *Politique et société*, 36–7, 153.

289. Francis, "Address of His Holiness Pope Francis to Participants in the Pilgrimage of Lutherans," Oct. 13, 2016, https://w2.vatican.va/content/francesco/en/speeches/2016/october/documents/papa-francesco_20161013_pellegrinaggio-luterani.html.

   During his visit to Rome's Evangelical Lutheran church, Francis had evoked that same idea that Catholics and Lutherans are already united. Answering a question from a woman who is married to a Catholic and who expressed bitterness that the two were not "able to partake together in the Lord's Supper," the pope answered ambiguously. He implied that it was a personal decision for her to take in conscience: "It is true that in a certain sense sharing is saying that there are no differences between us, that we have the same doctrine—I underline the word, a difficult word to understand—but I ask myself: don't we have the same Baptism? And if we have the same Baptism, we have to walk together. . . . When you pray together, that Baptism grows, it becomes strong; when you teach your children who Jesus is, why Jesus came, what Jesus did, you do the same, whether in Lutheran or Catholic terms, but it is the same. The question: and the Supper? There are questions to which

Previously, the pope allowed Fr. Raniero Cantalamessa, OFM, Cap., Preacher to the Papal Household, to assert in his presence during the 2016 Good Friday ceremony:

---

only if one is honest with oneself and with the few theological 'lights' that I have, one must respond the same, you see. . . . I respond to your question only with a question: how can I participate with my husband, so that the Lord's Supper may accompany me on my path? It is a problem to which each person must respond. A pastor friend of mine said to me: 'We believe that the Lord is present there. He is present. You believe that the Lord is present. So what is the difference?'—'Well, there are explanations, interpretations . . .' Life is greater than explanations and interpretations. Always refer to Baptism: 'One faith, one baptism, one Lord,' as Paul tells us, and take the outcome from there. I would never dare give permission to do this because I do not have the authority. One Baptism, one Lord, one faith. Speak with the Lord and go forward. I do not dare say more." Francis, "Responses of the Holy Father to the Questions of Three Members of the Evangelical Lutheran Community of Rome," Nov. 15, 2015, https://w2.vatican.va/content/francesco/en/speeches/2015/november/documents/papa-francesco_20151115_chiesa-evangelica-luterana.html.

Inspired by these words, the sixty German bishops present at the meeting of the German Bishops' Conference held February 19–22, 2018, approved, by an overwhelming majority (only 13 bishops voted against), the issuing of a pastoral handout prepared by the Commission for Ecumenism titled, "On the Path of Unity With Christ: Confessional Marriages and Joint Participation in the Eucharist." The document deems mixed Catholic-Lutheran couples a "practical laboratory of unity." It provides an opening for the reception of Holy Communion by the Protestant spouse, invoking the "grave spiritual necessity" mentioned in canon 844 of the 1983 *Code of Canon Law*. On the eve of this work's final editing, seven German bishops, including the cardinal-archbishop of Cologne, wrote a letter to the Congregation for the Doctrine of the Faith asking it to clarify if the desire to share the Eucharist in order to favor ecumenism could be considered, *yes* or *no*, as a "grave spiritual necessity," and whether the Bishops' Conference of a single country could take an isolated decision in a matter that affects the faith and practice of the universal Church. See Edward Pentin, "Complete Letter of Seven German Bishops on Holy Communion for Protestant Spouses Published," *National Catholic Register*, Apr. 25, 2018, http://www.ncregister.com/blog/edward-pentin/full-text-of-seven-german-bishops-letter-on-intercommunion-for-protestant-s.

The Holy See convened the leadership of the German Bishops' Conference to Rome for a meeting. During the same, the prefect of the Congregation for the Doctrine of the Faith officially declared, according to the communiqué issued by the Secretariat for Communications, that Pope Francis "appreciates the ecumenical commitment of the German bishops and asks them to find, in a spirit of ecclesial communion, a unanimous result, if possible." "Communiqué, 03.05.2018," *Holy See Press Office*, May 3, 2018, http://press.vatican.va/content/salastampa/en/bollettino/pubblico/2018/05/03/180503e.html.

Cardinal Willem Eijk, archbishop of Utrecht and president of the Bishops' Conference of The Netherlands, deemed the pope's answer "completely incomprehensible." The prelate said, "The Church's doctrine and practice regarding the administration of the Sacrament of the Eucharist to Protestants is perfectly clear. . . . The differences between faith in consubstantiation and that of transubstantiation are so great that one must really demand that someone who wishes to receive Communion explicitly and formally enters into full communion with the Catholic Church . . . and in this way explicitly confirms his acceptance of the faith of the Catholic Church, including the Eucharist." Edward Pentin, "Cardinal Eijk: Pope Francis Needed to Give Clarity on Intercommunion," *National Catholic Register*, May 7, 2018, http://www.ncregister.com/blog/edward-pentin/cardinal-eijk-pope-needed-to-give-clarity-to-german-bishops-on-intercommuni. As far as the cardinal is concerned, Pope Francis should have simply informed the German delegation of what the *Code of Canon Law* and the *Catechism of the Catholic Church* clearly stipulate in this matter.

For his part, Cardinal Gerhard Müller, prefect emeritus of the Congregation for the Doctrine of the Faith, pointed out that the possibly unanimous result the Vatican asked the German bishops to attain cannot contradict the Catholic faith: "One cannot separate the Catholic faith from a unanimous understanding. If that separation happened, we would then have a schism in the Catholic Church." Walter Sánchez Silva, "Cardeal Müller sobre comunhão para protestantes: Não se pode contradizer a fé católica," *ACIDigital*, May 8, 2018, https://www.acidigital.com/noticias/cardeal-muller-sobre-comunhao-para-protestantes-nao-se-pode-contradizer-a-fe-catolica-56387.

The righteousness of God is that by which God makes those who believe in his Son Jesus acceptable to him. It does not enact justice but makes people just.

Luther deserves the credit for bringing this truth back when its meaning had been lost over the centuries, at least in Christian preaching, and it is this above all for which Christianity is indebted to the Reformation, whose fifth centenary occurs next year.[290]

On October 31, 2016, just a fortnight after the disturbing meeting in the Paul VI Audience Hall, the pope went to Lund, Sweden, where the current secretary of the Lutheran World Federation resides. The pope went there to mark the beginning of the year of the quincentennial of Luther's rupture with the Church. The event's official aim was "expressing the gifts of the Reformation and asking forgiveness for the division which followed theological disputes."[291] Paolo Ricca, a Waldensian theologian and pastor, explained the journey's symbolic scope: "The participation at the commemoration is a gesture of great relevance. Because the pope is going to Lund, to the home of the Lutherans, as if he were one of the family. My impression is, in a way I wouldn't know how to define, that he also feels part of that portion of Christianity born of the Reform."[292] Commenting on the pope's homily in Lund, German Lutheran theologian Thomas Schirrmacher later stated that "from [his] point of view, on that occasion, Francis interpreted Luther's thinking better than most Lutheran bishops."[293]

---

290. Raniero Cantalamessa, OFM, Cap., "'Be Reconciled to God'–Good Friday Sermon, 2016, in St. Peter's Basilica," *Cantalamessa.org*, Mar. 26, 2016, http://www.cantalamessa.org/?p=3050&lang=en. This perspective had a bearing on Pope Francis's journey to Fatima, where he stated: "Great injustice is done to God's grace whenever we say that sins are punished by his judgment, without first saying—as the Gospel clearly does—that they are forgiven by his mercy! Mercy has to be put before judgment and, in any case, God's judgment will always be rendered in the light of his mercy. Obviously, God's mercy does not deny justice, for Jesus took upon himself the consequences of our sin, together with its due punishment. He did not deny sin, but redeemed it on the cross. Hence, **in the faith that unites us to the cross of Christ, we are freed of our sins**; we put aside all fear and dread, as unbefitting those who are loved (cf. 1 John 4:18)." Francis, "Greeting of the Holy Father: Blessing of the Candles—Pilgrimage of His Holiness Pope Francis to the Shrine of Our Lady of Fatima," May 12, 2017, https://w2.vatican.va/content/francesco/en/speeches/2017/may/documents/papa-francesco_20170512_benedizione-candele-fatima.html. (My emphasis.) For a deeper understanding of this convergence, see Fr. Stefano Carusi, "L'influsso di Lutero dietro la 'tesi Kasper'? Un aspetto del recente sinodo sulla famiglia," *Disputationes Theologicae*, Dec. 21, 2014, http://disputationes-theologicae.blogspot.fr/2014/12/linflusso-di-lutero-dietro-la-tesi.html; "Praise for Martin Luther at St. Peter's Basilica: 'Martin Luther Had Brought the Truth to Light Again,'" *The Eponymous Flower*, Mar. 27, 2016, http://eponymousflower.blogspot.com/search/label/Father%20Cantalamessa.

291. "Pope Francis to Go to Sweden for the 500th Anniversary of the Protestant Reformation," *L'Osservatore Romano*, Jan. 25, 2016, http://www.osservatoreromano.va/en/news/pope-francis-go-sweden-500th-anniversary-protestan.

292. Roberto de Mattei, "To Which Church Does Pope Bergoglio Belong?" trans. Francesca Romana, *Rorate Cæli*, Oct. 19, 2016, https://rorate-caeli.blogspot.com/2016/10/de-mattei-to-which-church-does-pope.html.

293. Thomas Schirrmacher, "Wie protestantisch ist der papst?" *Zeit*, Oct. 27, 2017, http://www.zeit.de/2017/44/thomas-schirrmacher-protestantismus-martin-luther-papst-franziskus.

In fact, the pope's sympathy for the German heresiarch was apparent during the press conference he gave on his return flight from Armenia. He stated:

> I think that Martin Luther's intentions were not mistaken; he was a reformer. . . . The Church was not exactly a model to emulate. There was corruption and worldliness in the Church; there was attachment to money and power. That was the basis of his protest. He was also intelligent, and he went ahead, justifying his reasons for it. . . .
>
> He offered a "remedy" for the Church, and then this remedy rigidified in a state of affairs, a discipline, a way of believing, a way of acting, a mode of liturgy.[294]

Pope Francis believes such stiffening is not an attack on unity, but an enrichment for the Church. He made this clear to members of the Pentecostal Church of Reconciliation during his July 28, 2014 visit to Caserta, Italy:

> The Church is one in diversity. And, to use a beautiful word of an Evangelist whom I love very much, a diversity "reconciled" by the Holy Spirit. . . .
>
> We are in the epoch of globalization, and we think about what globalization is and what unity would be in the Church: perhaps a sphere, where all points are equidistant from the center, all equal? No! This is uniformity. And the Holy Spirit doesn't create uniformity! What shape can we find? Let us consider a prism: the prism is unity, but all its parts are different; each has its own peculiarity, its charisma. This is unity in diversity. It is on this path that we Christians do what we call by the theological name of ecumenism.[295]

---

294. Francis, "In-Flight Press Conference of His Holiness Pope Francis From Armenia to Rome," Jun. 26, 2016, https://w2.vatican.va/content/francesco/en/speeches/2016/june/documents/papa-francesco_20160626_armenia-conferenza-stampa.html.

295. Francis, "Address of Pope Francis: Private Visit of the Holy Father to Caserta for a Meeting With the Evangelical Pastor Giovanni Traettino," Jul. 28, 2014, https://w2.vatican.va/content/francesco/en/speeches/2014/july/documents/papa-francesco_20140728_caserta-pastore-traettino.html.
    Many Protestants do not share the implicit relativism of this concept of ecumenism. For example, Pedro Tarquis, member of the committee for the celebration of the 500th anniversary of the Reformation in Spain, declared to *Religión Digital*: "In essence, nothing has changed. . . . If Luther were rehabilitated, the pope would cease to exist as such." Asked about the possibility of a communion without absorption, Tarquis replied, "I see this as impossible today, except in some very superficial evangelical denomination that does not care about the underlying problem. I would say that 90% of Protestant evangelicals worldwide, not only in Spain, would be absolutely against [it] because of the great differences [that remain]. It would be like saying that because the Partido Popular and Podemos have the same constitution they could unite in the same party." Jesús Bastante, "'Esperamos que los actos conmemorativos sean un testimonio de que somos una Iglesia viva," *Periodista Digital*, Jul. 8, 2017, http://www.periodistadigital.com/religion/otras-confesiones/2017/07/08/religion-iglesia-confesiones-500-anos-reforma-protestante-pedro-tarquis-esperamos-que-los-actos-conmemorativos-sean-un-testimonio-de-que-somos-una-iglesia-viva.shtml.

The contradiction between the errors of the Lutheran heresy and the dogmas of the Catholic faith seem of little importance to Pope Francis. Presumably, this is because he does not believe that Truth is abstract and absolute, but pragmatic and variable. In fact, in that same encounter with the Pentecostals, the pope stated, "Brother Giovanni [the local pastor who hosted the pope] said something that I completely share: The truth is an encounter, an encounter between people. Truth is not found in a laboratory, it is found in life."[296]

"The Word of God Is a Dynamic Reality"

Supposedly, this would also be true for understanding and adhering to Divine Revelation. As Pope Francis explained to Fr. Antonio Spadaro in a famous interview at the beginning of his pontificate, "Ours is not a 'lab faith,' but a 'journey faith,' a historical faith. God has revealed himself as history, not as a compendium of abstract truths."[297] Hence, the Church's new synodality would consist in "an attitude of listening and discernment of all that the Spirit moves in the consciousness of the people of God."[298]

Pope Francis developed this evolutionary conception of Divine Revelation further during a meeting to celebrate the 25th anniversary of the 1992 *Catechism of the Catholic Church*:

> Only a partial vision regards the "deposit of faith" as something static. The word of God cannot be mothballed like some old blanket in an attempt to keep insects at bay! No. The word of God is a dynamic and living reality that develops and grows because it is aimed at a fulfillment that none can halt. . . .
>
> Doctrine cannot be preserved without allowing it to develop, nor can it be tied to an interpretation that is rigid and immutable without demeaning the working of the Holy Spirit.[299]

On that occasion, in contrast with the Church's traditional teaching as reiterated in the *Catechism*—which, as seen, was the reason for the celebration—Pope Francis made a concrete application of his vision of a dynamic deposit of faith: "It must be clearly stated that the death penalty is an inhumane measure

---

296. Francis, "Private Visit to Caserta."

297. Spadaro, "A Big Heart."

298. Francis, "Il Papa: 'La Chiesa missionaria non si chiuda in se stessa,'" *Corriere della Sera*, Oct. 19, 2015, http://www.corriere.it/cronache/15_ottobre_19/papa-francesco-la-chiesa-missionaria-non-si-chiuda -se-stessa-2973aab8-7620-11e5-9086-b57baad6b3f4.shtml.

299. Francis, "Address of His Holiness Pope Francis to Participants in the Meeting Promoted by the Pontifical Council for Promoting the New Evangelization," Oct. 11, 2017, http://w2.vatican.va/content/francesco/en /speeches/2017/october/documents/papa-francesco_20171011_convegno-nuova-evangelizzazione.html.

that, regardless of how it is carried out, abases human dignity. It is per se contrary to the Gospel."[300]

The Death Penalty's Legitimacy Has Been Church Teaching for 2,000 Years

Edward Feser, co-author with Joseph Bessette of *By Man Shall His Blood Be Shed: A Catholic Defense of Capital Punishment*, reacted to Pope Francis's statement that the death penalty is "per se contrary to the Gospel," in an article published in *The Catholic Herald*.

He states that Revelation cannot teach errors in matters of faith and morals and "Yet there are a great many passages in Scripture that teach the legitimacy of capital punishment." He also affirms that "the Fathers of the Church understood such passages to be sanctioning capital punishment, and the Church has for two thousand years consistently followed this interpretation," and that the First Vatican Council teaches that "Catholics are obliged to interpret Scripture consistent with the way the Fathers understood it, and consistent with the Church's traditional interpretation."

He concludes, saying, "Taken together, these teachings logically entail that the legitimacy of capital punishment is regarded by the Church as a divinely revealed doctrine." (Edward Feser, "'The Pope's Remarks on Capital Punishment Need to Be Clarified," *The Catholic Herald*, Oct. 15, 2017, http://www.catholicherald.co.uk/commentandblogs/2017/10/15/the-popes-remarks-on-capital-punishment-need-to-be-clarified/.)

Also, Pope Innocent III required Waldensian heretics to affirm this teaching's legitimacy as a condition of their readmission to the Church.

Nothing above prevents public authority, at a given epoch, from making a prudential decision not to include the death penalty in its criminal code.

One finds another application of his understanding of Catholic teaching's evolutionary nature in his Wolton book-interview. Regarding just war, he said:

> Even today we must ponder well the concept of "just war." In political philosophy, we learned that to defend oneself, one can wage war and consider it as just. But, can we call it "just war"? Or rather

---

300. Ibid.

"defensive war"? Because peace is the only just thing. . . .
No war is just. The only thing just is peace.[301]

Such statements collide with no. 2309 of the *Catechism of the Catholic Church*. There, the *Catechism* reiterates the Church's traditional teaching going back to Saint Augustine. It lists the conditions for the moral legitimacy of just war.[302]

Truth as a Superior Synthesis of Real-Life Tensions
At the beginning of the dialogue between Eugenio Scalfari and Pope Francis, the pontiff responded to a Scalfari editorial with his "Letter to a Non-believer." The pope had been asked whether there is an absolute truth. He was asked further if it is wrong to think that there are only some relative and subjective truths. The pontiff replied: "I would not speak about 'absolute' truths, even for believers, in the sense that absolute is that which is disconnected and bereft of all relationship. Truth, according to the Christian faith, is the love of God for us in Jesus Christ. Therefore, truth is a relationship. As such each one of us receives the truth and expresses it from within, that is to say, according to one's own circumstances, culture and situation in life, etc."[303]

Aware of the relativistic implications of his thought, the pope had previously qualified, "This does not mean that truth is variable and subjective, quite the contrary. But it does signify that it comes to us always and only as a way and a life." However, this qualification does not eliminate the subjectivist perspective of the pontiff's concept of truth. If truth is not presented as an objective expression of reality (*esse id quod est*, as Saint Augustine says), but instead is "always and only" (i.e., exclusively) as a necessarily individual path and life, then it loses its universal and absolute character by which it is valid for all men, situations, and time. Each person would grasp truth exclusively according to his own situation and history. Truth *would* be variable and subjective. Logically speaking, Pope Francis's qualification is useless.

The pontiff's tendency to relativism becomes even more explicit in his final,

301. Wolton, *Politique et société*, 57–8.

302. See *Catechism*, no. 2309.

303. Francis, "Letter to a Non-believer: Pope Francis Responds to Dr. Eugenio Scalfari Journalist of the Italian Newspaper 'La Repubblica,'" Sept. 4, 2013, http://w2.vatican.va/content/francesco/en/letters/2013/documents/papa-francesco_20130911_eugenio-scalfari.html.
  In a sermon at Santa Marta, the pope expressed the same idea of truth being *situation-based*. He stated, "Paul did not tell the Athenians: 'This is the encyclopedia of truth. Study it and you will have the truth.' No! Truth does not fit into an encyclopedia. Truth is an encounter, an encounter with the Supreme Truth: Jesus, the great truth. No one owns the truth. Truth is received in the encounter." Kelen Galvan, "Papa diz que para evangelizar, cristãos devem construir pontes e não muros," *Cançao Nova*, May 8, 2013, https://noticias.cancaonova.com/especiais/Francis/papa-diz-que-para-evangelizar-cristaos-devem-construir-pontes-e-nao-muros/.

Hegelian-flavored appeal: "We must have a correct understanding of the terms and, perhaps, in order to overcome being bogged down by conflicting absolute positions, we need to redefine the issues in depth."[304]

In a part of the Wolton book-interview that deals with communication and ecumenism, one finds this insightful exchange:

> Pope Francis: [One must] not be afraid of tensions. How do you solve a tension? On the upper plane.
> Dominique Wolton: It is the German philosopher, Hegel, that . . .
> Pope Francis: Hegel makes the synthesis. I say something else: That the synthesis is done on a plane superior to the two parties. And what we find in the higher plane retains the two initial points of view at its root. Because life is always in tension, it is not in the synthesis. The synthesis is not really vital. The tension, yes, is vital.[305]

In another passage of this same book-interview, Francis affirms that he learned this mysterious concept of synthesis in the works of Romano Guardini, whom he considers the master of "bipolar tensions," which pave the way for "unity in diversity." However, he must explain how this is to be reconciled with the inviolable principle of non-contradiction (a synthesis that does not resolve the previous discrepancy).[306]

This relativism undergirding Pope Francis's thought was identified by agnostic intellectual Zygmunt Bauman. Commenting on the "Letter to a Non-believer," Bauman wrote:

> Employing "truth" in the singular in a polyphonic world is like trying to applaud with one hand. With one hand you can only slap or caress, but not applaud. Pope Francis not only preaches the need for dialogue but practices it. A true dialogue between people with explicitly different points of view who communicate to understand each other. . . . [307]

Scalfari agreed with Bauman's assessment:

> Pope Francis is, therefore, one of the very few vicars of Christ who

---

304. Francis, "Letter to a Non-believer."

305. Wolton, *Politique et société*, 240.

306. See page 138.

307. Zygmunt Bauman, "Se il Papa ama il dialogo vero più della verità," *La Repubblica*, Oct. 21, 2014, http://ricerca.repubblica.it/repubblica/archivio/repubblica/2014/10/21/se-il-papa-ama-il-dialogo -vero-piu-della-verita53.html.

guides the Church after two thousand years, one of the very few—in my view the only one—that deals in this way with the problem of Truth and, therefore, of the absolute. . . .

What about truth? The pope rejects the word "relativism," in the sense of a specific movement with characteristics of religious politics, but he does not reject the word "relative." No to relativism; but the Pope acknowledges the fact that the truth is relative.[308]

Truth as a Vital and Pragmatic Relationship

Based on these premises, one understands why Pope Francis wrote in the Apostolic Exhortation *Evangelii Gaudium* that "realities are greater than ideas."[309] The pope affirmed that this concept is one of the four principles which guide his actions.

In theory, this postulate can have a Thomistic interpretation.[310] Indeed, the pope quotes St. Thomas's adage, "*adaequatio intellectus ad rem*" in his exhortation. This means that conceptual elaborations are at the service of understanding and conducting reality. However, in the sociological-pastoral context in which it is inserted, the postulate takes on a very different connotation. As Fr. Giovanni Scalese explained, "It rather means that we should accept reality as it is, without intending to change it on the basis of absolute principles, for example, moral principles, which are only abstract 'ideas' that most of the time risk being turned into ideology."[311]

In fact, as Father Scalese pointed out, "this postulate is at the basis of Francis's

---

308. Eugenio Scalfari, "Il Vicario di Cristo e la verità relativa che conduce a Dio," *La Repubblica*, Oct. 28, 2014, http://www.repubblica.it/cultura/2014/10/28/news/il_vicario_di_cristo_e_la_verit_relativa_che_conduce_a_dio-99162795/.

309. Francis, *Evangelii Gaudium*, nos. 231, 233. Prof. Giovanni Turco says, "Taking a closer look at it, more than principles here you have presuppositions, undemonstrated and indemonstrable points of view that evoke nothing metaphysic but exist exclusively in function of praxis, as happens with ideologies: We can call it 'pragmatic 'transcendentalism.'" Giovanni Turco, "[Da leggere] alcune linee guida per la lettura filosfica del pontificato di Bergoglio," *Radio Spada*, Jun. 25, 2017, https://www.radiospada.org/2017/06/da-leggere-alcune-linee-guida-per-la-lettura-filosofica-del-pontificato-di-bergoglio/, republished summary of "Axes de lecture philosophique de textes du pontificat actuel," *Courrier de Rome* 593 (Nov. 2016), https://laportelatine.org/publications/presse/courrier_de_rome/2016/1611cdr593.pdf.

310. This is how Fr. Giovanni Cavalcoli interpreted it in his essay titled, "La dipendenza dell'idea dalla realtà nella *Evangelii Gaudium* di papa Francesco," *PATH* (2/2014), 13:287–316, http://www.cultura.va/content/dam/cultura/docs/pdf/accademie/path/2-2014.pdf.

311. Giovanni Scalese, "I postulati di papa Francesco," *Antiquo Robore*, May 10, 2016, no. 6b, http://querculanus.blogspot.fr/2016/05/i-postulati-di-papa-francesco.html.
    However, as Fr. Scalese adroitly puts it, "in human action, one is inevitably guided by some principles that are abstract by their nature. It is no use therefore to argue about the abstract character of 'doctrine,' opposing to it a 'reality' to which one should simply conform. If reality is not enlightened, guided, ordered by some principles, it risks breaking into chaos." Ibid., no. 8.

continuing polemic against doctrine."[312] According to Cardinal Carlo Caffarra, however, "A Church that doesn't pay enough attention to doctrine isn't a more pastoral Church, but a more ignorant Church."[313]

According to Prof. Giovanni Turco, the new pontifical language "gives rise to Bergoglio's profound thought: Truth is a relationship. It is not the relationship's criterion but its product. Therefore, truth is *relative* in the full sense of the word. It is clear that such a relationship is not understood in the Thomistic sense as *adequatio rei et intellectus*, but as a vital and pragmatic relationship that derives from a situation. Thus understood, truth has no content of its own. It cannot be 'absolute,' that is, 'always valid.' For this very reason, it ceases to be truth (and becomes mere opinion)!"[314]

This relativistic postulate also undergirds the pope's praxis and pastoralism. What Roberto de Mattei says of the new modernist's way of thinking can be applied to Pope Francis: "The traditional maxim according to which '*agire sequitur esse*' [action follows being] is stood on its head: action precedes Being, and man finds truth and faith itself in action," and, therefore, "the mysteries of faith starting from the consciousness of man, from his needs, his aspirations, from all that springs from his experience of life."[315]

---

312. Ibid., no. 6b.

    For example, he cites these phrases by the pope that show some aversion to doctrine: "It is true that in a certain sense sharing is saying that there are no differences between us, that we have the same doctrine—I underline the word, a difficult word to understand—but I ask myself: don't we have the same Baptism?" Francis, "Responses to Three Members"; "The view of the Church's teaching as a monolith to defend without nuance or different understandings is wrong." Spadaro, "A Big Heart"; "Rather than offering the healing power of grace and the light of the Gospel message, some would 'indoctrinate' that message, turning it into 'dead stones to be hurled at others.'" Francis, Apostolic Exhortation *Amoris Laetitia*, Mar. 19, 2016, no. 49, https://w2.vatican.va/content/dam/francesco/pdf/apost_exhortations/documents/papa-francesco _esortazione-ap_20160319_amoris-laetitia_en.pdf; "Our teaching on marriage and the family cannot fail to be inspired and transformed by this message of love and tenderness; otherwise, it becomes nothing more than the defense of a dry and lifeless doctrine." Ibid., no. 59. For more, see Giovanni Scalese, "Dottrina vs discernimento," *Antiquo Robore*, Apr. 18, 2017, http://querculanus.blogspot.fr/2017/04/dottrina-vs -discernimento.html.

313. Matteo Matzuzzi, "Only a Blind Man Can Deny That There's Now in the Church Great Confusion," trans. Juliana Freitag, *Caffarra.it*, Jul. 21, 2018, http://www.caffarra.it/eng140117.php.

314. Giovanni Turco, "[Da leggere] alcune linee guida."

315. Roberto de Mattei, "Roberto de Mattei Double-Post: 'Meltdown of the Church' and a Response: 'The Process That Has Led Us to the New Modernists,'" trans. Fr. Richard Cipolla, *Rorate Cœli*, Dec. 1, 2013, https://rorate-caeli.blogspot.com/2013/12/roberto-de-mattei-double-post-meltdown.html.

CHAPTER 6

A New, Subjective Morality
Without Absolute Imperatives

Public statements and gestures made by the Pontiff and those close to him reveal a drastic paradigm shift in the moral field. A new interpretation of the Encyclical Humanae Vitae—*now being debated—and countless openings in sexual matters, in general, plow a deep furrow in the Church's unchangeable magisterium and discipline. The copious use of ambiguous expressions leaves the ordinary faithful with a confused impression that the Church is caving into the Sexual Revolution.*

Philosophical relativism and the primacy of praxis inevitably lead to ethical relativism, according to which there are no moral absolutes.

Eugenio Scalfari posed a question, "Your Holiness, is there a single vision of the Good? And who decides what it is?"

The pope responded:

> Each of us has a vision of good and of evil. We have to encourage people to move toward what they think is Good. . . .
>
> [And the pope added, e]veryone has his own idea of good and evil and must choose to follow the good and fight evil as he conceives them.[316]

The controversial Apostolic Exhortation *Amoris Laetitia*, which will be analyzed later in more detail, welcomed this relativization of moral absolutes. For now, suffice it to note that paragraph 303 said that, "individual conscience needs to be better incorporated into the Church's praxis in certain situations which do not objectively embody our understanding of marriage." The papal document stated further that, in an objective situation of adultery, a person may find that continuing to live *more uxorio* (i.e., as husband and wife), "for now is the most generous response which can be given to God, and come to see with a certain moral security that it is what God himself is asking amid the concrete complexity of one's limits, while yet not fully the objective ideal."[317]

On August 5, 2017, Prof. Josef Seifert published an article in the German theological and philosophical journal *AEMAET* titled with the question: "Does

---

316. Eugenio Scalfari, "The Pope: How the Church Will Change," *La Repubblica*, Oct. 1, 2013, http://www.repubblica.it/cultura/2013/10/01/news/pope_s_conversation_with_scalfari _english-67643118/.

317. Francis, *Amoris Laetitia*, no. 303.

Pure Logic Threaten to Destroy the Entire Moral Doctrine of the Catholic Church?" He says that no. 303 of *Amoris Laetitia* is:

> a moral theological atomic bomb that threatens to tear down the whole moral edifice of the Ten Commandments and of Catholic moral teaching....
>
> [He goes on to explain this dramatic statement:] If only one case of an intrinsically immoral act can be permitted and even willed by God, must this not apply to all acts considered "intrinsically wrong"? . . .
>
> Must then not from pure logic euthanasia, suicide, or assistance to it, lies, thefts, perjuries, negations or betrayals of Christ, like that of St. Peter, or murder, under some circumstances and after proper "discernment," be good and praiseworthy because of the complexity of a concrete situation (or because of a lack of ethical knowledge or strength of will)?[318]

Regarding adultery, the bishop of Como, Italy, has already taken that step. In a pastoral note on "remarried" divorcees living *more uxorio* he stated that, "each conjugal act [*sic*] remains an 'objective disorder,' but it is not necessarily a 'grave sin' that prevents one from fully welcoming the life of grace."[319] In his turn, in an opinion titled "Moral Theological Deepening," which was attached to the bishop's Pastoral Note, moralist Msgr. Angelo Riva categorically stated that such adulterous relations "are not sins. They are good acts of conjugal life."[320]

High-Ranking Prelates Confirm Moral Paradigm Shift
The Vatican secretary of state, Cardinal Pietro Parolin, confirmed the radical nature of this new understanding of morality in an interview with *Vatican News*,

318. Josef Seifert, "Does Pure Logic Threaten to Destroy the Entire Moral Doctrine of the Catholic Church?" *AEMAET* 6, no. 2 (2017): 5–7, http://www.aemaet.de/index.php/aemaet/article/view/44/pdf_1. Because of that article, the archbishop of Granada illegitimately and illegally dismissed Prof. Seifert from the chair of Realist Phenomenology of the International Academy of Philosophy, of which he was the founder. It was a first example of what Prof. Claudio Pierantoni called "the beginning of the official persecution of orthodoxy within the Church." Claudio Pierantoni, "Josef Seifert, Pure Logic, and the Beginning of the Official Persecution of Orthodoxy Within the Church," *AEMAET* 6, no. 2 (2017): 22, http://www.aemaet.de/index.php/aemaet/article/view/46/pdf_1.

319. Diocesi di Como, "Nota pastorale per l'attuazione del cap. VIII di *Amoris Laetitia*: Accompagnare, discernere e integrare le fragilità," Feb. 14, 2018, no. 20, https://famigliechiesacomo.files.wordpress.com/2018/02/diocesicomo_notapastorale_capviii_al2.pdf.

320. Angelo Riva, "Approfondimento di teologia morale in margine alla nota pastorale per l'attuazione del cap. VIII di Amoris Laetitia," Jan. 30, 2018, p. 23, https://famigliechiesacomo.files.wordpress.com/2018/02/approfondimentoteologiamorale_30gennaio2018_donangeloriva.pdf; "Linee guida crescono da una periferia all'altra, i 'dubia' sempre più ignorati," *Chiesa e Post Concilio*, Mar. 18, 2018, https://chiesaepostconcilio.blogspot.fr/2018/03/linee-guida-crescono-da-una-periferia.html.

a media outlet launched by the Holy See's new Secretariat for Communication. He stated that *Amoris Laetitia* represents "a new paradigm" through which the pope calls for "a change in attitude," "a paradigm shift, and the text [of *Amoris Laetitia*] itself insists on this, that's what is asked of us—this new spirit, this new approach" to deal pastorally with the marital situations examined in the document.[321]

This idea had already been proposed by Cardinal Walter Kasper in an article published by the magazine *Stimmen der Zeit*, in November 2016, under the title, "*Amoris Laetitia*: Bruch oder aufbruch?" (*Amoris Laetitia*: Rupture or the beginning of a journey?). Cardinal Kasper says that "one only understands *Amoris Laetitia* if one understands the paradigm shift that it undertakes,"[322] which consists, he says, in shifting from a moral of the law to Saint Thomas Aquinas's moral of the virtues, or rather his own misreading of the latter.[323] The same idea of paradigm shift was already present in the book *Amoris Laetitia: Wendepunkt für die Moraltheologie?* (*Amoris Laetitia*: A turning point in moral theology?), written in 2016 by Stephan Goertz and Caroline Witting, professors of Moral Theology at the University of Mainz, Germany.

Cardinal Blase Cupich, archbishop of Chicago, made the same assessment in a February 2018 lecture at the University of Cambridge, England, titled, "Pope Francis's Revolution of Mercy: *Amoris Laetitia* as a New Paradigm of Catholicity." Six criteria underlie the new paradigm. The first is:

> families are a privileged place of God's self-revelation and activity, then no family should be considered deprived of God's grace. . . .

---

321. Alessandro Gisotti, "Card. Parolin: Il 2018 di Francesco all'insegna di giovani e famiglia," *Vatican News*, Jan. 11, 2018, 09:30, https://www.vaticannews.va/it/vaticano/news/2018-01/card--parolin--il-2018 -di-francesco-allinsegna-di-giovani-e-fami.html#play; Edward Pentin, "Cardinal Parolin: *Amoris Laetitia* Represents New Paradigm, Spirit and Approach," *National Catholic Register*, Jan. 11, 2018, http://www.ncregister.com/blog/edward-pentin/cardinal-parolin-amoris-represents-new -paradigm-new-spirit-new-approach.

322. Walter Kasper, "'Amoris Laetitia': Bruch oder aufbruch?" *Stimmen der Zeit* 11 (Nov. 2016), http://www.stimmen-der-zeit.de/zeitschrift/ausgabe/details?k_beitrag=4752128&cnid=13&k _produkt=4754046.

323. "Sometimes one opposes the moral of the law to the moral of virtue because one sees the former as the expression of an outward desire, and the latter, as a call to interiority. This opposition is not founded on the *Summa Theologiae*, in which the treatise on law follows the treatise on virtue, and in which virtuous works are the object of precepts and consist of instructions equally directed to the intellect and the will, thereby showing man how to achieve, with divine grace, the perfection of his created and redeemed being." Jacques Etienne, "Loi et grâce: Le concept de la loi nouvelle dans la *Somme théologique* de S. Thomas d'Aquin," *Revue théologique de Louvain* 16, no. 1 (1985): 18– 9, https://www.persee.fr/doc/thlou_0080-2654_1985_num_16_1_2089; see Basil Cole, OP, "Thomism, Moral Claim and Amoris Laetitia," *Anthropotes* 33 (2017): 313–26, http://www.istitutogp2.it/public/Basil%20Cole%20OP_Anthropotes%202017-1_estratto.pdf.

[since] whenever there is a family striving to live together and to love one another, the Spirit is already present.[324]

George Weigel is the well-known biographer of John Paul II. He replied to Cardinal Cupich in a *First Things* article, stating that the "evolution of the Church's understanding of the Gospel over the centuries is not a matter of 'paradigm shifts,' or ruptures, or radical breaks and new beginnings; it's a question of what theologians call the development of doctrine," which must be "organic and in continuity with 'the faith once . . . delivered to the saints.'"[325]

Loose Phrases and Symbolic Gestures
That, in Practice, Relativize Moral Mandates

Pope Francis confirms this moral relativism through highly symbolic gestures. The first was his response to a journalist's question on the return flight from Rio de Janeiro, after the World Youth Day. It has become a kind of motto of his pontificate. The journalist mentioned widely documented homosexual moral scandals in Montevideo, Uruguay involving Msgr. Battista Ricca, a close collaborator of the pope, and asked how the pope intended to:

> confront the whole question of the gay lobby? . . .
>
> [The pope replied:] I see that many times in the Church, over and above this case, but including this case, people search for "sins from youth," for example, and then publish them. . . . But if a person, whether it be a lay person, a priest or a religious sister, commits a sin and then converts, the Lord forgives, and when the Lord forgives, the Lord forgets. . . . So much is written about the gay lobby. I still haven't found anyone with an identity card in the Vatican with "gay" on it. They say there are some there. . . . If someone is gay and is searching for the Lord and has good will, then who am I to judge him?[326]

By shifting from the issue of sinful homosexual *relations*, at the heart of the question, to the homosexual *tendency*, which can be involuntary, the pope seemed to imply in his imprecise language that he judges neither same-sex attracted people nor those who engage in homosexual relations. That was how the media interpreted the phrase "who am I to judge?" and trumpeted it to the four corners

---

324. Cupich, "Revolution of Mercy," 6–7.

325. Weigel, "The Catholic Church Doesn't Do 'Paradigm Shifts.'"

326. Francis, "Press Conference of Pope Francis During the Return Flight: Apostolic Journey to Rio de Janeiro on the Occasion of the XXVIII World Youth Day," Jul. 28, 2013, http://w2.vatican.va/content/francesco /en/speeches/2013/july/documents/papa-francesco_20130728_gmg-conferenza-stampa.html.

of the world. This received no subsequent papal rectification. In several cases, both Catholic legislators and voting citizens approved bills and ballot measures favoring the legalization of homosexual unions. When doing so, they rationalized their actions claiming that they could not be "more papist than the pope."[327]

In January 2015, Francis received in audience at his Santa Marta residence a transsexual from Plasencia, Spain named Neria Lejárraga, who tried to assume a male identity. In a letter to the pontiff, she had complained that after having undergone sex-change surgery she was rejected by Catholics in her city. The pope called her by telephone and invited her to visit him at the Vatican, with all expenses paid by the Apostolic Nunciature in Madrid. He received her in the company of her so-called *fiancée*.[328] In his press conference on the plane returning from Georgia and Azerbaijan, the pope described the meeting in detail. In his narrative, the pope used the masculine pronoun when referring to Neria. "He, who had been she, but is he."[329] Never did he condemn her sex change and planned "marriage" to another woman.

Equally disconcerting, the pope granted an audience to his former student Yayo Grassi, accompanied by his homosexual partner, the Indonesian Iwan Bagus, at the Washington, D.C. Nunciature. The pontiff cordially embraced the two in front of the cameras. A subsequent note published by the Holy See Press Office aggravated this scandal. The communiqué stated, "The only real audience granted by the pope at the Nunciature was with one of his former students and his family [sic]."[330] The note thereby downgraded to the status of a "brief greeting" the pope's meeting with Kim Davis, the renowned Rowan County Clerk, from Kentucky, who suffered jail time for having refused to register homosexual unions.

Even more egregious was the official reception at the Apostolic Palace of Xavier Bettel, Prime Minister of Luxembourg, who was accompanied by his homosexual partner, architect Gauthier Destenay. The two contracted a civil union in 2010, then "married" in 2015, when same-sex "marriage" was legalized in the Grand Duchy. The visit's pretext was the meeting of European leaders in the Eternal City to celebrate the 60th anniversary of the Treaty of Rome (the

327. Lisa Bourne, "Pope Francis: Don't Be 'More Papist Than the Pope,'" *LifeSiteNews*, Apr. 28, 2017, https://www.lifesitenews.com/news/francis-blasts-critics-for-defending-catholic-teaching-dont-be-more-papist.

328. See "El Papa recibe en audiencia privada a un transexual español," *El País*, Jan. 27, 2015, http://politica.elpais.com/politica/2015/01/27/actualidad/1422355975_624238.html.

329. Francis, "In-Flight Press Conference of His Holiness Pope Francis From Azerbaijan to Rome," Oct. 2, 2016, http://w2.vatican.va/content/francesco/en/speeches/2016/october/documents/papa-francesco_20161002_georgia-azerbaijan-conferenza-stampa.html.

330. Fr. Federico Lombardi, dir., "Statement Regarding a Meeting of Pope Francis and Mrs. Kim Davis at the Nunciature in Washington, DC," *Holy See Press Office*, Oct. 2, 2015, https://press.vatican.va/content/salastampa/it/bollettino/pubblico/2015/10/02/0749/01616.html.

first building block for today's European Union).[331] Pablo Iglesias, leader of the Spanish ultra-leftist party Podemos, immediately tweeted a photo of the reception, with the caption, "Xavier Bettel, Prime Minister of Luxembourg, received at the Vatican with his husband. And here [cardinal] Cañizares [archbishop of Valencia] says that gays go to hell." Bettel responded immediately with his own tweet: "It was a pleasure and an honor for me and Gauthier to be welcomed by the leader of the Catholic Church."[332]

Similar anomalies have taken place regarding artificial birth control methods. The pope has allowed unchallenged circulation of statements attributed to him that are contrary to Church teaching. The statement of Sr. Martha Pelloni, a Teresian Carmelite Missionary nun, was a disturbing example. She is a teacher and founder of aid organizations for peasants. During a talk show on the decriminalization of abortion in Argentina, she stated to *Radio Cut* (Corrientes, Argentina), "There must be responsible parenthood, planning." She went on to add, "Speaking of this theme, Pope Francis used three words with me: *preservativo, transitorio, reversible* [meaning contraceptive, temporary, reversible]. A diaphragm, and, if there is no alternative, we counsel peasant women to have . . . a tubal ligation."[333]

Another Argentine nun, Sr. Lúcia Caram, who lives in Catalonia, Spain, and defends abortion and same-sex "marriage,"[334] asserted to the media that in a meeting with the pope he told her to "keep wreaking havoc."[335]

The Vatican Publishes Scandalous Sex Education Textbook
Relativistic preaching from a pope's lips, highlighted by extremely symbolic gestures, only aggravates the "moral fluidity"[336] of society today. This moral

331. See Cecilia Rodriguez, "Pope Francis' Welcome to World's Only Openly Gay Prime Minister Rekindles Vatican Controversy," *Forbes*, Apr. 9, 2017, https://www.forbes.com/sites/ceciliarodriguez/2017/04/09/pope-franciss-welcome-to-worlds-only-openly-gay-prime-minister-rekindles-vatican-controversy.

332. "Pablo Iglesias cree que los obispos españoles no entenderían esta foto," *HuffingtonPost.es*, Mar. 25, 2017, http://www.huffingtonpost.es/2017/03/25/pablo-iglesias-obispos-foto_a_22011379/.

333. Hemos Visto, "Martha Pelloni: El Papa le habría recomendado el preservativo," *Adelante la Fe*, Apr. 3, 2018, 8:52–9:10, https://adelantelafe.com/martha-pelloni-el-papa-le-habria-recomendado-preservativos-diafragma-o-ligadura-de-trompas/; Martha Pelloni: 'En Corrientes el índice de pobreza es muy grande," *Radiocut.fm*, 8:52–9:10, https://radiocut.fm/audiocut/martha-pelloni-en-corrientes-el-indice-de-pobreza-es-muy-grande/.

334. See Ignacio A. Castillo, "La Iglesia no debe meterse en la decisión de una mujer de abortar; ni siquiera Dios, que por algo nos hizo libres," *La Opinión de Málaga*, Jan. 23, 2014, http://www.laopiniondemalaga.es/sociedad/2014/01/23/iglesia-debe-meterse-decision-mujer/647536.html.

335. German Parga, "El Papa Francisco le pide a Lucía Caram que 'siga armando lío,'" *20Minutos.es*, Oct. 6, 2016, https://www.20minutos.es/noticia/2856412/0/papa-Francis-sor-lucia-caram-lio/.

336. "'La Verità' intervista Aldo Maria Valli: 'Un papa non può guidare la Chiesa con i 'forse,' i 'dipende,' i 'però,'" *Le Cronache di Papa Francesco*, Jan. 7, 2017, https://cronicasdepapafrancisco.com/2017/01/07/la-verita-intervista-aldo-maria-valli-un-papa-non-puo-guidare-la-chiesa-con-i-forse-i-dipende-i-pero/. The expression is Aldo Maria Valli's.

relativism in society is reaching unimagined levels with disastrous consequences for the individual faithful, families, and for public morality—the foundation of life together.

The publication of an unusual sex education textbook was yet another
harmful case. Printed in several languages, it was made available to participants of the 2016 World Youth Day, in Krakow, Poland.

The Pontifical Council for the Family produced the noxious book before its
merger into a new mega-dicastery. At the time, Archbishop Vincenzo Paglia
led the Council. The Catholic University of Saint Anthony of Murcia, in Spain,
collaborated in the book's writing. Titled *The Meeting Point*, it is divided into
six units. It claims to be a "Project for Affective and Sexual Formation," in response to Pope Francis's call in *Amoris Laetitia*,[337] from which it quotes extensively. It supposedly takes into account progress made in the fields of
psychology and pedagogy. However, it makes no mention of the Ten Commandments (not even the Sixth and Ninth). Nor does it mention the sinful and
unnatural character of homosexual relations.

Movements that fight hedonistic sexual education programs promoted by international organizations and against the pro-abortion lobby have been rightly
scandalized by the textbook's sensual and graphically explicit character.[338]

American psychiatrist Rick Fitzgibbons is an assistant professor at the John
Paul II Institute for Marriage and Family Studies at the Catholic University of
America, with forty years of professional experience. He wrote:

> In a culture in which youth are bombarded by pornography, I was
> particularly shocked by the images contained in this new sex educa-
> tion program, some of which are clearly pornographic. My immediate
> professional reaction was that this obscene or pornographic ap-
> proach abuses youth psychologically and spiritually.
>
> Youth are also harmed by the failure to warn them of the long-
> term dangers of promiscuous behaviors and contraceptive use. As a
> professional who has treated both priest perpetrators and the victims
> of the abuse crisis in the Church, what I found particularly troubling
> was that the pornographic images in this program are similar to

337. Pontifical Council for the Family, *The Meeting Point: Project for Affective and Sexual Formation*, July
19, 2016.

338. See Pete Baklinski, "Vatican Sex Ed 'Surrenders' to Sexual Revolution: Life and Family Leaders React,"
LifeSiteNews, Jul. 29, 2016, https://www.lifesitenews.com/news/vatican-surrenders-to-sexual-revolution-
with-release-of-sex-ed-program-life; Stephanie Block, "The Poverty That Is the Vatican's New Sexual Education Program," *Spero Forum*, Aug. 4, 2016, http://www.speroforum.com/a/BZZBFMQVUF52/78494
-The-poverty-that-is-the-Vaticans-new-sexual-education-program.

those used by adult sexual predators of adolescents.[339]

Judy Brown, president of the American Life League, said in a press release, "It's bad enough when Planned Parenthood pushes perverse forms of sex education into our schools. For the Vatican to jump on that bandwagon is a nightmare scenario. Someone must be asleep at the wheel, and it's high time for them to wake up."[340]

"Reinterpreting" *Humanae Vitae* to Legitimize Artificial Birth Control

This year is the fiftieth anniversary of *Humanae Vitae*. Thus the Holy See set up a work team to study the history of the encyclical's writing, coordinated by Msgr. Gilfredo Marengo. In September 2015, he wrote an article for *Vatican Insider* that was meaningfully titled, "*Humanae Vitae* and *Amoris Laetitia*: Parallel stories." In it, the author wondered if "the controversial game 'yes to the pill—no to the pill' as well as the current 'yes to Communion for remarried divorcees—no to Communion for remarried divorcees' is nothing but the surfacing of much more discomfort and fatigue in the fabric of ecclesial life."[341]

According to Prof. Roberto de Mattei, this initiative is part of an orchestrated plan to "reinterpret" *Humanae Vitae* to accept the use of artificial methods of birth control in some cases.[342]

The encyclical's golden anniversary was marked by a lecture series at the Gregorian University in Rome. The third lecture of the series, titled, "Re-reading *Humanae Vitae* (1968) in Light of *Amoris Laetitia* (2016),"[343] was delivered on December 14, 2017, by moralist Fr. Maurizio Chiodi. He is a member of the abovementioned special work team. In his talk, he defended the thesis that "one can understand how in situations in which these [methods] are impossible or impracticable other forms of responsibility must be found: these

339. Rick Fitzgibbons, "Psychiatrist: The Vatican's Sex Ed Is the Most Dangerous Threat to Youth I've Seen in 40 Years," *LifeSiteNews*, Sept. 2, 2016, https://www.lifesitenews.com/opinion/exclusive-the-new-threat-to-catholic-youth-the-meeting-point.

340. Pete Baklinski, "Petition Urges Pope Francis to Withdraw 'Nightmare' Vatican Sex-Ed Program," *LifeSiteNews*, Aug. 22, 2016, https://www.lifesitenews.com/pulse/catholic-pro-life-org-launches-petition-asking-pope-francis-to-withdraw-nig.

341. Gilfredo Marengo, "'Humanae Vitae e Amoris Laetitia, storie parallele,'" *La Stampa–Vatican Insider*, Mar. 23, 2017, http://www.lastampa.it/2017/03/23/vaticaninsider/ita/commenti/humanae-vitae-e-amoris-laetitia-storie-parallele-Mqg9RCXIpwtYnj9ajItpdO/pagina.html.

342. Roberto de Mattei, "De Mattei: The Plan of 'Reinterpretation' for Humanae Vitae," trans. Francesca Romana, *Rorate Cæli*, Jun. 14, 2017, https://rorate-caeli.blogspot.com/2017/06/de-mattei-plan-of-reinterpretation-for.html.

343. Diane Montagna, "New Academy for Life Member Uses Amoris to Say Some Circumstances 'Require' Contraception," *LifeSiteNews*, Jan. 8, 2017, https://www.lifesitenews.com/news/new-academy-for-life-member-uses-amoris-to-say-some-circumstances-require-c.

'circumstances,' for responsibility, require other methods of birth control. In these cases, 'technological' intervention [that is, the artificial methods condemned by the encyclical] does not deny the responsibility of the procreating relationship."[344]

In a January 9, 2018 statement, Prof. Josef Seifert commented, "The situation ethics Fr. Chiodi defends would also deny the intrinsic wrongness of abortion and euthanasia, and of many other acts listed in *Veritatis Splendor* as acts that are morally wrong under all circumstances and in all situations." He expressed the hope that "Pope Francis, Archbishop Paglia, and the large majority of members of PAV will ask Father Chiodi to revoke these grave errors, or to resign immediately his membership in this illustrious Academy."[345] Unfortunately, so far nothing has happened. . .

Toward *De Facto* Acceptance of Same-Sex Unions
Following Italy's approval of the Cirinnà law, which legalized same-sex civil unions, Pope Francis, in his book-interview with French intellectual Dominique Wolton, declared himself favorable to them:

> What to think of same-sex marriage? "Marriage" is a historical word. It has always been a man and a woman in humanity and not only in the Church. That cannot be changed. . . .
> That cannot be changed. It's the nature of things. They are like this. Let's call it civil unions. . . .
> Let's say things as they are: Marriage is a man with a woman. That is the precise term. Let's call the same-sex union a "civil union."[346]

It is surprising that Francis affirms that "marriage is a historical word" as if it were a human, not a divine institution. The immutability of marriage does not derive from the fact that it has always been this way in history, but from the Divine will. This is all the more so since Our Lord Jesus Christ Himself restored marriage to its original dignity, elevating it to the dignity of Sacrament. His proposal to call a partnership founded on unnatural vice a "civil union" is equally disconcerting, for it legitimizes such unnatural unions in the eyes of

344. Sandro Magister, "Goodbye, 'Humanae Vitae.' Francis Liberalizes the Pill," trans. Matthew Sherry, *L'Espresso–Settimo Cielo*, Jan. 30, 2018, http://magister.blogautore.espresso.repubblica.it/2018/01/30/goodbye-humanae-vitae-francis-liberalizes-the-pill/.

345. Maike Hickson, "Professor Seifert Comments on Fr. Chiodi's 'Re-Reading of Humanae Vitae,'" *OnePeterFive*, Jan. 9, 2018, https://onepeterfive.com/professor-seifert-comments-fr-chiodis-re-reading-humanae-vitae/.

346. Wolton, *Politique et société*, 321–2.

the public, especially the youth.[347]

In this context, one understands better the announcement by Bishop Brendan Leahy of Limerick, Ireland: "Gay couples must be made welcome at next year's World Meeting of Families in Ireland." Organized by the new Dicastery for the Laity, Family, and Life, the meeting is scheduled for August 21–26, 2018, and the pope is expected to attend. "We are living in changing times and family too is changing," the bishop said.[348]

The organizing committee released a promotional video in which Most Rev. David Gerard O'Connell, a native of Cork, Ireland who is now auxiliary bishop of Los Angeles, states:

> Pope Francis, he gets it. He gets it that our society has changed so much in the last couple of generations.
>
> We have all sorts of configurations of families now, whether it's just the traditional family of mum and dad together, or it's now mum on her own or dad on his own, or a gay couple raising children, or people in second marriages.[349]

Due to protests by the *Lumen Fidei* movement, that part of the video was excluded by the meeting organizers.

The same thing happened with a promotional booklet for the event. It originally had five pictures of homosexual couples. They were later removed together with this statement: "While the Church upholds the ideal of marriage as a permanent commitment between a man and a woman, other unions exist which provide mutual support to the couple. Pope Francis encourages us never to exclude but to accompany these couples also, with love, care and support."[350]

U.S. Jesuit James Martin's Bridge to the Homosexual Community

Pope Francis's April 12, 2017 appointment of Fr. James Martin, SJ as a consultant

---

347. Congregation for the Doctrine of the Faith, "Considerations Regarding Proposals to Give Legal Recognition to Unions Between Homosexual Persons," Jul. 31, 2003, no. 6, http://www.vatican.va/roman_curia /congregations/cfaith/documents/rc_con_cfaith_doc_20030731_homosexual-unions_en.html.

348. Sarah MacDonald, "Gay Couples Must Be Made Welcome at World Meeting of Families, Insists Bishop," *The Irish Independent*, Oct. 13, 2017, https://www.independent.ie/irish-news/gay-couples -must-be-made-welcome-at-world-meeting-of-families-insists-bishop-36222730.html.

349. Sarah MacDonald, "Welcome to Gay Parents Edited Out of Church Video," *The Irish Independent*, Mar. 5, 2018, https://www.independent.ie/irish-news/welcome-to-gay-parents-edited-out-of-church -video-36669007.html.

350. Patsy McGarry, "Images of Same-Sex Couples Removed From World Meeting of Families Booklet," *The Irish Times*, Jan. 30, 2018, https://www.irishtimes.com/news/social-affairs/religion-and-beliefs /images-of-same-sex-couples-removed-from-world-meeting-of-families-booklet-1.3372908.

to the Holy See's Secretariat of Communications was equally telltale of this gradual acceptance of homosexual relationships. Just months before, on October 30, 2016, New Ways Ministry honored the Jesuit with its Build Bridges Award. Years earlier, this group was condemned by the Holy See and by the United States Bishops' Conference for favoring homosexual relations and unions. At the bestowal, the organization's executive director stated, "Being mentioned by Fr. Martin is better than being mentioned by *The New York Times* or CNN," because when he links to a post by the group the number of visits increases twentyfold.[351]

For decades, Father Martin has been laboring to force Church acceptance of the homosexual community and its lifestyle. He authored *Building a Bridge: How the Catholic Church and the LGBT Community Can Enter Into a Relationship of Respect, Compassion, and Sensitivity*. In it, he argued that the Church must acknowledge that "the L.G.B.T. community brings unique gifts to the Church." He said the Church must treat homosexuals like any other group, without fear of appearing to be in "a tacit agreement with everything that anyone in the L.G.B.T. community says or does." The Church must do this, he emphasized, because "L.G.B.T. people are beloved children of God with gifts—both as individuals and as a community."[352]

Father Martin has condemned Catholic institutions that fire employees who enter into same-sex unions. He approved of Cardinal Schönborn, archbishop of Vienna, when the prelate praised such unions. Similarly, he has called for the elimination of the expressions "objectively disordered" and "intrinsically disordered," which the *Catechism of the Catholic Church* employs when referring to homosexuality, for their presumed cruelty.[353]

In a video released in September 2017, Father Martin stated that the Church's teaching that homosexuals should remain celibate throughout their lives is not binding on conscience because it was not "received" [by the People of God] "for it to be really authoritative."[354] And in a September 19, 2017

351. Jim Russell, "New Ways Ministry's 'Fr. James Martin Effect,'" *Crisis Magazine*, Apr. 12, 2017, http://www.crisismagazine.com/2017/new-ways-ministrys-fr-james-martin-effect.

352. James Martin, SJ, "We Need to Build a Bridge Between LGBT Community and the Catholic Church," *America*, Oct. 30, 2016, https://www.americamagazine.org/faith/2016/10/30/james-martin-sj-we-need-build-bridge-between-lgbt-community-and-catholic-church.

353. Ibid. See *Catechism of the Catholic Church*, nos. 2357, 2358; Jonathan Merritt, "This Vatican Adviser Is Moving Catholics Toward LGBT Inclusion," *Religion News Service*, Jun. 6, 2017, http://religionnews.com/2017/06/06/this-top-vatican-official-is-quietly-moving-catholics-toward-lgbt-inclusion/.

354. "Brandon Ambrosino Interviews James Martin, SJ, Villanova University, Aug. 29, 2017," Joseph Sciambra, "James Martin on Same-Sex Marriage, Humanae Vitae and Ex-gays," *YouTube*, Sept. 20, 2017, https://www.youtube.com/watch?v=wfbYRJN-jWE&feature=youtu.be, 3:03, 3:20–22; Marco Tosatti, "'Insegnamento non ricevuto', liberi i cristiani LGBT," *La Nuova Bussola Quotidiana*, Sept. 22, 2017, http://lanuovabq.it/it/insegnamento-non-ricevuto-liberi-i-cristiani-lgbt.

Facebook post, he wrote to his half-million followers: "The Holy Spirit knows what She's doing."[355]

When Obama's executive order imposing transgender restrooms on schools was reversed by the Trump White House, Father Martin sent his followers a tweet saying he disapproved: "It saddens me that a #trans student cannot choose what bathrooms to use."[356]

Cardinal Kevin Farrell, the prefect of the Vatican Dicastery for the Laity, Family, and Life, praised Father Martin's *Building Bridges*, saying it is "much-needed." For his part, Cardinal Joseph Tobin, archbishop of Newark, called it "brave, prophetic."[357]

Toward a Liturgical Blessing for Homosexual Unions?

The Vatican Secretariat for Communications' hiring of Accenture is another indication of the growing rapprochement with the homosexual movement. This company was commissioned to reorganize and unify all of the Holy See's current channels of communication. This includes *Vatican Media*, *Vatican Radio*, and *Vatican News*. Accenture is known worldwide for promoting the homosexual lobby's political agenda. In 2013, it received the award of Britain's most "gay friendly" employer, and, in 2016, Ireland's "best LGBT workplace" award.[358] Accenture produces videos proposing strategies to promote homosexual rights worldwide. It co-signed an *amicus curiae* brief for Obergefell *v.* Hodges, favoring the approval of same-sex "marriage" by the U.S. Supreme Court.

Moreover, last Christmas, the Holy See installed a crèche in Saint Peter's Square with neither ox nor donkey. The figures of the Holy Family were placed in the background while many others in the foreground evoked the corporal works of mercy. The secular media saw this, too, as a sign of this rapprochement. The most talked about scene was called: "Clothe the naked." It featured a naked man, with a shaved body, seemingly forged by bodybuilding. The secular media referred to it as favorable to homosexuality and as

355. James Martin, SJ, *Facebook*, Sept. 19, 2017, https://www.facebook.com/FrJamesMartin/posts/10154760118671496?pnref=story.

356. James Martin, SJ, *Twitter*, Feb. 22, 2017, 9:40 PM, https://twitter.com/JamesMartinSJ/status/834578641698844674. On July 29, 2018, Fr. Martin had 226,000 Twitter followers.

357. Claire Chretien, "Francis-Appointed Cardinals Back Jesuit's Pro-LGBT Book," *LifeSiteNews*, Apr. 7, 2017, https://www.lifesitenews.com/news/francis-appointed-cardinals-back-jesuits-pro-lgbt-book.

358. Matthew Cullinan Hoffman, "Vatican Hires LBGT Activist Company to Create and Run New Internet News Platform," *LifeSiteNews*, Dec. 20, 2017, https://www.lifesitenews.com/news/vatican-hires-lgbt-activist-company-to-create-and-run-new-internet-news-pla.

having "homoerotic allusions."[359]

The president of Arcigay Naples admitted that "the presence of the Vatican Nativity Scene for us is a reason to be even happier this year. For the homosexual and transsexual community of Naples, it is an important symbol of inclusion and integration." In fact, the crib was a gift from the Abbey of Montevergine (Avellino), in whose vicinity homosexuals celebrate an "'ancestral gay pride' pilgrimage" [*sic*] with references to the pagan cult of Cybele, the goddess symbol of androgyny.[360]

Pope Francis's and the Holy See's direct actions in this matter go hand-in-hand with the Vatican's silence on initiatives that encourage acceptance of homosexual unions in the Church. An example of this is the statement of Cardinal Reinhard Marx, president of the German Bishops' Conference and member of the small circle of the pope's advisors on the reform of the Curia, known as C9. Questioned by Bavarian public radio on the proposal to have a Church blessing ceremony for homosexual couples, the archbishop of Munich said,

> "One must also encourage priests and pastoral workers to give people in concrete situations encouragement. I do not really see any problems there."
>
> The specific liturgical form such blessings—or other forms of "encouragement"—should take is a quite different question . . . that requires further careful consideration. . . .
>
> [The cardinal repeated] there could be "no general solutions."
>
> "It's about pastoral care for individual cases."[361]

359. "Vaticano, papa Francesco e il presepe gay in piazza San Pietro: Scandalo mondiale, mai vista una roba così," *Libero Quotidiano*, Dec. 31, 2017, http://www.liberoquotidiano.it/news/italia/13295190/vaticano-papa-francesco-presepe-gay-scandalo-piazza-san-pietro-rivolta-cristiana.html.; Fabrizio D'Esposito, "Vaticano, il presepe filogay scatena la destra clericale," *Il Fatto Quotidiano*, Dec. 31, 2017, https://www.ilfattoquotidiano.it/premium/articoli/vaticano-il-presepe-filogay-scatena-la-destra-clericale/; Diane Montagna, "Vatican's 'Sexually Suggestive' Nativity Has Troubling Ties to Italy's LGBT Activists," *Life-SiteNews*, Dec. 20, 2017, https://www.lifesitenews.com/news/vaticans-sexually-suggestive-nativity-has-troubling-ties-to-italys-lgbt-act.

360. Ibid.

361. Anian Christoph Wimmer, "Cardinal Marx Endorses Blessing Ceremonies for Same-Sex Couples," *Crux*, Feb. 4, 2018, https://cruxnow.com/global-church/2018/02/04/cardinal-marx-endorses-blessing-ceremonies-sex-couples/.

CHAPTER 7
An Example of the Paradigm Shift: Holy Communion for "Remarried" Divorcees

The Apostolic Exhortation Amoris Laetitia *is undoubtedly the document-symbol of the ongoing paradigm shift and cultural revolution. It opened the possibility for civilly "remarried" divorcees to receive Holy Communion on a "case-by-case basis." Great Catholic theologians and scholars see it as the "straw that breaks the back" of moral theology as a whole. Four cardinals respectfully raised* dubia *on the subject, but the pope never responded. Dozens of bishops, priests, religious, theologians, and laymen have taken a public stand in defense of traditional Catholic doctrine, a front of resistance unseen in Church history for centuries.*

There is one application of the moral relativism denounced earlier that is dramatic beyond description. Indeed, it entails the serious risk of multiplying sacrileges. It is the issue of marriage indissolubility, and the Church's *de facto* acceptance of adulterous unions in the name of a pastoral policy informed by people's actual lives.

The Church's centuries-old discipline denies Holy Communion for civilly "remarried" divorcees. They are in an objective state of mortal sin. Their fault is further aggravated by scandal if their adulterous situation is public and notorious. Whatever their subjective intentions may be, such persons are objectively in the state of "manifest grave sin." Consequently, they cannot receive the Holy Eucharist.[362] To receive Holy Communion they must first repent of their sins and abandon their illicit relations. If "remarried" divorcees cannot leave the house where they live with the adulterous partner because, for example, they must raise their children, then they must commit to living chastely, i.e., under the same roof, but not in the same bed.

However, there are growing numbers of divorced Catholics who civilly "remarry." Because of this, efforts have been made since the seventies to relativize the prohibition of their receiving Holy Communion. Such efforts have been

---

362. See *Code of Canon Law*, can. 915, http://www.vatican.va/archive/ENG1104/_P39.HTM. "If the divorced are remarried civilly, they find themselves in a situation that objectively contravenes God's law. Consequently, they cannot receive Eucharistic communion as long as this situation persists. For the same reason, they cannot exercise certain ecclesial responsibilities. Reconciliation through the sacrament of Penance can be granted only to those who have repented for having violated the sign of the covenant and of fidelity to Christ, and who are committed to living in complete continence." *Catechism of the Catholic Church*, no. 1650.

seen primarily in the United States and Canada.[363]

Solemn Magisterial Reaffirmation of
Eucharistic Exclusion for Civilly "Remarried" Divorcees

The issue was raised during the 1980 Synod on the family because of these liberal efforts. After the synod, John Paul II published the Apostolic Exhortation *Familiaris Consortio*. In paragraph 84, he confirmed the exclusion of divorced and "remarried" persons from Holy Communion. The undergirding principles were approved by a majority of the Synod Fathers:

> However, the Church reaffirms her practice, which is based upon Sacred Scripture, of not admitting to Eucharistic Communion divorced persons who have remarried. They are unable to be admitted thereto from the fact that their state and condition of life objectively contradict that union of love between Christ and the Church, which is signified and effected by the Eucharist.
>
> Besides this, there is another special pastoral reason: if these people were admitted to the Eucharist, the faithful would be led into error and confusion regarding the Church's teaching about the indissolubility of marriage.[364]

Test of Strength Between the Leadership
of the German Episcopate and the Holy See

Despite the text's clarity, the three German bishops of the ecclesiastical province of the Upper Rhine published a joint pastoral letter in July 1993. They claimed

---

363. These attempts began in diocesan groups specializing in pastoral care for divorcees, including those civilly "remarried." Group chaplains sustained that if, in conscience, "remarried" divorcees considered themselves to be free from their first marriage bond, then they could receive Communion even without a canonical declaration of marriage nullity.

In 1971, under the pretext of respect for conscience, a committee of the Catholic Theological Society of America presented a study that endorsed this so-called pastoral practice. The condition was that the "remarried" divorcees present themselves for Communion "after proper consultation, reflection and prayer."

In 1972, in the name of a solution in the internal forum, Most Rev. Robert Tracy, bishop of Baton Rouge, wrote a pastoral letter proposing a diocesan tribunal that would issue a "decree of good conscience." Kenneth R. Himes, OFM, and James A. Coriden, "Notes on Moral Theology 1995: Pastoral Care of the Divorced and Remarried," *Theological Studies* 57 (1996): 100, http://cdn.theologicalstudies.net/57/57.1/57.1.6.pdf.

In September 1972, the Administrative Board of the National Conference of [U.S.] Catholic Bishops sent the Vatican a study raising the possibility of admitting to Communion "remarried" divorcee couples who did not live as brothers and sisters. Accordingly, in March 1975, the secretary of the Congregation for the Doctrine of the Faith wrote the president of the United States Catholic Conference reiterating that couples living in irregular unions can receive Communion only if they (a) live in chastity, and (b) receive it in churches where they are unknown, to avoid scandal. See ibid.

364. John Paul II, Apostolic Exhortation *Familiaris Consortio*, Nov. 22, 1981, no. 84, http://w2.vatican.va/content/john-paul-ii/en/apost_exhortations/documents/hf_jp-ii_exh_19811122_familiaris-consortio.html.

that the Church should treat divorced and civilly "remarried" couples with mercy. They asserted that Canon Law's prescriptions are general but fail to take into account complex individual cases. They suggested that each "remarried" divorcee could discern his or her situation with the aid of a priest, and decide, in conscience, whether or not to receive Holy Communion. The celebrant or Eucharistic minister would be forbidden to refuse Communion to the divorcee.[365]

That pastoral letter had an enormous impact because of its authors' fame. Two of them were well-known theologians, the Most Rev. Walter Kasper, bishop of Rottenburg-Stuttgart, and Most Rev. Karl Lehmann, archbishop of Mainz and president of the German Bishops' Conference. The third was the Bishops' Conference vice-president, Most Rev. Oskar Saier, a respected canonist and archbishop of Freiburg im Breisgau.

The impact was such that it prompted a Vatican response. After a series of meetings between Cardinal Joseph Ratzinger and the German bishops, the Congregation for the Doctrine of the Faith published a year later a Curia document titled "Letter to the Bishops of the Catholic Church Concerning the Reception of Holy Communion by the Divorced and Remarried Members of the Faithful." It emphatically stated: "Members of the faithful who live together as husband and wife with persons other than their legitimate spouses may not receive Holy Communion. Should they judge it possible to do so, pastors and confessors, given the gravity of the matter and the spiritual good of these persons as well as the common good of the Church, have the serious duty to admonish them that such a judgment of conscience openly contradicts the Church's teaching. Pastors in their teaching must also remind the faithful entrusted to their care of this doctrine."[366]

Some ignored the Church's teaching. They argued erroneously, for example, that Eucharistic ministers cannot make an external judgment on the subjective conditions of a civilly "remarried" divorcee being in mortal sin. Addressing this claim, the Pontifical Council for Legislative Texts published

---

365. "The [Rhine] bishops suggest eight criteria for discernment: (1) Responsibility for the collapse of the first marriage 'must be acknowledged and repented'; (2) it must be clear 'that a return to the first partner is really impossible'; (3) 'restitution must be made for wrongs done'; (4) any 'obligations to the wife and children of the first marriage' must be met; (5) 'scandal should be taken into consideration'; (6) the second relationship 'must have proved itself over a long period of time to represent a decisive and also publicly recognizable will to live together permanently'; (7) whether or not there exist moral obligations of 'fidelity to the second relationship' should be determined; (8) it should be clear that 'the partners seek truly to live according to the Christian faith and with true motives.'" Himes and Coriden, "Pastoral Care of the Divorced and Remarried," 104.

366. Congregation for the Doctrine of the Faith, "Letter to the Bishops of the Catholic Church Concerning the Reception of Holy Communion by the Divorced and Remarried Members of the Faithful," Sept. 14, 1994, no. 6, http://www.vatican.va/roman_curia/congregations/cfaith/documents/rc_con_cfaith_doc _14091994_rec-holy-comm-by-divorced_en.html.

a June 2000 document titled "Declaration Concerning the Admission to Holy Communion of Faithful Who Are Divorced and Remarried." This Holy See document reaffirmed, "The prohibition found in the cited canon [915], by its nature, is derived from divine law and transcends the domain of positive ecclesiastical laws: the latter cannot introduce legislative changes which would oppose the doctrine of the Church."[367]

Pope Francis Nods to a Change in the Church's Position
This firm and clear position became a victim of the paradigm shift. In his very first Angelus address, from the balcony of the papal palace, newly-elected Pope Francis praised Cardinal Walter Kasper, calling him "a good theologian."[368]

The second sign of paradigm shift came on the return flight from Rio de Janeiro, after the World Youth Day. The pope was asked if there is any possibility of changing Church discipline regarding access to the sacraments by divorced and "remarried" people. Francis responded: "The Orthodox have a different practice. They follow the theology of what they call *oikonomia*, and they give a second chance, they allow it. But I believe that this problem . . . must be studied within the context of the pastoral care of marriage."[369]

The expectation of change mushroomed, even more, when the media carried statements by an Argentine woman and her divorced companion. They claimed that Pope Francis had phoned her and authorized her to receive Holy Communion. The condition was, not to do so in her parish. That way there would be no conflict with her pastor.[370] The Holy See Press Office did not deny her story. It merely stated that such conversations should be understood in the context of the pope's personal pastoral relations. They should not be seen as events with "consequences for the teachings of the Church."[371]

The "Kasper Report" Triggers Chain Reactions
On October 8, 2013, the Third Extraordinary General Assembly of the Synod of Bishops was convoked in this atmosphere charged with mixed signals. The

---

367. Pontifical Council for Legislative Texts, "Declaration: II. Concerning the Admission to Holy Communion of Faithful Who Are Divorced and Remarried," Jun. 24, 2000, no. 1, http://www.vatican.va/roman_curia /pontifical_councils/intrptxt/documents/rc_pc_intrptxt_doc_20000706_declaration_en.html.

368. Francis, "Angelus," Mar. 17, 2013, http://w2.vatican.va/content/francesco/en/angelus/2013 /documents/papa-francesco_angelus_20130317.html.

369. Francis, "Returning From Rio's World Youth Day."

370. See "Franicsco llamó a una divorciada para decirle que puede comulgar," *Cronista*, Apr. 22, 2014, https://www.cronista.com/informaciongral/Francis-llamo-a-una-divorciada-para-decirle-que-puede -comulgar-20140422-0117.html.

371. "Santa Sede. Le telefonate del papa, non trarre conclusioni su insegnamento della Chiesa," *Avvenire*, Apr. 24, 2014, https://www.avvenire.it/chiesa/pagine/papa-divorziati-eucaristia-lombardi.

announcement stated the synod would be held in October of the following year. Its delegates would address "Pastoral Challenges to the Family in the Context of Evangelization."[372] This theme would also be the subject of the next Ordinary Synod, in 2015, which would discuss "The Vocation and Mission of the Family in the Church and Contemporary World."[373] There would also be broad consultation with the grassroots.

Cardinal Lorenzo Baldisseri, secretary general of the Synod of Bishops, sent out a preparatory document to the world's bishops. It included a 38-question survey on "new situations" surrounding the family. Four of these were particularly controversial. They dealt with unions between same-sex persons[374] and pastoral care, especially access to Holy Communion for divorced couples in a second union.[375]

Papal speeches encouraged the grassroots to respond to the Baldisseri questionnaire proposing Church pastoral and doctrinal changes. The so-called grassroots were really progressive lay groups and bishops' conferences. For example, the Office of Pastoral Care for the Freiburg Archdiocese issued an official document that encouraged "remarried" divorcees to immediately and unscrupulously present themselves for Holy Communion. They could do so based on a simple "decision taken responsibly and according to one's

---

372. Synod of Bishops, Third Extraordinary General Assembly, "Pastoral Challenges to the Family in the Context of Evangelization—Preparatory Document," Nov. 5, 2013, http://www.vatican.va/roman_curia /synod/documents/rc_synod_doc_20131105_iii-assemblea-sinodo-vescovi_en.html.

373. Synod of Bishops, Fourteenth Ordinary General Assembly, "The Vocation and Mission of the Family in the Church and Contemporary World—*Lineamenta*," Dec. 9, 2014, http://www.vatican.va/roman_curia /synod/documents/rc_synod_doc_20141209_lineamenta-xiv-assembly_en.html.

374. Here are this topic's questions:
    5. On Unions of Persons of the Same Sex
    a) Is there a law in your country recognizing civil unions for people of the same-sex and equating it in some way to marriage?
    b) What is the attitude of the local and particular Churches toward both the State as the promoter of civil unions be- tween persons of the same sex and the people involved in this type of union?
    c) What pastoral attention can be given to people who have chosen to live in these types of union?
    d) In the case of unions of persons of the same sex who have adopted children, what can be done pastorally in light of transmitting the faith?
Synod of Bishops, Third Extraordinary General Assembly, "Preparatory Document," III–5

375. Here are the survey's controversial questions on this matter:
    4. Pastoral Care in Certain Difficult Marital Situations . . . .
    c) Are separated couples and those divorced and remarried a pastoral reality in your particular Church? Can you ap- proximate a percentage? How do you deal with this situation in appropriate pastoral programs?
    d) In all the above cases, how do the baptized live in this irregular situation? Are [they] aware of it? Are they simply indifferent? Do they feel marginalized or suffer from the impossibility of receiving the sacraments?
    e) What questions do divorced and remarried people pose to the Church concerning the Sacraments of the Eu- charist and of Reconciliation? Among those persons who find themselves in these situations, how many ask for these sacraments?
Ibid., III–4.

conscience."[376] At the time, Freiburg's archbishop was Most Rev. Robert Zollitsch, president of the German Bishops' Conference.

With most cardinals present in Rome for the February 2014 consistory, Pope Francis asked them to discuss the family, using an introductory report he had commissioned from Cardinal Walter Kasper. As seen, Cardinal Kasper was the German prelate who issued a 1993 joint pastoral with two other Rhine bishops, proposing to remove the prohibition of communion for divorced and "remarried" persons.

Cardinal Kasper's 2014 report again suggested a paradigm shift for the Church regarding communion for "remarried" divorcees. He said the issue should be considered from the perspective of those who are suffering and requesting help. He claimed (falsely) that in the early Church, Christians who separated from their still-living spouse and entered into a second union were not allowed to marry a second time but that, after a certain period of penance, they received a life raft in the form of Communion. He went on to say that while the Latin Church had abandoned this custom, the (schismatic) Orthodox had retained it with the principle of *oikonomia*, as Pope Francis mentioned during the press conference returning from Rio de Janeiro.

In subsequent weeks, renowned historians refuted Cardinal Kasper's thesis that the early Church admitted "remarried" divorcees to Communion. They conclusively proved that councils had approved Communion for remarried *widows* and *widowers*, not for "remarried" divorcees.

Many cardinals reacted to the dissemination of the Kasper thesis. Among

---

376. Birger Menke, "Diocese Opens Door to Communion for the Remarried," *Spiegel Online*, Aug. 10, 2013, http://www.spiegel.de/international/germany/freiburg-catholic-diocese-opens-door-to-communion-for-remarried-people-a-926645.html.

In response to this scandalous initiative, German Archbishop Gerhard L. Müller reaffirmed the indissolubility of marriage and the prohibition of Communion for public sinners. See Gerhard Ludwig Müller, "Testimony to the Power of Grace: On the Indissolubility of Marriage and the Debate Concerning the Civilly Remarried and the Sacraments," Oct. 23, 2013, http://www.vatican.va/roman_curia/congregations/cfaith/muller/rc_con_cfaith_20131023_divorziati-risposati-sacramenti_en.html. In this article, first published in *L'Osservatore Romano*, the prefect of the Congregation for the Doctrine of the Faith condemned, in passing, the pastoral leniency of *oikonomia* practiced by the Orthodox schismatics. However, statements from two other prelates overshadowed Archbishop Müller's intervention: Cardinal Reinhard Marx, archbishop of Munich, and Cardinal Oscar Maradiaga, archbishop of Tegucigalpa, Honduras—both very close to Pope Francis and members of the C9, the group of cardinals who assist the pope in the reform of the Curia. Cardinal Marx declared that this article could not "stop discussions." "'Müller Cannot Stop Discussions' Relating to Remarried Divorcees," *La Stampa–Vatican Insider*, Nov. 11, 2013, http://www.lastampa.it/2013/11/11/vaticaninsider/mller-cannot-stop-discussions-relating-to-remarried-divorcees-xPpiKwGFyq80O1a7QoxGqM/pagina.html. Cardinal Maradiaga pontificated that Archbishop Müller "'is a professor of German theology,' 'he sees things in black-and-white terms . . . in terms of good and bad. . . .' But, 'the world isn't like that, my brother. You should be a bit flexible.'" "Maradiaga Says Müller Needs to 'Be a Bit More Flexible,'" *La Stampa–Vatican Insider*, Jan. 21, 2014, http://www.lastampa.it/2014/01/21/vaticaninsider/maradiaga-says-mller-needs-to-be-a-bit-more-flexible-vZdAXTfW8PCqOqYloLM4oM/pagina.html.

them were Cardinals Burke, Müller, Brandmüller, De Paolis, Caffarra, and Pell. Historians, theologians, canonists, and moralists all weighed in. Eight U.S. Dominican professors published a notable work in which they highlighted that Cardinal Kasper's report would entail suppressing the obligation of chastity according to one's state in life. It would be as if the faithful could not be sure of the help of grace in the practice of the virtue of purity.[377]

On the eve of the Extraordinary Synod, the first five of the above-noted cardinals published their assessments together with those of four experts in a book titled, *Remaining in the Truth of Christ: Matrimony and Communion in the Catholic Church*. In it, the authors recounted the centuries-old history of Catholic opposition to Communion for "remarried" divorcees. They also showed there is no argument supporting the kind of tolerance Cardinal Kasper was proposing. The latter deplored the book's publication as "an ideological war" aimed at Pope Francis.[378] *National Catholic Register*'s well-known Rome correspondent Edward Pentin reported that "reliable and high-level sources allege the head of the secretariat of the synod of bishops, Cardinal Lorenzo Baldisseri, ordered they [copies of the book] be intercepted [removed from the Synod Fathers' mail boxes] because they would 'interfere with the synod.'"[379]

Maneuvers to Impose the "Kasper Thesis" at the Extraordinary Synod
On October 5, 2014, the Extraordinary Synod opened, but with various anomalies.[380] When the intermediate report was read, many protested that it did not reflect the actual content of most speeches but only the Kasper minority thesis. They pointed out that the thesis included a surprising moral principle—the

---

377. "Although the present proposals concern only the divorced-and-remarried, adopting them—even as a 'merely' pastoral practice—requires that the Church accept in principle that sexual activity outside of a permanent and faithful marriage is compatible with communion with Christ and with the Christian life. If accepted, however, it is hard to see how the Church could resist admitting to Holy Communion unmarried cohabiting couples, or persons in homosexual unions, and so forth. Indeed, the logic of this position suggests that the Church should bless such relationships (as the Anglican communion is now doing), and even accept the full gamut of contemporary sexual 'liberation.' Communion for the divorced-and-remarried is only the beginning." John Corbett, OP, et al., "Recent Proposals for the Pastoral Care of the Divorced and Remarried: A Theological Assessment," *Nova et Vetera* 12, no. 3 (Summer 2014): 615–6, http://www.laikos.org/recent-proposals-a-theological-assessment.pdf.

378. Antonio Manzo, "Intervista al cardinale Kasper: 'Voglione la guerra al Sinodo, il papa è il bersaglio,'" *Il Mattino*, Sept. 18, 2014, https://www.ilmattino.it/primopiano/cronaca/cardinale_kasper_intervista_mattino-595778.html.

379. Edward Pentin, "Vatican Alleged to Have Intercepted Synod Book," *Newsmax*, Feb. 25, 2015, https://www.newsmax.com/edwardpentin/pope-francis-cardinal-walter-kasper-cardinal-gerhard-muller-vatican/2015/02/25/id/626811/.

380. The two main anomalies were the failure to make public the speeches given during the Synod's meetings and the addition of six progressive prelates to the drafting committee of the intermediate and final reports. For an overview of the anomalies, see Edward Pentin, *The Rigging of a Vatican Synod? An Investigation Into Alleged Manipulation at the Extraordinary Synod on the Family* (San Francisco: Ignatius, 2015).

so-called principle of gradualness. That principle would supposedly allow one to gather positive elements from objectively sinful situations. For example, one should see "seeds of the Word that have spread beyond its visible and sacramental boundaries"[381] in premarital relations or homosexual unions. In other words, any sin would become just an imperfect form of good. One should practice a kind of ecumenism with evil or sin. "According to official sources, at least forty-one bishops who [were] involved in the Synod were quite surprised—and quite 'agitated'—at the appearance of the document Monday."[382]

In subsequent workshops, the intermediate report was literally shredded by the sheer number of proposed amendments, some seven hundred. Most of them recommended that the final report should emphasize above all that there is only one marriage model: The indissoluble union of one man and one woman, open to having children and raising them in the Faith. Despite the pope's presence, discontent exploded in the Synod hall when it was announced that reports from the language groups[383] would not be communicated to the Synod Fathers. Naturally, this increased the risk that the final report would merely disregard their proposed changes.[384] Faced with such strong opposition, and after a vote, the texts were finally communicated to the participants.

Although the drafting committee was compelled to draw up a compromise text for the final vote, three paragraphs failed to muster the required two-thirds majority for approval and inclusion in the final report. One dealt with the pastoral care of persons with same-sex attraction. The other two concerned Communion for "remarried" divorcees. These paragraphs' failure to secure the votes needed proves the existence of divergent positions among the Synod Fathers. Despite their rejection and contrary to the Synod rules, Pope Francis ordered that they be included in the final report. This report would be sent to dioceses and parishes to inspire grassroots proposals for the Ordinary Synod the following year.[385] Commenting on this, Cardinal Reinhard Marx told the daily *Die Zeit*, "The

381. Synod of Bishops, III Extraordinary General Assembly, "*Relatio post disceptationem*," 4.

382. Robert Royal, "Synod Day 9—Bishops to World: 'Never Mind,'" *The Catholic Thing*, Oct. 15, 2014, https://www.thecatholicthing.org/2014/10/15/synod-day-9-bishops-to-world-never-mind/.

383. "From October 13 to 16, [2014] the assembly was divided into 10 *Circoli minori* (small working groups), composed of an average 25 persons each, divided according to language groups. These groups discussed the content of the RPD [*Relatio Post Disceptationem*] and made recommendations for changes and other inputs." The Servant General, "Report and Reflections on the III Extraordinary General Assembly of the Synod of Bishops," *Couples for Christ*, Oct. 24, 2014, http://cfcffl.net/report-and-reflections-on-the-iii-extraordinary-general-assembly-of-the-synod-of-bishops/.

384. Reportedly, Cardinal Pell stood up, slammed his hand on the table, and said, "You must stop manipulating this Synod." Robert Royal, "Synod Day 11: Some Numbers," *The Catholic Thing*, Oct. 17, 2014, https://www.thecatholicthing.org/2014/10/17/synod-day-11-some-numbers/.

385. See Brian Williams, "Baldisseri: Pope Francis Approved Controversial Midterm Relatio," *OnePeterFive*, Jan. 29, 2015, https://onepeterfive.com/baldisseri-pope-francis-approved-controversial-midterm-relatio/.

synod debates were just a starting point. Francis wants to get things moving, to push processes forward. The real work is about to begin."[386]

The secretary general of the Synod of Bishops, Cardinal Lorenzo Baldisseri, expressed similar ideas to the newspaper *Avvenire*: "In fact, we believe that this period between the two Synods is the most important. . . . There are study groups at various levels here in Rome that will study the most sensitive issues, especially those that touch on points that have not received a qualified majority."[387] In turn, when in the U.K. launching his book, *Pope Francis's Revolution of Tenderness and Love*, Cardinal Walter Kasper stated, "We should all pray for it because a battle is going on."[388]

Nearly 900,000 Faithful Ask for an Enlightening Word, but the Vatican Is Silent

The pope, himself, described that battle in an interview with the Argentine newspaper *La Nación*: "'The German Cardinal Walter Kasper said we should look for hypotheses, that is, he paved the way. And some people got frightened.'"[389] He continued: "In the case of divorcees who have remarried, we posed the question, what do we do with them? What door can we allow them to open? This was a pastoral concern: will we allow them to go to Communion? Communion alone is no solution. The solution is integration. They have not been excommunicated, true. But they cannot be godfathers to any child being baptized, Mass readings are not for divorcees, they cannot give Communion, they cannot teach Sunday school, there are about seven things they cannot do, I have the list over there. Come on!'"[390]

Faced with this threat to Church teaching, a group of organizations and laity under the name Filial Appeal promoted a message to Pope Francis which stated:

We see widespread confusion arising from the possibility that a

---

386. Christa Pongratz-Lippitt, "Cardinal Marx: Pope Francis Has Pushed Open the Doors of the Church," *National Catholic Reporter*, Oct. 28, 2014, https://www.ncronline.org/blogs/ncr-today/cardinal-marx -pope-francis-has-pushed-open-doors-church.

387. Mimmo Muolo, "Sinodo. Baldisseri: 'Sinodo scelte coraggiose,'" *Avvenire*, Jan. 23, 2015, https://www.avvenire.it/chiesa/pagine/scelte-coraggiose-attesa-del-sinodo.

388. Cindy Wooden, "Cardinal Kasper Asks for Prayers for Synod, Saying 'a Battle Is Going on,'" *Catholic Herald*, Mar. 23, 2015, http://www.catholicherald.co.uk/news/2015/03/23/cardinal-kasper-asks-for -prayers-for-synod-saying-a-battle-is-going-on/.

389. Elisabetta Piqué, "Pope Francis: 'God Has Bestowed on Me a Healthy Dose of Unawareness,'" *La Nación*, Dec. 7, 2014, https://www.lanacion.com.ar/1750350-pope-francis-god-has-bestowed-on -me-a-healthy-dose-of-unawareness.

390. Elisabetta Piqué, "The Synod on the Family: 'The Divorced and Remarried Seem Excommunicated,'" *La Nación*, Dec. 7, 2014, https://www.lanacion.com.ar/1750351-the-synod-on-the-family-the -divorced-and-remarried-seem-excommunicated.

breach has opened within the Church that would accept adultery—
by permitting divorced and then civilly remarried Catholics to receive
Holy Communion—and would virtually accept even homosexual
unions when such practices are categorically condemned as being
contrary to Divine and natural law.

Paradoxically, our hope stems from this confusion. Truly, in these
circumstances, a word from Your Holiness is the only way to clarify
the growing confusion amongst the faithful.[391]

Nearly nine hundred thousand Catholics—including 211 cardinals, archbishops, and bishops—signed the petition. The petition was delivered personally by a commission and followed specific instructions received from one of
the pope's close collaborators. However, the Holy See did not even acknowledge
receipt. In an interview with the *Frankfurter Allgemeine Zeitung*, on October
28, 2017, Cardinal Walter Brandmüller stated, "The mere fact that a petition
with 870,000 signatures addressed to the pope asking him for clarification remains unanswered . . . raises questions. It's really hard to understand."[392]

At the same time, the Filial Appeal coalition published and sent to all the
world's bishops a copy of the booklet, *Preferential Option for the Family—100
Questions and Answers Relating to the Synod*, authored by Most Rev. Aldo
Pagotto, archbishop of Paraíba (Brazil), Most Rev. Robert Vasa, bishop of Santa
Rosa, Calif., and Most Rev. Athanasius Schneider, auxiliary bishop of Astana
(Kazakhstan). Cardinal Jorge Medina Estévez, prefect emeritus of the Congregation for Divine Worship, wrote the preface. The questions in this guide presented the most common objections to the themes raised by the Extraordinary
Synod on the Family (sexuality, indissolubility, divorce, homosexuality, Communion for "remarried" divorcees, and so on) and provided clear and straightforward answers.[393] Published in six languages and widely disseminated among
the faithful, this booklet helped increase the number of signers of the Filial Appeal to Pope Francis.

Meanwhile, three other scholarly publications came out in defense of the indissolubility of marriage. First, eleven cardinals authored a book of essays titled,

391. "Filial Appeal to His Holiness Pope Francis on the Future of the Family," accessed Jul. 23, 2018,
https://www.tfpstudentaction.org/assets/imgs/inline/filialpetition-en.pdf.

392. Christian Geyer and Hannes Hintermeier, "Das christentum hechelt nicht nach applaus," *Frankfurter
Allgemeine Zeitung*, Oct. 28, 2017, http://www.faz.net/aktuell/feuilleton/debatten/kardinal-walter-brand
mueller-ueber-den-streit-um-amoris-laetitia-15266671.html.

393. Aldo di Cillo Pagotto, SSS, Robert F. Vasa, and Athanasius Schneider, *Preferential Option for the
Family: 100 Questions and Answers Relating to the Synod* (Rome: Supplica Filiale, 2015),
http://www.tfp.org/images/stories/PDF_files/Preferential_Option_for_the_Family_English.pdf.

Eleven Cardinals Speak on Marriage and the Family.[394] The signed contributions were compiled by Prof. Winfried Aymans, a Canon Law specialist at the University of Munich. Second, a book was published containing the lectures from a seminar organized by the Pontifical Council for the Family, titled, *Family and Church.* Finally, the International Union of Catholic Jurists published essays by nine internationally-renowned experts under the direction of its president Miguel Ayuso, a professor at the University of Comillas, Spain. These experts state that admitting civilly "remarried" divorcees and homosexual couples to Holy Communion "represents the most serious challenge posed to the integrity of Catholic doctrine from the sixteenth century to the present day."[395]

Reforming the Canonical Process of Nullity to Influence the Debate

There was also the mobilization of what came to be known as the "Kasper group." Their main initiative was a behind closed doors symposium at the Gregorian University, organized by the presidents of the bishops' conferences of Germany, France, and Switzerland. It was attended by Cardinal Reinhard Marx, five bishops, fifty experts, and just one journalist, from *La Repubblica.* Two of the topics discussed were "Marriage and divorce" and "Sexuality as an expression of love." A German bishop commented, "The dogmatists say that the teaching of the Church is fixed. On the contrary, there is a development. And we need a development on sexuality, even if not sticking to this one alone." Another participant commented on Communion for "remarried" divorcees: "How can we deny it, as if it were a punishment, to people who failed and found a new partner with whom to start a new life?"[396] Two months before the Synod, the German Bishops' Conference posted a dossier on its website containing the main speeches from that off-limits symposium.

The pope's main intervention favoring the "Kasper thesis" was the promulgation and disclosure of two Motu Proprios: *Mitis Iudex Dominus* and *Mitis et Mis-*

---

394. Winfried Aymans, ed., *Eleven Cardinals Speak on Marriage and the Family* (San Francisco: Ignatius, 2015). The chapter authors were Cardinals Carlo Caffarra, Baselios Cleemis, Paul Josef Cordes, Dominik Duka, Willem Jacobus Eijk, Joachim Meisner, John Olorunfemi Onaiyekan, Antonio Maria Rouco Varela, Camillo Ruini, Robert Sarah, and Jorge Liberato Urosa Savino.

395. The experts are Danilo Castellano (Università degli Studi of Udine, Italy); Ricardo Dip (São Paulo Justice Tribunal, Brazil); Brian McCall (Oklahoma University, U.S.A.); Wolfgang Waldstein (former Dean of the University of Salzburg, Austria); Bernard Dumont (France); Alejandro Ordóñez (Attorney General of Colombia); José María Sánchez (University of Seville, Spain); Luis María de Ruschi (Interdiocesan Tribunal of Buenos Aires); Miguel Ayuso (University of Comillas, Spain, also president of the International Union of Catholic Jurists). See Carmelo López-Arias, "La Unión Internacional de Juristas Católicos aportará, con vistas al sínodo, un libro contundente," *Religión en Libertad*, Aug. 18, 2015, https://www.religionenlibertad.com/la-union-in ternacional-de-juristas-catolicos-aportara-con-vistas-al-sinodo-44358.htm.

396. "'La Chiesa deve riconoscere il valore dell'amore gay,' voilà l'agenda del sinodo 'ombra,'" *Il Timone*, May 27, 2015, http://www.iltimone.org/news-timone/la-chiesa-deve-riconoscere-il-valore-dellamore-gay/.

ericors Iesus. They made profound changes to the legal proceedings for declaring marriage nullity in the Latin and Eastern-rite Codes of Canon Law. The changes introduced by this reform included: Cases would now be decided by a single judge; the bishop was allowed to personally assume nullity causes; the obligatory double decree of nullity was eliminated; and the possibility of a fast-track process was introduced. Voices were raised, warning about the possibility that grounds for nullity would not be scrutinized with the required care, thus risking that legally valid marriages might be improperly declared null and void.[397] The papal initiative was interpreted as a means of avoiding that a majority of Synod Fathers would suggest a mere simplification of marriage nullity procedures as a solution for divorcees. Such a procedural simplification maintains the prohibition of Holy Communion for those whose marriages were judged valid.

In the meantime, the *Instrumentum laboris*, the basic text for the Synod's discussions, was distributed. Surprisingly, paragraph no. 123 erroneously claimed that "a great number agree that a journey of reconciliation or penance, under the auspices of the local bishop, might be undertaken by those who are divorced and civilly remarried, who find themselves in irreversible situations."[398]

The 2015 Ordinary Synod Opens With Denunciations of Manipulation and Ends in Failure

Before the 2015 Synod's opening, Cardinal George Pell delivered a letter, signed by thirteen cardinals including himself, to the pope. All the signatories would be participants in the Ordinary Synod. They called the pope's attention to "concerns" shared by other participants regarding the synodal process. In their judgment, the process appeared to be "designed to facilitate predetermined results on important disputed questions." A major concern was that the members of the drafting committee and the rapporteurs for the various language groups were chosen, not by the Synod Fathers but by the Synod Secretariat. They also deemed the *Instrumentum laboris* inadequate as a "guiding text or the foundation of a final document."

During the first debate, with the pope present, Cardinal Pell and other Synod Fathers raised some of the issues addressed in the letter without mentioning it. When Francis spoke the next day, he rejected all the requests made in the letter. At a later press conference, Cardinal Tagle, a prominent figure in the progressive

---

397. See, for example, Sandro Magister, "Forbidden to Call It Divorce. But It Sure Looks Like It," trans. Matthew Sherry, *L'Espresso–Settimo Cielo*, Sept. 15, 2015, http://chiesa.espresso.repubblica.it/articolo/1351199.html; Sandro Magister, "Nullity of Marriage. A Reform That Risks Sinking in the Dock," trans. Matthew Sherry, *L'Espresso–Settimo Cielo*, Dec. 31, 2015, http://chiesa.espresso.repubblica.it/articolo/1351131.html.

398. Synod of Bishops, Fourteenth Ordinary General Assembly, "The Vocation and Mission of the Family in the Church and the Contemporary World—*Instrumentum Laboris*," 2015, no. 123, http://www.vatican.va /roman_curia/synod/documents/rc_synod_doc_20150623_instrumentum-xiv-assembly_en.html.

faction, stated with visible satisfaction, "The new method adopted by the Synod has definitely caused a bit of confusion, but it is good to be confused once in a while. If things were always clear, then we might not be in real life anymore."[399]

As in the 2014 Synod, the development of the *Relatio finalis* was manipulated. To the Synod Fathers' great surprise, the text they received came with an absolute prohibition of disclosure that extended to the fifty-one auditors and other participants in the assembly. It was distributed in the afternoon, and only in Italian, a language which few participants had mastered. Italian is also little known in the geographical areas most opposed to a change in Church discipline such as Africa, Poland, and the United States. Moreover, the text completely ignored the 1,355 Synod Father–proposed corrections. It substantially reiterated the *Instrumentum laboris*, including its most criticized paragraphs on homosexuality and "remarried" divorcees. The debate was set for the following morning. Only written suggested amendments were allowed.

Despite the sleight of hand, Pope Francis faced an unexpected refusal of the document. Fifty-one Synod Fathers participated in the debate, most of whom opposed the text. Among them were prominent prelates such as Cardinals Ouellet, Bagnasco, and Caffarra, as well as Archbishops Kurtz and Gadecki, presidents of the Bishops' Conferences of the United States and Poland, respectively. Plainly, the document could not be reintroduced the next day. It ran the risk of being rejected.

The drafting committee spent the night preparing a new text from which all references to homosexual couples were removed. Regarding Communion for "remarried" divorcees, it presented a compromise solution in an ambiguous paragraph from the report of the *Germanicus* language group, which included Cardinal Walter Kasper and Cardinal Gerhard Müller, prefect of the Congregation for the Doctrine of the Faith. The text was read to the assembly in the morning and voted on in the early afternoon, leaving insufficient time to thoroughly analyze the content of the most controversial proposals. The text obtained a qualified majority for 94 paragraphs. Paragraph 85 contained the German group's new proposal. It implied a back door opening to the possibility for civilly "remarried" divorcees to receive Holy Communion.[400] It was approved

399. Sandro Magister, "Thirteen Cardinals Have Written to the Pope. Here's the Letter," trans. Matthew Sherry, *L'Espresso–Settimo Cielo*, Oct. 12, 2015 http://chiesa.espresso.repubblica.it/articolo/1351154.html.

400. Addressing what the *Relatio finalis* would contain, during a press briefing on the eve of its release, Cardinal Schönborn stated, "'Discernment' is the key word, and I invite you to think this is not black and white, a simple yes or no; one must discern [each case]." Iacopo Scaramuzzi, "Sui divorziati risposati il Sinodo indica la via del 'discernimento,'" *La Stampa–Vatican Insider*, Oct. 24, 2015, http://www.lastampa.it/2015 /10/24/vaticaninsider/sui-divorziati-risposati-il-sinodo-indica-la-via-del-discernimento-tRfmF7sDD6DYB c0nVp2CCK/pagina.html. Indeed, the *Relatio finalis* does not affirm the *right* of divorced and civilly "remarried" people to receive Holy Communion. Instead, it denies the Church's right to publicly define their lifestyle as adulterous, leaving it up to pastors to make that assessment.

with a single vote over the required two-thirds majority (178 for, 80 against, and 7 abstentions).

Pope Francis's final address expressed no enthusiasm for the Synod's outcome and contained repeated disapproval of the Synod Fathers who defended the Church's traditional teaching and pastoral practice. Concluding, he said this Synod, "was also about laying closed hearts, which bare the closed hearts which frequently hide even behind the Church's teachings or good intentions, in order to sit in the chair of Moses and judge, sometimes with superiority and superficiality, difficult cases and wounded families."[401]

Contradictory interpretations of the document began the day after the Synod's end.

Defending the traditional meaning, Cardinal Raymond Burke told the *National Catholic Register* that the *Relatio finalis*'s section on Discernment and Integration "is of 'immediate concern because of its lack of clarity in a fundamental matter of the faith: the indissolubility of the marriage bond which both reason and faith teach all men.'"[402] For his part, Bishop Athanasius Schneider published a statement deploring the document's "highly skillful, elaborated ambiguity," whereby "All parties, both the promoters of the so-called 'Kasper agenda' and their opponents are apparently satisfied stating, 'All is OK. The Synod did not change the doctrine.' Yet, such a perception is quite naive, because it ignores the back door and the pending time bombs in the abovementioned text section, which become manifest by a careful examination of the text by its internal interpretive criteria."[403]

Confirming Bishop Schneider's fears, Cardinal Kasper portrayed the final report as a green light for his thesis: "I am satisfied. The door has been opened to the possibility of giving communion to remarried divorcees. Yes, there has been some opening, but one does not speak about the consequences. Everything is in the hands of the pope, who will decide what to do."[404]

401. Francis, "Address of His Holiness Pope Francis—Conclusion of the Synod of Bishops," Oct. 24, 2015, http://w2.vatican.va/content/francesco/en/speeches/2015/october/documents/papa-francesco_20151024_sinodo-conclusione-lavori.html.

402. Edward Pentin, "Cardinal Burke: Final Report Lacks Clarity on Indissolubility of Marriage," *National Catholic Register*, Oct. 26, 2015, http://www.ncregister.com/blog/edward-pentin/cardinal-burke-final-report-lacks-clarity-on-indissolubility-of-marriage.

403. "Bishop Athanasius Schneider Reaction to Synod: Door to Communion for Divorced & Remarried Officially Kicked Open," *Rorate Cæli*, Nov. 4, 2015, https://rorate-caeli.blogspot.com/2015/11/rorate-exclusive-bishop-athanasius.html.

404. Serena Sartini, "Ostia ai divorziati se pentiti e i gay non sono famiglia," *Il Giornale*, Oct. 26, 2015, http://www.ilgiornale.it/news/politica/ostia-ai-divorziati-se-pentiti-e-i-gay-non-sono-famiglia-1186816.html.

In *Amoris Laetitia*, Situation Ethics
Triumph With a Strategy "Typical of a Jesuit"

That papal decision came very quickly. Pope Francis published the post-synodal Apostolic Exhortation *Amoris Laetitia* on the feast of Saint Joseph, patron of the family, just five months after the Synod's closure.

It claimed not to have changed Church doctrine on the indissolubility of marriage. Nevertheless, the exhortation introduced a tremendous change in pastoral practice for civilly "remarried" divorcees. It allowed them to be absolved in confession and receive Holy Communion without the commitment to live chastely, as brother and sister.

That permission was not given in general terms. *Amoris Laetitia* says nothing about canon 915, which forbids giving communion to those who obstinately persevere in "manifest grave sin." However, *Amoris Laetitia* encouraged shepherds of souls to "accompany" people living in irregular marriages. It told pastors to "discern" their situation, aiming to integrate them fully into the life of the Church. A simple footnote said that such integration could include reception of the sacraments. In other words, sacramental absolution and the Eucharist can be given to "remarried" divorcees provided it is done on a "case by case" basis.

It is, therefore, a substantial change. Its chief promoter, Cardinal Walter Kasper, welcomed it in advance as "the first step in a reform that will turn a page in the Church after 1,700 years."[405] In language typical of situation ethics adepts, the cardinal justified the step taken in *Amoris Laetitia*, saying, "God's law and commandments are valid forever, for all situations, but all situations are different and one cannot tell each person that he lives in adultery or that he or she is a sinner. One needs to take the situation into account and apply God's commandment to the specific situation: this is the tradition of the Church."[406]

Archbishop Bruno Forte was one of the vice presidents of the Extraordinary and Ordinary Synods. He was also a close collaborator of Pope Francis in writing the exhortation. He explained that the moral paradigm shift followed a strategy that was elaborated by the Supreme Pontiff himself whereby solutions would be given on a "case by case" basis. "If we speak explicitly about Communion for the divorced and remarried," Pope Francis is reported to have told Archbishop Forte, "you do not know what a terrible

405. Tommaso Bedini Crescimanni, "Kasper elogia Fratel Paoli e la diocesi," *Il Tirreno*, Mar. 16, 2016, http://iltirreno.gelocal.it/lucca/cronaca/2016/03/16/news/kasper-elogia-fratel-paoli-e-la-diocesi-1.13136909. Cardinal Kasper's allegation that the Council of Nicaea, in 325, authorized Communion to people living in a "second union" is baseless. In fact, as has been said, in its canon 8, that Council confirmed only that *widowed* persons who remarry are in full communion with the Church.

406. "Amoris Laetitia, parla il cardinale Kasper," *Stanze Vaticane*, Apr. 2, 2018, http://stanzevaticane.tgcom24.it/2018/04/02/amoris-laetitia-parla-il-cardinale-kasper/.

mess we will make. So we won't speak plainly, do it in a way that the premises are there, then I will draw out the conclusions." "Typical of a Jesuit," Archbishop Forte quipped.[407]

Numerous and authoritative churchmen have stated the exhortation is simply ambiguous because it did not create a clear general rule and left the conclusion implicit. Consequently, they requested an official interpretation that confirms traditional discipline.[408] Other analysts took an even more unfavorable view. They stated that the exhortation contained ambiguous teachings whose natural sense is at variance with traditional teaching. One such analyst was Bishop Athanasius Schneider.[409] Others affirmed that *Amoris Laetitia* collided head-on with Catholic dogma. Professors Robert Spaemann[410] and Josef Seifert

407. "Incontro con monsignor Forte sull'esortazione di papa Francesco, 'Amoris Laetitia,'" *Zona Locale*, May 3, 2016, http://www.zonalocale.it/2016/05/03/-nessuno-si-deve-sentire-escluso-dalla-chiesa-/20471. See also Steve Skojec, "Forte: Pope Did Not Want to Speak 'Plainly' of Communion for Remarried," https://onepeterfive.com/pope-speaking-plainly-communion-divorced-messy/.

408. See Raymond Burke, "'Amoris Laetitia' and the Constant Teaching and Practice of the Church," *National Catholic Register*, Apr. 12, 2016, http://www.ncregister.com/daily-news/amoris-laetitia-and-the-constant-teaching-and-practice-of-the-church/; Athanasius Schneider, "Official Response of Bishop Athanasius Schneider to Amoris Laetitia," *Rorate Cæli*, Apr. 26, 2016, https://rorate-caeli.blogspot.com/2016/04/official-response-of-bishop-athanasius.html; Edward Pentin, "Livi: 'Amoris Laetitia' Is Vulnerable to 'Every Malevolent Interpretation,'" *National Catholic Register*, Apr. 14, 2016, http://www.ncregister.com/blog/edward-pentin/livi-amoris-laetitia-is-vulnerable-to-every-malevolent-interpretation; Redazione, "Il preside dell'Istituto Giovanni Paolo II: 'L'esortazione è un documento positivo, non c'è alcun cambiamento," *Il Foglio*, Apr. 11, 2016, http://www.ilfoglio.it/chiesa/2016/04/11/il-preside-dellistituto-giovanni-paolo-ii-lesortazione-post-sinodale-un-documento-positivo-non-c-alcun-cambiamento___1-v-140538-rubriche_c868.htm; Thibaut Collin, "Couples non mariés, divorcés remariés: le pari osé du pape François," *Le Monde*, Apr. 6, 2016, https://www.lemonde.fr/idees/article/2016/04/08/couples-non-maries-divorces-remaries-le-pariose-du-pape-francois_4898896_3232.html; Robert Royal, "Beautiful, Moving, and Divisive," *The Catholic Thing*, Apr. 8, 2016, https://www.thecatholicthing.org/2016/04/08/beautiful-moving-and-divisive/.

409. On July 2, 2016, Bishop Athanasius Schneider wrote a letter to *The Remnant* commenting on *Amoris Laetitia*'s "ambiguous expressions" that, "contain a real spiritual danger, which will cause doctrinal confusion, a fast and easy spreading of heterodox doctrines concerning marriage and moral law, and also the adoption and consolidation of the praxis of admitting divorced and remarried to Holy Communion, a praxis which will trivialize and profane, as to say, at one blow three sacraments: the sacrament of Marriage, of Penance, and of the Most Holy Eucharist." Athanasius Schneider, "Bishop Athanasius Schneider Replies to *The Remnant*'s Open Letter on Amoris Laetitia," *The Remnant*, Jun. 2, 2016, http://remnantnewspaper.com/web/index.php/articles/item/2558-bishop-athanasius-schneider-replies-to-the-remnant-s-open-letter-on-amoris-laetitia.

410. In an interview with *Catholic News Service*, he stated: "Article 305 together with footnote 351 . . . directly contradicts article 84 of Pope John Paul II's exhortation *Familiaris consortio*. . . . It cannot be expected in a papal exhortation that people will rejoice in a pleasant text and ignore decisive sentences, which change the teachings of the Church. There is actually only a clear yes or no decision: to give Communion or not. . . . That it is an issue of a breach emerges doubtlessly for every thinking person, who knows the respective texts." Anian Christoph Wimmer, "Full Text: Interview With Robert Spaemann on Amoris Laetitia," *Catholic News Agency*, Apr. 29, 2016, https://www.catholicnewsagency.com/news/full-text-interview-with-robert-spaemann-on-amoris-laetitia-10088.

are included in this group.[411] Others, similarly claiming that the change implied a serious breach with Church traditional teaching, called for the repeal of *Amoris Laetitia* by the current pope or a successor.[412]

Nevertheless, numerous diocesan bishops and some Bishops' Conferences have published documents to implement the Apostolic Exhortation. Some did this in a sense that maintains traditional discipline. Others authorized civilly "remarried" divorcees to receive Holy Communion after a period of discernment. Due to this work's limited scope, I will not list them here. The number of documents and the various grounds alleged for their pastoral applications is substantial.

From the "Declaration of Fidelity to the Church's Unchangeable Teaching on Marriage" to the *Correctio Filialis*

In September 2016, promoters of the Filial Appeal issued a petition titled, "Declaration of Fidelity to the Church's Unchangeable Teaching on Marriage and to Her Uninterrupted Discipline." Its 36,049 signatories included three cardinals, nine bishops, 636 diocesan and religious priests, 46 deacons, 25 seminarians, 51 lay religious, 150 cloistered and active nuns, as well as 458 academics, professors of theology and religion, catechists, and pastoral workers. The Declaration stated that:

> . . . irregular unions of cohabitating Catholics who never married in the Church, or divorcees who have attempted a civil marriage, radically contradict and cannot express the good of Christian marriage, neither

---

411. Josef Seifert published an article titled, "*Amoris Laetitia*: Joy, Sadness and Hopes" in the German philosophy and theology journal *AEMAET*. He stated: "I think that some passages of AL, *particularly* those that are likely to have the greatest effect, are cause of great concern and even of deep sadness, not only because some of them can easily lead to misunderstandings and in their consequence to abuse, but also because others—at least apparently—stand in sharp conflict with the word of God and the teaching of the Catholic Church on the moral order, on intrinsically wrong and disordered actions, on the divine commandments and on our ability to keep them with the help of divine grace, on the indissolubility of marriage, on the sanctity of the sacraments of the Eucharist and marriage, on eternal damnation (hell), and on the sacramental discipline and pastoral care of the Church that derives from the Word of God and from a 2000 year old sacred tradition of the Church." Josef Seifert, "*Amoris Laetitia*: Joy, Sadness and Hopes," *AEMAET* 5, no. 2 (2016): 169, http://www.aemaet.de/index.php/aemaet/article/view/35/pdf.

412. See, for example, Claude Barthe, "L'instinct de la foi," *L'Homme Nouveau*, Apr. 6, 2016, http://www.hommenouveau.fr/1647/tribune-libre/l-instinct-de-la-foi.htm; James V. Schall, SJ, "In *Amoris Laetitia*, Who Is Admonishing Whom?" *Catholic World Report*, Apr. 8, 2016, https://www.catholicworldreport.com/2016/04/08/in-who-is-admonishing-whom/; Roberto de Mattei, "L'esortazione post-sinodale Amoris Laetitia: Prime riflessioni su un documento catastrofico," *Corrispondenza Romana*, Apr. 13, 2016, http://www.corrispondenzaromana.it/lesortazione-post-sinodale-amoris -laetitia-prime-riflessioni-su-un-documento-catastrofico/; Luíz S. Solimeo, "Because of Its Grave Errors 'Amoris Laetitia' Should Be Rejected," *TFP.org*, May 4, 2016, http://www.tfp.org/tfp-home/catholic -perspective/because-of-its-grave-errors-amoris-laetitia-should-be-rejected.html; Matthew McCusker, "Key Doctrinal Errors and Ambiguities of Amoris Laetitia," *Voice of the Family*, May 7, 2016, http://voiceofthefamily.com/key-doctrinal-errors-and-ambiguities-of-amoris-laetitia/.

partially nor analogously, and should be seen as a sinful way of life or
as a permanent occasion of grave sin. . . .

[from which is deduced] the impossibility of giving absolution and
Holy Communion to Catholics living manifestly in an objective state
of grave sin.[413]

Earlier, in July 2016, forty-five Catholic theologians and scholars sent a circular letter to every cardinal and the prefect of the Congregation for the Doctrine of the Faith. Their missive included a "Theological Critique" of *Amoris Laetitia*. The analysis stigmatized many of the Apostolic Exhortation's passages with a theological censure: Eleven propositions were censured as *haeretica* (heretical), five as *erronea in fide* (erroneous in the Faith), three as false. Most others incur the censures of *aequivoca* (equivocal), *ambigua* (ambiguous), *obscura* (obscure), *praesumptuosa* (presumptuous), *anxia* (causing uneasiness), *dubia* (doubtful), *captiosa* (captious), *malesonans* (evil-sounding), *piarum aurium offensiva* (offensive to pious ears).[414]

A year later, on September 24, 2017, sixty-two Catholic priests and intellectuals from twenty nations (most of them signatories of the circular letter to the College of Cardinals) made public a letter they had sent to Pope Francis. The public version was titled, *Correctio filialis de haeresibus propagatis* (Filial correction due to the propagation of heresies). After publication, additional signatories joined, for a combined total of 250 distinguished individuals. This *Filial Correction* stated that the pope—through his Apostolic Exhortation *Amoris Laetitia* and other statements, deeds, and omissions—has upheld seven heretical positions on marriage, moral life, and the reception of the sacraments, and promoted the spreading of such heretical opinions within the Church.[415] Questioned about the *Correctio filialis*, the secretary of state, Cardinal Pietro Parolin, declared, "It is important to dialogue, even within the Church."[416]

---

413. "Declaration of Fidelity to the Church's Unchangeable Teaching on Marriage and to Her Uninterrupted Discipline," *Filial Appeal*, nos. 6, 26, accessed Jul. 23, 2018, http://www.filialappeal.org/full.

414. The "Theological Critique" says that it "does not deny or question the personal faith of Pope Francis." Instead, it affirms that *Amoris Laetitia* contains "many statements whose vagueness or ambiguity permit interpretations that are contrary to faith or morals, or that suggest a claim that is contrary to faith and morals without actually stating it. It also contains statements whose natural meaning would seem to be contrary to faith or morals." Joseph Shaw, et al., "The Apostolic Exhortation *Amoris Laetitia*: A Theological Critique," *OnePeterFive*, p. 2, accessed Jul. 24, 2018, https://onepeterfive.com/wp-content/uploads/2016/07/45 -theologians-censure-AL.pdf.

415. "*Correctio filialis de haeresibus propagatis*," Jul. 16, 2017, http://www.correctiofilialis.org/wp-content /uploads/2017/08/Correctio-filialis_English_1.pdf.

416. "Parolin, lettera eresie? Occorre dialogo," *ANSA*, Sept. 28, 2017, http://www.ansa.it/sito/notizie/cronaca/2017/09/28/parolin-lettera-eresie-occorre-dialogo_3ec88a16 -fa2a-463a-b94a-d80747159e61.html.

Four Cardinals Present Five *Dubia* and Pope Francis Does Not Respond
Meanwhile, four well-known cardinals undertook an even more critical initiative with enormous repercussion.

The diametrically opposite interpretations of *Amoris Laetitia*, and its practical guidelines, as well as the confusion swirling among the faithful, prompted another action. On September 19, 2016, Cardinals Walter Brandmüller, Raymond Burke, and the later deceased Carlo Caffarra and Joachim Meisner sent a private letter to the pope, with a copy to the Congregation for the Doctrine of the Faith. In their letter, they expounded five doubts concerning *Amoris Laetitia*'s chapter 8.[417] These *dubia* were:

> It is asked whether . . . it has now become possible to grant absolution in the sacrament of penance and thus to admit to holy Communion a person who, while bound by a valid marital bond, lives together with a different person *more uxorio* [as husband and wife]. . . .
>
> [D]oes one still need to regard as valid the teaching . . . on the existence of *absolute moral norms* that prohibit intrinsically evil acts and that are binding without exceptions? . . .
>
> [I]s it still possible to affirm that a person who habitually lives in contradiction to a commandment of God's law . . . finds him or herself in an *objective situation of grave habitual sin*? . . .
>
> [D]oes one still need to regard as valid the teaching . . . according to which "circumstances or intentions can never transform an act intrinsically evil by virtue of its object into an act 'subjectively' good or defensible as a choice"? . . .
>
> [D]oes one still need to regard as valid the teaching . . . that conscience can never be authorized to legitimate exceptions to absolute moral norms that prohibit intrinsically evil acts by virtue of their object?[418]

Once the letter became public, several prelates expressed their support and desire that the pope respond clearly to the *dubia*. Among them were Chinese

---

417. Acknowledging that confirming the baptized in the Faith and dissipating ambiguities that can create divisions in the Church are at the core of the Petrine ministry is an act of fidelity to the papacy. In addition, every cardinal has the duty to assist the pope in his solicitude for the universal Church. The practice called *dubia* (Latin for "doubts"), of sending formal questions to the pope and to the Congregation for the Doctrine of the Faith that are formulated to elicit a straightforward *yes* or *no* answer, without theological arguments, has existed in the Church for hundreds of years.

418. Edward Pentin, "Full Text and Explanatory Notes of Cardinals' Questions on 'Amoris Laetitia,'" *National Catholic Register*, Nov. 14, 2016, http://www.ncregister.com/blog/edward-pentin/full-text -and-explanatory-notes-of-cardinals-questions-on-amoris-laetitia.

Cardinal Joseph Zen Ze-kiun, bishop emeritus of Hong Kong;[419] Most. Rev. Jan Watroba, bishop of Rzeszów and chairman of the Polish Bishops' Conference's Committee for the Family;[420] Most Rev. Józef Wróbel, auxiliary bishop of Lublin, Poland;[421] and Most Rev. Athanasius Schneider, auxiliary bishop of Astana, Kazakhstan.[422]

The "Welcoming" Pope Denies the *Dubia* Cardinals an Audience

Since the Holy Father decided not to respond, the four cardinals interpreted his silence as an invitation to continue the discussion calmly and respectfully. However, eight months after the *dubia* were first presented, Pope Francis gave indications that he would not respond since he felt that the *dubia* do not allow for categorical responses.[423]

Perhaps this explains why the pope did not respond to the sorely missed Cardinal Caffarra's request for an audience on the four cardinals' behalf. The request was made through a letter dated April 25, 2017. In that audience, the cardinals would have personally talked with the pope about the *dubia*, because of *Amoris Laetitia*'s varying interpretations, whereby, "What is sin[ful] in Poland is good in Germany ... what is prohibited in the archdiocese of Philadelphia is permitted in Malta. And so on." Moreover, the cardinal wished to speak with the Holy Father, because of the "numerous

---

419. See Raymond Arroyo, "The World Over With Raymond Arroyo," Feb. 16, 2017, *Twitter*, 16:05–16:18, https://twitter.com/RaymondArroyo/status/833679507668230144; *YouTube*, 16:05–16:18, https://www.youtube.com/watch?v=xHQc7rQeY_U&t=2s.

420. See "Streit um 'Amoris Laetitia,'" *Die Tagespost*, Oct. 18, 2017, https://www.die-tagespost.de/politik /Streit-um-bdquo-Amoris-laetitia-ldquo;art315,174099.

421. See Michele M. Ippolito, "Il vescovo Wrobel: 'La Amoris Laetitia non é stata scritta bene,'" *La Fede Quotidiana*, Nov. 21, 2016, http://www.lafedequotidiana.it/vescovo-wrobel-la-amoris-laetitia-non -stata-scritta-bene/.

422. See Athanasius Schneider, "Una nuova voce si leva: Il vescovo Athanasius Schneider in difesa dei quattro cardinali," *Corrispondenza Romana*, Nov. 24, 2016, https://www.corrispondenzaromana.it /speciale-una-nuova-voce-si-leva-il-vescovo-athanasius-schneider-in-difesa-dei-quattro-cardinali/.

423. Just three days after the *dubia*'s disclosure, in an interview with the newspaper *Avvenire*, on November 17, 2016, Pope Francis stated, "Some—think of certain replies to *Amoris Laetitia*—continue not to understand; white or black, even if it is in the flow of life that one must discern." Stefania Falasca, "L'intervista ad *Avvenire*. Papa Francesco: Non svendo la dottrina, seguo il Concilio," *Avvenire*, Nov. 17, 2016, https://www.avvenire.it/papa/pagine/giubileo-ecumenismo-concilio-intervista-esclusiva-del-papa -ad-avvenire. Fr. Antonio Spadaro spoke in the same sense in answer to *Crux*'s question, "Why hasn't the pope responded to the cardinals?" He stated: "The pope doesn't give binary answers to abstract questions. But that doesn't mean he hasn't responded. His response is to approve and to encourage positive pastoral practices." Further on, he added, "The ones who really understand Catholic doctrine are the pastors, because doctrine does not exist for the purpose of debate but for the *salus animarum* ['the health of souls']—for salvation rather than intellectual discussion." Austen Ivereigh, "Jesuit Close to Pope Says Attacks on 'Amoris' Are 'Part of the Process,'" *Crux*, Dec. 4, 2016, https://cruxnow.com/interviews /2016/12/04/jesuit-close-pope-says-many-attacks-amoris-result-bad-spirit/.

statements [that] have appeared from individual bishops, cardinals, and even Bishops' Conferences, approving what the magisterium of the Church has never approved."[424]

Prominent individuals close to Pope Francis have argued that a response to the *dubia* would be superfluous. They claim it has already been given during the Synod's discussions and that the answer can be found in the Apostolic Exhortation itself.[425] However, this borders on a fallacious circular argument: To interpret *Amoris Laetitia*'s ambiguities, one must look at *Amoris Laetitia*'s ambiguous terms . . .

One could readily respond to such claims with journalist Phil Lawler, editor of *Catholic World News*. He wrote, "If the papal teaching is clear, how can it mean one thing in Poland, and another in Germany? If the final answer to that vexed question is No in Philadelphia and Portland, how can it be Yes in Chicago and San Diego? If some bishops are interpreting the papal document incorrectly, why have they not been corrected?"[426]

In the an interview with the Crux website (see footnote 423), Father Spadaro said: "The questions of the four cardinals have actually already had an answer during the Synod, where the dialogue was broad, profound and above all frank . . . *Amoris Laetitia* is the ripe fruit of the Synod. And in the Synod, all the necessary answers were given more than once."

A Papal Statement Adds to the Confusion

Just weeks after the four cardinals' audience request, a rescript—an administrative act issued by a competent authority—dated June 5, 2017, and signed by the cardinal secretary of state, ordered the publication of two documents on the Vatican website and in the *Acta Apostolicae Sedis* (AAS). Described as authentic magisterium, the two documents were: (a) A note containing the criteria drawn up by the bishops of the Buenos Aires pastoral

---

424. Sandro Magister, "Another Letter from the Four Cardinals to the Pope. This Too With No Response," *L'Espresso–Settimo Cielo*, Jun. 20, 2017, http://magister.blogautore.espresso.repubblica.it/2017/06/20 /another-letter-from-the-four-cardinals-to-the-pope-this-too-with-no-response/.

425. Cardinal Oscar Rodríguez Maradiaga told Swiss Italian Radio "I think, first, that they have not read *Amoris Laetitia*, because unfortunately, this is the case!" Ettore Gotti Tedeschi, "Cadinali, guerre di religione e dubia," *La Nuova Bussola Quotidiana*, Apr. 14, 2017, http://www.lanuovabq.it/it/articoli-cardinali-guerre -di-religione-e-dubia-19547.htm. Interviewed in Alcalá de Henares, Spain, the prefect of the Apostolic Penitentiary, Cardinal Mauro Piacenza said that the pontiff did not respond to the *dubia* "simply because he believed that he had responded in practice through his document." Marco Tosatti, "Da Hong Kong al Kazakistan, adesione ai 'dubia,'" *La Nuova Bussola Quotidiana*, Feb. 26, 2017, http://www.lanuovabq.it/it /articoli-da-hong-kong-al-kazakistan-adesione-ai-dubia-19066.htm.

426. Phil Lawler, "On Request for Clarification of Amoris Laetitia, the Pope's Silence Speaks Volumes," *Catholic Culture*, Nov. 16, 2016, https://www.catholicculture.org/commentary/otn.cfm?id=1185.

region,[427] and (b) Pope Francis's letter of approval to such criteria stating that "there are no other interpretations."[428] On December 6, 2017, Andrea Tornielli, a journalist close to the pope, announced in *Vatican Insider* that Cardinal Parolin's rescript containing both documents had been published on the AAS website and in its printed issue as an October 2016 document, the month of its promulgation.

The rescript's disclosure increased the confusion even more because the Argentine Bishops' criteria would admit divorced and "remarried" Catholics to Holy Communion. On December 5, 2017, Cardinal Francesco Coccopalmerio, president of the Pontifical Council for Legislative Texts, told *Catholic News Service*:

> The fact that the pope requested that his letter and the interpretations of the Buenos Aires bishops be published in the AAS means that His Holiness has given these documents a particular qualification that elevates them to the level of being official teachings of the Church....
>
> Thus together the two documents became the Holy Father's authentic magisterium for the whole Church.[429]

For his part, veteran Vatican analyst Marco Tosatti wrote:

> The news can only serve to further feed the confusion and uncertainty surrounding the controversial apostolic exhortation and the pope's way of doing things....
>
> For what purpose? To oblige everyone to give religious assent to a magisterium expressed in oblique and ambiguous forms or to reply without committing himself in a direct response that would

---

427. On Sept. 5, 2016, the bishops of the Pastoral Region of Buenos Aires sent their priests a note with "minimal criteria" according to which "5) When the concrete circumstances of a couple make it feasible . . . one can propose they commit to live in continence." But, "6) In other, more complex circumstances . . . the aforementioned option may not be feasible. . . . [so that] when a person judges that he would commit another fault by harming the offspring of the new union, *Amoris Laetitia* opens the possibility of access to the sacraments of Reconciliation and the Eucharist." "Obispos de la Región Buenos Aires dan criterios pastorales sobre los divorciados en nueva unión," *AICA*, Sept. 13, 2016, nos. 5–6, http://www.aica.org/25025-obispos-de-la-region-buenos-aires-dan-criterios-pastorales-sobre.html.

428. Francis, "Carta del Santo Padre Francisco a los Obispos de la Región Pastoral de Buenos Aires," Sept. 5, 2016, http://w2.vatican.va/content/francesco/es/letters/2016/documents/papa-francesco_20160905 _regione-pastorale-buenos-aires.html. See also, *Acta Apostolicae Sedis*, vol. 108, no. 10, pp. 1071–4, http://www.vatican.va/archive/aas/documents/2016/acta-ottobre2016.pdf; Andrea Tornielli, "Amoris Laetitia, il papa rende ufficiale la lettera ai vescovi argentini," *La Stampa–Vatican Insider*, Dec. 6, 2017, http://www.lastampa.it/2017/12/06/vaticaninsider/ita/vaticano/amoris-laetitia-il-papa-rende -ufficialela-lettera-ai-vescovi-argentini-7Uzx2Ijt6sIYUdZNAQl0wI/pagina.html.

429. Cindy Wooden, "Pope's Letter to Argentine Bishops on 'Amoris Laetitia' Part of Official Record," *Catholic News Service*, Dec. 6, 2017, http://www.catholicnews.com/services/englishnews/2017/popes -letter-to-argentine-bishops-on-amoris-laetitia-part-of-official-record.cfm.

unequivocally reveal the pope's mind to the doubtful and perplexed?[430]

Brave Reaction by Three Kazakh Bishops

After an official stamp was given to the bishops of the Buenos Aires Pastoral Region's interpretation of *Amoris Laetitia*, on December 31, 2017, feast of the Holy Family, three Kazakhstan shepherds—Most Rev. Tomasz Peta, metropolitan archbishop of Astana; his auxiliary bishop Most Rev. Athanasius Schneider; and the archbishop emeritus of Karaganda, Most Rev. Jan Pawel Lenga—published a "Profession of the Immutable Truths About Sacramental Marriage." They observed that, after the publication of the Apostolic Exhortation, various Bishops' Conferences and individual bishops issued norms allowing some civilly "remarried" divorcees to receive Holy Communion. They stated further that those norms received an approval:

> . . . even from the supreme authority of the Church. . . .
> [These norms] caused a considerable and ever increasing confusion among the faithful and the clergy. . . .
> [And they are] a means of . . . . spreading the 'plague of divorce' even in the life of the Church.

Accordingly, these prelates felt obliged to reiterate seven immutable truths on the sacrament of marriage to the faithful. They end, saying, "It is not licit (*non licet*) to justify, approve, or legitimize either directly or indirectly divorce and a non-conjugal stable sexual relationship through the sacramental discipline of the admission of so-called 'divorced and remarried' to Holy Communion, in this case a discipline alien to the entire Tradition of the Catholic and Apostolic faith."[431] Afterward, one cardinal and five more bishops endorsed "Profession of the Immutable Truths."

A "Multi-Speed" Church Based on Geographically Differentiated Pastoral Disciplines

Neither the "Profession" nor any of the earlier initiatives—Filial Appeal, *Dubia*, *Correctio filialis*, and so on—received an answer from Pope Francis or any

---

430. Marco Tosatti, "Vatican. Una notizia ambigua; Un'indiscrezione e una voce che speriamo non sia confermata su mons. Gaenswein," *Stilum Curiæ*, Dec. 1, 2017, http://www.marcotosatti.com/2017/12/01/vaticano-una-notizia-ambigua-unindiscrezione-e-una-voce-che-speriamo-non-sia-confermata-su-mons-gaenswein/; see Dorothy Cummings McLean, "Confusion Explodes as Pope Francis Throws Magisterial Weight Behind Communion for Adulterers," *LifeSiteNews*, Dec. 4, 2017, https://www.lifesitenews.com/news/pope-upgrades-guidelines-allowing-communion-for-adulterers-to-authentic-mag.

431. "Full Text of Kazakhstan Catholic Bishops Statement on Amoris Laetitia," *LifeSiteNews*, Jan. 2, 2018, https://www.lifesitenews.com/news/full-text-of-kazakhstan-catholic-bishops-statement-on-amoris-laetitia.

agency of the Holy See. Senior Vatican analyst and *Crux* editor, John L. Allen, Jr., speculated that "the pope's strategic silence," was due to an "apparent willingness to tolerate a bit of pastoral chaos at the moment." According to Allen, the varying implementations "will allow people to do some comparing and contrasting," and thus "find out which side has the better read on reality."[432]

That interpretation of the developments would not be arbitrary since, in *Amoris Laetitia*, Pope Francis himself said that, "not all discussions of doctrinal, moral or pastoral issues need to be settled by interventions of the magisterium. Unity of teaching and practice . . . does not preclude various ways of interpreting some aspects of that teaching or drawing certain consequences from it. . . . Each country or region, moreover, can seek solutions better suited to its culture and sensitive to its traditions and local needs."[433] Incidentally, the pope declared himself aware of the risk of confusion that such differentiated interpretations and solutions entail: "I understand those who prefer a more rigorous pastoral care which leaves no room for confusion. But I sincerely believe that Jesus wants a Church attentive to the goodness which the Holy Spirit sows in the midst of human weakness."[434]

Also, in the Synod's closing speech, the pope expressed himself in favor of different solutions for various geographical areas: "And—apart from dogmatic questions clearly defined by the Church's magisterium—we have also seen that what seems normal for a bishop on one continent, is considered strange and almost scandalous—almost!—for a bishop from another; . . . what for some is freedom of conscience is for others simply confusion. Cultures are in fact quite diverse, and every general principle—as I said, dogmatic questions clearly defined by the Church's magisterium—every general principle needs to be inculturated."[435]

The papal promotion of geographically differentiated practices inaugurated a multi-speed Church where a single moral problem is regulated differently, depending on where one is. German-speaking, so-called *adult* Catholics are allowed to follow the fast-track missionary evangelization, while *backward* Catholics attached to their traditions, be they Africans or Poles, are permitted to follow a slower pace.[436]

---

432. John L. Allen, Jr., "Does Francis Have an 'R&D Strategy' on the Divorced/Remarried?" *Crux*, Nov. 14, 2016, https://cruxnow.com/analysis/2016/11/14/francis-rd-strategy-divorcedremarried/.

433. Francis, *Amoris Laetitia*, no. 3.

434. Ibid., no. 308.

435. Francis, "Conclusion of the Synod of Bishops," Oct. 24, 2015.

436. See Roberto de Mattei, "The Failed Synod: Everyone Defeated, and Catholic Morality in Particular," trans. Francesca Romana, *Rorate Cœli*, Oct. 27, 2015, https://rorate-caeli.blogspot.com/2015/10/de-mattei-failed-synod-everyone.html?m=1.

Regardless of Pope Francis's intentions, his refusal to respond to the *dubia* and to other initiatives by paradigm shift opponents has objectively increased the confusion among the faithful and division within the Church.[437]

Serious Threats of Division Among Catholics

In the face of this situation, prelates with lofty responsibilities or who are respected for their learning agree that the confusion among the faithful could lead to a schism.

"Uncertainty, confusion and disorientation among many faithful" is the expression used by the *dubia* cardinals in their September 19, 2016 letter to Pope Francis. Later, in a note explaining their disclosure of the letter, they added, "We have noted a grave disorientation and great confusion of many faithful regarding extremely important matters for the life of the Church."[438]

"It is a fact—which only a blind man can deny—that there exists in the Church, a great confusion, uncertainty, and insecurity," Cardinal Caffarra later asserted to the newspaper *Il Foglio*.[439] Likewise, in an interview with the newspaper *The Remnant*, Cardinal Burke stated, "There's great danger of a continued confusion in the Church, which is leading souls into error with regard to

---

437. In an interview to EWTN, Cardinal Burke responded to Fr. Antonio Spadaro's accusation that the *dubia* promoters were creating division in the Church. The cardinal stated: "Only when these questions, which we have raised according to the traditional manner of resolving questions in the Church which have to do with very serious matters, only when these questions are adequately answered will the division be dissipated. But as is happening right now, as long as this continues, the division will only grow and of course the fruit of division is error. And here we're talking about the salvation of souls, people being led into error in matters which have to do with their eternal salvation. And so Father Spadaro is very much in error in that affirmation." Claire Chretien, "Cardinal Burke Defends Dubia Signers in Blockbuster EWTN Interview," *LifeSiteNews*, Dec. 16, 2016, https://www.lifesitenews.com/news/cardinal-burke-responds-to -dubia-critics-not-a-sign-of-illness-to-care-abou.

On November 1, 2017, the moderately progressive *Crux* published a letter sent to the pope by Fr. Thomas G. Weinandy, OFM, Cap., professor emeritus at Oxford and the Gregorian University, a member of the International Theological Commission, and the former executive director of the Secretariat on Doctrine of the United States Catholic Conference. The theologian stated: "In *Amoris Laetitia*, your guidance at times seems intentionally ambiguous, thus inviting both a traditional interpretation of Catholic teaching on marriage and divorce as well as one that might imply a change in that teaching. . . . The Holy Spirit is given to the Church, and particularly to yourself, to dispel error, not to foster it. . . . Yet you seem to censor and even mock those who interpret Chapter 8 of *Amoris Laetitia* in accord with Church tradition as Pharisaic stone-throwers who embody a merciless rigorism. This kind of calumny is alien to the nature of the Petrine ministry." Thomas G. Weinandy, OFM, Cap., "July 31, 2017 Letter to the Holy Father," *Crux*, Nov. 1, 2017, https://cruxnow.com/wp-content/uploads/2017/10/Francis-Letter-Final.pdf.

438. Pentin, "Cardinals' Questions on Amoris Laetitia."

439. CWR Staff, "'Only a Blind Man Can Deny That There Is Great Confusion in the Church," trans. Andrew Guernsey, *Catholic World Report*, Jan. 15, 2017, https://www.catholicworldreport.com/2017/01/15/only -a-blind-man-can-deny-that-there-is-great-confusion-in-the-church/, translation of Matteo Matzuzzi, "'Solo un cieco può negare che nella Chiesa ci sia grande confusione'. Intervista al cardinale Caffarra," *Il Foglio*, Jan. 14, 2017, http://www.ilfoglio.it/chiesa/2017/01/14/news/carlo-caffarra-papa-sinodo-famiglia -coscienza-newman-chiesa-114939/.

questions that have to do with their very salvation."[440] He reiterated that position during a talk in Virginia:

> There continues to spread a very harmful confusion in the Church. . . .
> Many people because of this confusion are becoming very upset, and understandably so.[441]

In turn, Cardinal Robert Sarah, prefect of the Congregation for Divine Worship, warned, "Without a common faith, the Church is threatened by confusion and then, progressively, she can slide into dispersion and schism."[442] His assessment is similar to that of Bishop Schneider: "In our day, we see an ambiguity whose breadth is comparable only to the general confusion during the fourth-century Arian crisis. . . . There is not only a risk of schism, but a kind of schism already exists in the Church."[443]

"It Is Not to Be Excluded That I Will Enter History as the One Who Split the Catholic Church"

Even lay observers and analysts of Catholic life have commented on this division. In an interview with *Catholic News Agency*, well-known German philosopher Robert Spaemann stated, "Chaos has been erected as a principle, with the stroke of a pen. The pope should have known that with such a step he splits the Church and leads her toward a schism."[444] *The New York Times* columnist Ross Douthat spoke of a "low-grade civil war"[445] and "a submerged schism."[446] Guido Horst in the headline of an editorial in *Die Tagespost* referred to "de facto

440. Michael Matt, "The Remnant Interview of Cardinal Raymond Burke," *The Remnant*, Jan. 9, 2017, https://remnantnewspaper.com/web/index.php/articles/item/2980-the-remnant-interview-of-cardinal-raymond-burke.

441. Charles Collins, "Burke Again Says Pope Must Answer 'Amoris' Questions," *Crux*, Mar. 27, 2017, https://cruxnow.com/vatican/2017/03/27/burke-says-pope-must-answer-amoris-questions/.

442. Pete Baklinski, "Cardinal Sarah: Church Is Facing 'Grave Risk' of Schism Over Morality," *LifeSiteNews*, Apr. 24, 2017, https://www.lifesitenews.com/news/card.-sarah-a-decentralized-church-would-face-confusion-then-dispersion-the.

443. Athanasius Schneider, "Interview With TV-Libertés—'Terres de Mission,' Program no. 10," *TV-Libertés*, Dec. 4, 2016, 11:28–11:38, 13:06–13:16, https://gloria.tv/video/3TPZg1Enfkw9D7qULW8ejhcdY.

444. Robert Moynihan, "Letter #37, 2016–The Danger of Schism," *Inside the Vatican*, Apr. 28, 2016, https://insidethevatican.com/news/newsflash/letter-37-2016-danger-schism/.

445. Ross Douthat, "The New Catholic Truce," *The New York Times*, Apr. 9, 2016, https://www.nytimes.com/2016/04/10/opinion/sunday/the-new-catholic-truce.html.

446. Ross Douthat, "The End of Catholic Marriage," *The New York Times*, Dec. 1, 2016, https://douthat.blogs.nytimes.com/2016/12/01/the-end-of-catholic-marriage/.

schism."[447] More incisively, philosopher Marcello Pera, former president of the Italian Senate, told the Naples daily *Il Mattino* that, "there is a schism hidden in the Catholic world, which is pursued by Bergoglio with determination and obstinacy."[448] Measuring his words, *EWTN* lead anchor Raymond Arroyo said in a panel discussion that the climate in the Church "gives the feeling of a schism. It's not a schism, but it gives the feeling of one."[449] Even Charles Collins, *Crux*'s managing editor and a journalist favorable to the current pontificate's orientation admitted: "It is difficult not to acknowledge the confusion in the Church."[450]

Indeed, the idea that the Church is enveloped in confusion and moving toward schism is widespread. Thus, *Der Spiegel*'s Italy correspondent did not fear being dubbed a fake news source when he reported that, in a moment of self-criticism, the pope is alleged to have said: "It is not to be excluded that I will enter history as the one who split the Catholic Church."[451]

447. Guido Horst, "Leitartikel: Faktisches schisma," Oct. 18, 2017, *Die Tagespost*, https://www.die-tagespost.de/politik/Leitartikel-Faktisches-Schisma;art315,175459.

448. Niccolò Magnani, "Marcello Pera vs papa Francesco/'Bergoglio fa politica, è in atto uno scisma nella Chiesa,'" *Il Sussidiario*, Jul 10, 2017, http://www.ilsussidiario.net/News/Cronaca/2017/7/10/Marcello-Pera-vs-Papa-Francesco-Bergoglio-fa-politica-e-in-atto-uno-scisma-nella-Chiesa-/773071/.

449. Claire Chretien, "'It Gives the Feeling of a Schism': EWTN Panel Analyzes Current 'Disaster' in the Church," *LifeSiteNews*, Feb. 17, 2017, https://www.lifesitenews.com/news/it-gives-the-feeling-of-a-schism-ewtn-panel-analyzes-current-disaster-in-th.

450. Collins, "Burke Again Says Pope Must Answer."

451. Walter Mayr, "Der papst kocht," *Der Spiegel*, Dec. 23, 2016, http://www.spiegel.de/panorama/gesellschaft/vatikan-kritik-an-papst-franziskus-nimmt-vor-weihnachten-zu-a-1127247.html.

CHAPTER 8

The Paradigm Shift's Common Denominator: Adapting to Revolutionary and Anti-Christian Modernity

Whatever the field affected by Pope Francis's paradigm shift, a shared trait is always the desire to embrace modernity and align the Church with the secular and anti-Christian Revolution which most popes over the last two centuries condemned in various ways. Thus, preaching on God is increasingly replaced with preaching human values.

While each change described in previous chapters is grave, even more so is this pontificate's overall direction. Adapting to the "spirit of the world" seems to be its common denominator. Regarding Western civilization, this specifically means adjusting to a revolutionary process that has been destroying its Christian character in the name of modernity since the Renaissance.

Modernity's Profound Moral Unity Is the Mentality of the Anti-Christian Revolution

It is often said in progressive environments that a Catholic must be a man of his time. Such progressives claim that Catholics must accept the transformations and progress that make society today different from previous times. What they forget to say is that such changes must conform to the spirit and doctrine of the Gospel if they are to be acceptable to the faithful. Only then will change promote authentic social progress. Thus, discerning the good and evil that exist in today's world is needed.

> The features of an age cannot be broken down into mutually autonomous, good and bad aspects. Every historical period has its own mentality, which simultaneously results from good and bad elements. If the former predominate and the latter are only secondary, the epoch, without being excellent, can be called good. On the contrary, if evil aspects dominate and good is found just in one or another detail, then the epoch must be called bad. In the problem of relationships between Catholics and their time, it is not enough to take a stand in the face of fragmentary aspects of the world in which they live. The faithful must consider the characteristics of the time in their profound moral unity and take

a stand in the face of it.[452]

Jean Baudrillard, Jacinto Lageira, and Alain Brunn recognize that profound moral unity of modern culture:

> Modernity is neither a sociological, political nor properly speaking a historical concept. It is a characteristic mode of civilization that opposes that of tradition, that is, all other previous or traditional cultures. . . .
> Inextricably entangled in both myth and reality, modernity is specified in all fields: modern state, modern technology, modern music and painting, modern customs and ideas—as a kind of general category and cultural imperative. . . . Variable in its forms, contents, in time and space, it is unstable and irreversible except as a value system, a myth—and in this sense, one needs to write it with a capital letter: Modernity. In this, it looks like Tradition. . . .
> It acts as a force-idea and a dominant ideology, sublimating the contradictions of history into the effects of civilization.[453]

From what Tradition did modernity seek to free itself and thus become the dominant ideology and historical path trodden over the last centuries? Clearly, it was the Catholic culture and civilization that prevailed in the Middle Ages.

Stages in the Process of De-Christianization of the West
Pope Pius XII succinctly described the stages of this philosophical and religious emancipation when he spoke of a subtle and mysterious *enemy* that has sought to effect the intellectual, moral, and social disintegration of Christendom:

> It has sought nature without grace [the Renaissance], reason without faith [Protestantism and the Enlightenment], freedom without authority [the French Revolution], and, at times, authority without freedom [Communism]. It is an "enemy" that has become more and more apparent with an absence of scruples that still surprises: Christ yes; the Church no! [Protestantism]. Afterward: God yes; Christ no! [the French Revolution's Enlightenment]. Finally the impious shout: God is dead and, even,

---

452. Antônio de Castro Mayer, *Carta pastoral sobre problemas do apostolado moderno: Contendo um catecismo de verdades oportunas que se opõem a erros contemporâneos*, 2nd ed. (Campos, Brazil: n. p., 1953), 55–6, https://www.pliniocorreadeoliveira.info/Carta%20Pastoral%20sobre%20os%20Erros%20do%20Apostolado%20Moderno.pdf.

453. Jean Baudrillard, Jacinto Lageira, and Alain Brunn, "Modernité," in *Encyclopédie Universalis*, accessed Jul. 24, 2018, https://www.universalis.fr/encyclopedie/modernite/.

God never existed! [Communism]. And behold now the attempt to build the structure of the world on foundations which we do not hesitate to indicate as the main causes of the threat that hangs over humanity: economy without God, law without God, politics without God.[454]

Plinio Corrêa de Oliveira called this enemy *the Revolution* with a capital *R*:

> Its profound cause is an explosion of pride and sensuality that has inspired, not one system, but, rather, a whole chain of ideological systems. Their wide acceptance gave rise to the three great revolutions in the history of the West: the Pseudo-Reformation, the French Revolution, and Communism.
>
> Pride leads to hatred of all superiority and, thus, to the affirmation that inequality is an evil in itself at all levels, principally at the metaphysical and religious ones. This is the egalitarian aspect of the Revolution.
>
> Sensuality, *per se*, tends to sweep aside all barriers. It does not accept restraints and leads to revolt against all authority and law, divine or human, ecclesiastical or civil. This is the liberal aspect of the Revolution.
>
> Both aspects, which in the final analysis have a metaphysical character, seem contradictory on many occasions. But they are reconciled in the Marxist utopia of an anarchic paradise.[455]

It would be wrong to think that the Revolution subverts only the political order: "A process so profound, vast, and prolonged cannot develop without encompassing every domain of human activity, such as culture, art, laws, customs, and institutions."[456]

---

454. Pius XII, "Allocation to the Union of Men of the Italian Catholic Action," Oct. 12, 1952, https://w2.vatican.va/content/pius-xii/it/speeches/1952/documents/hf_p-xii_spe_19521012_uomini-azione-cattolica.html.

455. Plinio Corrêa de Oliveira, *Revolution and Counter-Revolution*, 3rd English ed. (York, Penn.: The American Society for the Defense of Tradition, Family and Property, 1993), intro., 3, http://www.tfp.org/revolution-and-counter-revolution/. In his essay, Plinio Corrêa de Oliveira summarizes the historic stages of this centuries-long process as follows:

The Pseudo-Reformation was a first revolution. It implanted, in varying degrees, the spirit of doubt, religious liberalism, and ecclesiastical egalitarianism in the different sects it produced.

The French Revolution came next. It was the triumph of egalitarianism in two fields: the religious field in the form of atheism speciously labeled as secularism; and the political field through the false maxim that all inequality is an injustice, all authority a danger, and freedom the supreme good.

Communism is the transposition of these maxims to the socioeconomic field.

These three revolutions are episodes of one single Revolution, within which socialism, liturgicism, the *politique de la main tendue* (policy of the extended hand), and the like are only transitional stages or attenuated manifestations. Ibid., 3–4.

456. Ibid., 4.

From Clash to Dialogue With Revolutionary Modernity

Since the dawn of Christianity, clergy and faithful alike have been tempted to conform to the spirit of the world (see Rom. 12:2). This did not change when, from the Renaissance on, the revolutionary spirit of modernity began to dominate the cultural, intellectual, and political life of the West. Mainly from the nineteenth century on, the Church was pressured to adapt to the new emerging world. "It is not a matter of choosing between the principles of 1789 and the dogmas of the Catholic religion," exclaimed Duke Albert de Broglie, one of the leaders of the liberal Catholic bloc, "but to purify principles with dogmas and make both walk side by side. It is not a question of confronting each other in a duel but of making peace."[457]

Seeing the danger that Revolutionary principles would infiltrate society and Catholic circles, Pius IX[458] and Pius X[459] issued explicit condemnations against the attempt to reconcile the Church with modern errors. They urged Catholics to courageously confront the secular, liberal, and egalitarian offensives unleashed

---

457. Albert de Broglie, *Questions de religion et d'histoire* (Paris: Michel Lévy Frères, 1860), 2:199, https://books.google.com/books?id=9JUTIdKex-QC.

458. In his *Syllabus* (or Index of the main errors of his time), Pius IX condemned this proposition: "The Roman Pontiff can, and ought to, reconcile himself, and come to terms with progress, liberalism and modern civilization" (prop. 80). The condemned proposition is from the allocution *Iamdudum Cernimus,* given by Pius IX at the secret consistory of March 18, 1861. It states:

 Civil society in Our unhappy times is more than ever thrown into agitation and turmoil. Some defend principles they call the principles of modern civilization; others defend the rights of justice and of Our most holy religion. The former ask that the Roman Pontiff reconcile and make an alliance with what they call progress, liberalism, the new civilization. The latter rightly ask that the immutable and unshakable principles of eternal justice be kept inviolable in their integrity and that the salutary force of Our divine religion be fully safeguarded. . . .

 Therefore, We ask those who invite Us to extend a friendly hand to today's civilization, if the facts are such as to induce the Vicar of Christ on Earth—supernaturally established by Christ Himself to defend the purity of His heavenly doctrine and feed His lambs and sheep, confirming both in it—to make an alliance with the present-day civilization, from which come great evils that are never deplored enough, so many horrible opinions, and so many errors and false principles entirely contrary to the Catholic religion and its doctrine, without seriously injuring his conscience, and without great scandal for all the good. . . .

 If civilization were to be understood as a system expressly combined to weaken and perhaps overthrow the Church of Christ, it is certain that neither the Holy See nor the Roman Pontiff could ever come to an understanding with this civilization. Pius IX, Allocution *Iamdudum Cernimus,* Mar. 18, 1861, https://w2.vatican.va/content/pius-ix/it/documents/allocuzione-iamdudum-cernimus-18-marzo-1861.html.

459. Addressing the secret cause of disciplinary infractions in the behavior of followers of the popular, modernist-inspired educational movement *Le Sillon,* St. Pius X explained to the French bishops:

 You are the past; they are the pioneers of the civilization of the future. You represent the hierarchy, social inequalities, authority, and obedience—worn out institutions to which their hearts, captured by another ideal, can no longer submit. Occurrences so sad as to bring tears to Our eyes bear witness to this frame of mind. And we cannot, with all Our patience, overcome a just feeling of indignation. Now then! Distrust of the Church, their Mother, is being instilled into the minds of Catholic youth; they are being taught that after nineteen centuries She has not yet been able to build up in this world a society on true foundations; She has not understood the social notions of authority, liberty, equality, fraternity and human dignity; they are told that the great bishops and kings, who have made France what it is and governed it so gloriously, have not been able to give their people true justice and true happiness because they did not possess the Sillonist Ideal! Pius X, Encyclical *Notre Charge Apostolique,* Aug. 25, 1910, http://www.papalencyclicals.net/pius10/p10notre.htm.

by the promoters of the Revolution. Other pontiffs were less energetic. Others were even conciliatory. With John XXIII and the opening of the Second Vatican Council, that position of combat against modernity and its errors was officially abandoned and replaced with an attitude of benevolent dialogue with the modern world.

In his speech closing the Council, Pope Paul VI expressed very clearly the meaning of this change of attitude:

> Yes, the Church of the council has been concerned, not just with herself and with her relationship of union with God, but with man— man as he really is today. . . .
>
> Secular humanism, revealing itself in its horrible anti-clerical reality has, in a certain sense, defied the council. The religion of the God who became man has met the religion (for such it is) of man who makes himself God. And what happened? Was there a clash, a battle, a condemnation? There could have been, but there was none. The old story of the Samaritan has been the model of the spirituality of the council. A feeling of boundless sympathy has permeated the whole of it. The attention of our council has been absorbed by the discovery of human needs (and these needs grow in proportion to the greatness which the son of the earth claims for himself). But we call upon those who term themselves modern humanists, and who have renounced the transcendent value of the highest realities, to give the council credit at least for one quality and to recognize our own new type of humanism: we, too, in fact, we more than any others, honor mankind. . . .
>
> A wave of affection and admiration flowed from the council over the modern world of humanity. Errors were condemned, indeed, because charity demanded this no less than did truth, but for the persons themselves there was only warning, respect and love. Instead of depressing diagnoses, encouraging remedies; instead of direful prognostics, messages of trust issued from the council to the present-day world. The modern world's values were not only respected but honored, its efforts approved, its aspirations purified and blessed.[460]

Despite these candid intentions, the Catholic Faith at the time of the Council did not purify modernity's humanistic values. Instead, many, and especially the youth of the time, took these humanistic values to their final consequences.

---

460. Paul VI, "Address of Pope Paul VI During the Last General Meeting of the Second Vatican Council," Dec. 7, 1965, http://w2.vatican.va/content/paul-vi/en/speeches/1965/documents/hf_p-vi_spe _19651207_epilogo-concilio.html.

They leaped into postmodernity, that is, the current stage of the Revolution. There, "the height of individual liberty and of consentaneous collectivism"[461] was represented by the structuralist dream of the dissolution of all large social organizations. Small, self-managed urban and rural communities were to replace the destroyed institutions. Molded by the hippie generation, the members of these communes were to give up "the old standards of individual reflection, volition, and sensibility. These w[ould] be gradually replaced by forms of thought, deliberation, and sensibility that are increasingly collective."[462]

The May 1968 student revolt at Paris's Sorbonne University can be seen as the beginning of that profound change. Its most enduring cultural change has been the evaporation of authority in the family, school, business, and so forth. It also led to the loosening of morals with the Sexual Revolution. In the opinion of those who lived through the Sorbonne Revolution and analysts who later studied it, the Second Vatican Council to some extent anticipated and even favored the Sorbonne's outbreak by refusing to employ a language of dogmatic affirmations and a reiteration of moral prohibitions.[463]

---

461. Corrêa de Oliveira, *Revolution and Counter-Revolution*, 158.

462. Ibid.

463. "The demands of the movement of May '68," writes Mariologist and Council expert Fr. René Laurentin, "coincided to a great extent with the major ideas of the council, in particular of the conciliar constitution on the Church and the world." In his opinion, "Vatican II was already to some extent the dissent of a group of bishops who banded together against the curia that was trying to stage an institutionally prefabricated council." René Laurentin, *Enjeu du deuxième synode: Et contestation dans l'Église* (Paris: Seuil, 1969), 14, 16.

Religion sociologist Jean-Louis Schlegel writes: "Even before 1968, rebellion became widespread and extended to the Church herself, to her structures and behavior, as well as to the holders of religious power. . . .

"A post-conciliar climate of Christian 'insurrection' or 'subversion,' which tends to cast into outer darkness all that we had worshiped before, with the feeling that the Church has 'deceived us' thus joins the more general cultural, social, and political effervescence that has been developing since the early 1960s. . . .

"When Cardinal Marty, newly installed in Paris, stated that 'God is not conservative,' he winked at Catholics who indeed were so and who attacked the unbearable revolution. Philosopher Maurice Clavel took another step: he saw the [May 1968] events as an irruption of the Spirit." Jean-Louis Schlegel, "Changer l'Église en changeant la politique," in *À la gauche du Christ: Les chrétiens de gauche en France de 1945 à nos jours*, ed. Denis Pelletier and Jean-Louis Schelegel (Paris: Seuil, 2012), 279–80, 282.

In his book, *Principles of Catholic Theology*, Cardinal Joseph Ratzinger wrote about the post-council period, "The interdenominational communion that took place during the ecumenical Mass celebrated on the barricades was long regarded as a kind of salvation-historical event, as a revelation-event that introduced a new era of Christianity." Cardinal Joseph Ratzinger, *Principles of Catholic Theology: Building Stones for a Fundamental Theology*, trans. Mary Frances McCarthy, SND (San Francisco: Ignatius, 1987), 387–8.

As the editing of this work was wrapping up, historian Agostino Giovagnoli gave an interview to the *Servizio Informazione Religiosa* news agency. Questioned on the connection between the Second Vatican Council and the May '68 student revolts, he stated: "The '68 [revolution] was above all an anti-institutional challenge and it is on this terrain that one can recognize the nexus linking the two phenomena." He added, "The Catholic Church anticipated a transformation that later, in May 1968 presented itself in a convulsive way in the sense of a re-dimensioning of the weight of institutions within society." Giovanna Pasqualin Traversa, "Il Sessantotto. Agostino Giovagnoli (storico): 'Profondo legame con il Concilio che ne ha antecipato alcuni tratti,'" *Servizio Informazione Religiosa*, Apr. 26, 2018, https://agensir.it/italia/2018/04/26/il-sessantotto -agostino-giovagnoli-storico-profondo-legame-con-il-concilio-che-ne-ha-antecipato-alcuni-tratti/.

Pope Paul VI's Encyclical *Humanae Vitae* reiterated long-established Church doctrine and forbade the use of artificial methods of birth control. Rome then began to distance itself from the Sexual Revolution and to reaffirm moral principles. This was especially seen during the pontificate of John Paul II with the Encyclicals *Evangelium Vitae* and *Veritatis Splendor*, and the documents on homosexuality published by the Congregation for the Doctrine of the Faith, led by Cardinal Joseph Ratzinger.

However, with the election of Cardinal Jorge Mario Bergoglio that red line seems to have been crossed. As described in Chapter 6, Pope Francis's teachings and gestures show openness to postmodernity in the realm of sexual morals as well.

It seems this paradigm shift's remote origin can be found in the same positive stance vis-à-vis the evolution of contemporary society that John XXIII held regarding social change during his time. In his Apostolic Exhortation *Evangelii Gaudium*, Francis explains:

> Fifty years after the Second Vatican Council, we are distressed by the troubles of our age and far from naive optimism; yet the fact that we are more realistic must not mean that we are any less trusting in the Spirit or less generous. In this sense, we can once again listen to the words of Blessed John XXIII on the memorable day of 11 October 1962: "At times we have to listen, much to our regret, to the voices of people who, though burning with zeal, lack a sense of discretion and measure. In this modern age they can see nothing but prevarication and ruin ... We feel that we must disagree with those prophets of doom who are always forecasting disaster, as though the end of the world were at hand. In our times, divine Providence is leading us to a new order of human relations which, by human effort and even beyond all expectations, are directed to the fulfilment of God's superior and inscrutable designs, in which everything, even human setbacks, leads to the greater good of the Church."[464]

John Paul II established a red line regarding abortion and indissoluble marriage. The immediate origins for Francis's crossing of this line seem to be the agenda laid out by the late Cardinal Carlo Maria Martini. Indeed, Francis (also a Jesuit) considered himself to be the cardinal's disciple.[465] The spiritual testament

---

464. Francis, *Evangelii Gaudium*, no. 84.

465. In the foreword to the first volume of the controversial cardinal's *opera omnia*, titled *The Chair of Non-Believers*, Pope Francis says that "the legacy Cardinal Martini has left us is a precious gift. . . . How many of us, in Argentina, at the 'end of the world,' did the Spiritual Exercises from his texts. . . . He was a teacher to many of us who have heard his words and read his texts." Francis, "Il papa: 'La Chiesa missionaria non si chiuda in se stessa,'" *Corriere Della Sera*, Oct. 19, 2015, http://www.corriere.it/cronache/15_ottobre_19/papa-francesco-la-chiesa-missionaria-non-si-chiuda-se-stessa-2973aab8-7620-11e5-9086-b57baad6b3f4.shtml.

of this former archbishop of Milan was entrusted to his Jesuit confrere Georg Sporschill (with whom he wrote *Night Conversations With Cardinal Martini*) and journalist Federica Radice Fossati Confalonieri.[466] It was published in Milan's daily *Corriere della Sera* and contains this comment:

> The Church must recognize her own mistakes and walk a radical path of change, starting with the pope and bishops. Pedophilia scandals force us to tread the road of conversion. Questions about sexuality and all issues involving the body are an example. These themes are important to each person and are sometimes too important. We should ask ourselves if people still listen to the advice of the Church on sexual matters.... Neither the clergy nor Church Law can replace man's inner self.[467]

> All the external rules, the laws, the dogmas, are there to clarify this internal voice and for the discernment of spirits.
>
> Who are the sacraments for? . . . Are we carrying the sacraments to the people who need new strength? I think of all the divorced and remarried couples, to extended families.... The question of whether the divorced [and "remarried"] can receive Communion ought to be turned around. How can the Church reach people who have complicated family situations . . . ?
>
> The Church is 200 years behind the times. Why doesn't it stir? Are we afraid? Is it fear rather than courage?[468]

A "Church on the Move" That Overcomes Her Defensiveness Toward Today's World

To force the Church to conform to the modern world, Pope Francis uses keywords that have a talismanic effect. He talks of "building bridges." He mentions the need to dialogue instead of being a "builder of walls."[469] Being faithful

466. See Cardinal Carlo M. Martini and Georg Sporschill, *Night Conversations With Cardinal Martini* (Mahwah, N.J.: Paulist, 2012).

467. Georg Sporschill, SJ and Federica Radice Fossati Confalonieri, "'Chiesa indietro di 200 anni': L'ultima intervista: 'Perché non si scuote, perché abbiamo paura?'" *Corriere Della Sera*, Sept. 1, 2012, http://www.corriere.it/cronache/12_settembre_02/le-parole-ultima-intervista_cdb2993e-f50b-11e1-9f30-3ee01883d8dd.shtml.

468. John L. Allen, Jr., "Translated Final Interview With Martini," *National Catholic Reporter*, Sept. 4, 2012, https://www.ncronline.org/blogs/ncr-today/translated-final-interview-martini.

469. During a homily at Santa Marta, the pope said that today's Christians are like the Apostle Paul in the Aeropagus. "He did not say, 'Idolaters! You will go to hell! . . .'" No, he "tried to reach their hearts; he did not condemn from the outset but sought dialogue. 'Paul is a pope, a builder of bridges. He did not want to become a builder of walls.'" Francis, "Jesus Excludes No One: Morning Meditation in the Chapel of Domus Sanctae Marthae," May 8, 2013,

means "going out to the outskirts."[470] "An evangelizing community is also supportive, standing by people at every step of the way, no matter how difficult or
lengthy this may prove to be."[471] In this evangelizing effort, the bishop must
"sometimes go before his people, pointing the way." In some circumstances
though, he must "walk after them . . . allowing the flock to strike out on new
paths."[472] Catholics must be "a Church on the move."[473]

It is also necessary to "dialogue with states, dialogue with society—including
dialogue with cultures and the sciences—and dialogue with other believers."[474]
"In a culture which privileges dialogue as a form of encounter, it is time to de-
vise a means for building consensus and agreement."[475] This is all the more so
since "Seeing reality with the eyes of faith, we cannot fail to acknowledge what
the Holy Spirit is sowing." Not only "where great numbers of people have received baptism,"[476] but also where they practice "new ways of relating to God,
to others and to the world around us. . . . the places where new narratives and
paradigms are being formed."[477] This is important, "to overcome suspicion, habitual mistrust, fear of losing our privacy, all the defensive attitudes which
today's world imposes on us."[478]

Paradoxically, according to Francis, resisting today's spiritual and moral collapse would be an expression of "worldliness." Not locking step with the modern world would be a "self-absorbed Promethean neo-Pelagianism of those
who ultimately trust only in their own powers and feel superior to others because they observe certain rules or remain intransigently faithful to a particular

---

http://w2.vatican.va/content/francesco/en/cotidie/2013/documents/papa-francesco-cotidie_20130508
_non-exclusion.html.

   Pope Francis went on to say, "Now is a favorable time in the life of the Church: the last 50, 60 years are a
favorable time because, I remember when I was a child that one would hear in Catholic families, in my
family: 'No, we cannot go to their home because they are not married in the Church, they are socialist,
atheist eh!' It was like an exclusion. Now—thanks be to God—one no longer says that, isn't it so? One does
not say it! This existed as a defense of the faith, but with walls." Kelen Galvan, "Papa diz que para evangelizar, cristãos devem construir pontes e não muros," *Canção Nova–Notícias*, May 8, 2013,
https://noticias.cancaonova.com/especiais/pontificado/Francis/papa-diz-que-para-evangelizar
-cristaos-devem-construir-pontes-e-nao-muros/.

470. Francis, *Evangelii Gaudium*, no. 31.

471. Ibid., no. 24.

472. Ibid., no. 31.

473. John L. Allen, Jr., "In 2016, Pope Francis Wants a Church on the Move," *Crux*, Jan. 6, 2016,
https://cruxnow.com/church/2016/01/06/in-2016-pope-francis-wants-a-church-on-the-move/.

474. Francis, *Evangelii Gaudium*, no. 238.

475. Ibid., no. 239.

476. Ibid., no. 68.

477. Ibid., no. 74.

478. Ibid., no. 88.

Catholic style from the past. A supposed soundness of doctrine or discipline leads instead to a narcissistic and authoritarian elitism, whereby instead of evangelizing, one analyzes and classifies others."[479] Hence, "we have often been on the defensive, wasting pastoral energy on denouncing a decadent world."[480] Such actions, in the eyes of the world turn Catholics "into querulous and disillusioned pessimists, 'sourpusses.'"[481]

According to Francis, not even social developments that inevitably provoke the gradual disappearance of indissoluble marriage and the family should inspire Catholics to resist. Thus, *Amoris Laetitia* stated: "Neither today's society nor that to which we are progressing allow an uncritical survival of older forms and models."[482] All that would be left for the Church to do is adapt to the "anthropological and cultural changes" that today "influence all aspects of life."[483] For example, the need for pre-matrimonial and matrimonial pastoral care should not be confined to "the defense of a dry and lifeless doctrine"[484] or merely "solid doctrinal and spiritual convictions."[485] Instead, they should turn to "teachers and counselors, family and community physicians, social workers, juvenile and family advocates . . . drawing upon the contributions of psychology, sociology, marital therapy and counseling."[486]

An Immanentistic and Hegelian View of History
Like the late nineteenth century modernists did, Pope Francis rationalizes adapting the Church to "anthropological and cultural changes." According to him, the justification for change today is the divine impulse present in humanity's progress. In the previously mentioned interview with Fr. Antonio Spadaro, Pope Francis seemed to suggest an immanentistic and Teilhardian view of the universe and history. He attributed to *divine* action the impulses of new dynamics in *human* action:

> God manifests himself in historical revelation, in history . . . God is in history, in the processes. . . .
> God manifests himself in time and is present in the processes of

479. Ibid., no. 94.

480. Francis, *Amoris Laetitia*, no. 38.

481. Francis, *Evangelii Gaudium*, no. 85.

482. Francis, *Amoris Laetitia*, no. 32.

483. Ibid.

484. Ibid., no. 59.

485. Francis, *Evangelii Gaudium*, no. 80.

486. Francis, *Amoris Laetitia*, no. 204.

history. This gives priority to actions that give birth to new historical dynamics.[487]

Thus, in *Amoris Laetitia* the pope pointed out the need "to focus on concrete realities, since 'the call and the demands of the Spirit resound in the events of history.'"[488]

From that perspective, everything leads to the conclusion that this is an immanentist conception that would also include a dialectical dimension derived from the Hegelian notion of a relative truth. Accordingly, to advance toward the new world, one must also rely on the "constant tensions present in every social reality,"[489] "tensions and oppositions [which] can achieve a diversified and life-giving unity,"[490] always remembering that "the principal author, the historic subject of this process, is the people as a whole and their culture."[491] He has told the flock to ever remember that "in the constant tension between fullness and limitation," and in the "brighter horizon of the utopian future,"[492] time is greater than space, because "time governs spaces, illumines them and makes them links in a constantly expanding chain, with no possibility of return. What we need, then, is to give priority to actions which generate new processes in society."[493]

Therefore, a historical epoch cannot be judged by an absolute standard—the demands of truth revealed by God. Instead, it should be assessed by the humanistic and relativistic "criterion set forth by Romano Guardini: 'The only measure for properly evaluating an age is to ask to what extent it fosters the development and attainment of a full and authentically meaningful human existence, in accordance with the peculiar character and the capacities of that age.'"[494]

Embracing the Revolution at Every Stage
Consistent with Guardini's criterion, Pope Francis predictably sympathizes with each stage of the Revolution in the context of its time.

His goodwill toward its first stage (the Pseudo-Reformation) is evident in the already mentioned statements and gestures regarding Luther. His position

---

487. Spadaro, "A Big Heart."

488. Francis, *Amoris Laetitia*, no. 31.

489. Francis, *Evangelii Gaudium*, no. 221.

490. Ibid., no. 228.

491. Ibid., no. 239.

492. Ibid., no. 222.

493. Ibid., no. 223.

494. Ibid., no. 224.

regarding the second stage (the French Revolution) is ambivalent. He approved State secularization[495] and the human rights[496] it enshrined, but, on the other hand, the pope reckons that the democratic, bourgeois, and liberal political regime it promoted has turned against the lower classes and has been superseded by the ideal of participatory democracy. He believes further that nationalism is now a hindrance to the "dream of a new European humanism"[497] and to the new, globalized, multiethnic, and multicultural humanity. Lastly, he believes that the myth of progress promoted by Enlightenment philosophers in the revolutionary salons of 1789 has been overcome by a green worldview.[498]

By contrast, his appeal for the utopias of the third stage of the revolutionary process (Communism), and even for those of the Fourth Eco-tribalist Revolution, seems to be increasingly expressed by his efforts to bring together all popular and indigenist movements in the Vatican-sponsored World Meetings and collaboration with international bodies to promote ecological global governance.

The Church's Definitive *Ralliement* With the Revolution

The founder of *La Repubblica* had good reasons for titling his article on *Laudato Sì*: "Francis, the pope-prophet who meets modernity."[499] He said that the pope told him in a later meeting, "I will not have much time to finish the work to which I must dedicate myself, which is the fulfillment of the goals prescribed by Vatican II and particularly that of having the Church meet with modernity."[500]

According to Nicola di Bianco, professor of Theology at the Salernitano

---

495. "Confessional states end badly.... I believe that secularism accompanied by a strong law that guarantees religious freedom provides a framework for moving forward. We are all equal, as sons of God or [creations] of our personal dignity. But everyone should have the freedom to display their own faith publicly." Guillaume Goubert and Sébastien Maillard, "Le Pape François à *La Croix*: 'Un État doit être laïque,'" *La Croix*, May 16, 2016, http://www.la-croix.com/Religion/Pape/Le-pape-Francois-a-La-Croix-Un-Etat-doit-etre-laique-2016-05-16-1200760526.

496 "What has happened to you, the Europe of humanism, the champion of human rights, democracy and freedom?" Francis, "Conferral of the Charlemagne Prize."

497. Ibid.

498. In *Laudato Sì*, he states, "At one extreme, we find those who doggedly uphold the myth of progress and tell us that ecological problems will solve themselves simply with the application of new technology and without any need for ethical considerations or deep change....

"Whereas in the beginning [environmental education] was mainly centered on scientific information, consciousness-raising and the prevention of environmental risks, it tends now to include a critique of the 'myths' of a modernity grounded in a utilitarian mindset (individualism, unlimited progress, competition, consumerism, the unregulated market)." *Laudato Sì*, nos. 60, 210.

499. Eugenio Scalfari, "Francesco, papa profeta che incontra la modernità," *La Repubblica*, Jul. 1, 2015, http://www.repubblica.it/cultura/2015/07/01/news/francesco_papa_profeta_che_incontra_la_modernita_-118048516/.

500. Eugenio Scalfari, "Conservatori e temporalisti lo frenano ma Francesco non si fermerà," *La Repubblica*, Oct. 25, 2015, http://www.repubblica.it/politica/2015/10/25/news/conservatori_e_temporalisti_lo_frenano_ma_francesco_non_si_fermera_-125834299/.

Theological Institute, that meeting will actually go beyond the claims of modernity.

This becomes clear, considering that Freud attributed to modernity three "insults" to human narcissism:

- the Cosmic-Copernican: the earth is not the center of the universe;
- the biological-Darwinist: man is not the crowning of creation;
- the psychological-Freudian: affirmed the impotence of reason before the subconscious and the libido.

To these three "insults," Niklas Luhmann added a fourth: the sociological, modernity's present-day inability to model society.

Alluding to these "insults," Prof. Di Bianco says that the current pontiff wants to settle accounts with the history of the last few centuries. Francis's Church would recover the evolutionary stance by promoting processes and being Herself permanently "under construction." It would recover Freudian subjectivism by "declaring that the severity of guilt cannot be separated from the subject's imputability." And, finally, it would recover the sociological stance by upholding "the claims of the oppressed, marginalized, poor" and by denouncing "models of economic development that produce 'exclusions' and 'inequalities' and generate a 'throw-away' culture." Di Bianco concludes, saying that, "With his gestures, style and teaching Francis is reforming the Church, going beyond the 'insults' of 'modernity.'"[501]

The abundant documentation in previous chapters and the comments of Catholic intellectuals and agnostics who are friendly to Pope Francis suffice to reach a conclusion.

Thus, I conclude that this pontificate can be characterized as attempting to carry out a definitive *ralliement*[502] of the Church with the Revolution and its secularized humanism. Moreover, that this surrender of the Church to the Revolution is being done while the latter is at an impasse because, in its current stage, its final steps, the Revolution can no longer disguise the full stench and evil of its ultimate goal.

If consummated, this *ralliement* will produce catastrophic consequences for souls. Suffice it to consider this statement of Eugenio Scalfari: "The impulse [Francis] is giving the Ecclesia will have profoundly changed the concept

---

501. Nicola di Bianco, "Oltre gli 'insulti' della modernità," *La Stampa–Vatican Insider*, May 14, 2016, http://www.lastampa.it/2016/05/14/vaticaninsider/ita/commenti/oltre-gli-insulti-della-modernit -k3IrJh5mm8CBxVKgbAFDRM/pagina.html.

502. With the Encyclical *Au milieu des sollicitudes*, of February 1892, Pope Leo XIII called on French Catholics—most of whom were monarchists—to rally to the Republic in order to defend the interests of the Church from within. In this regard, see Roberto de Mattei, *Le ralliement de Léon XIII: L'échec d'un projet pastoral* (Paris: Cerf, 2016).

of religion and divinity, and that will be a cultural change that can hardly be modified."[503]

However, the consequences for the remnants of Christianity in Western society will be no less catastrophic.

---

503. Scalfari, "Francesco, papa profeta."

CHAPTER 9
The Flip Side of the Coin: Praise From Worldly Powers and Anti-Christian Currents

Friendliness between Francis and the progressive, secular world is undeniable. However, through its promotion of modernity, this world was generally hostile to the Church until his accession to the papacy.

Pope Francis's magisterial, pastoral, and political choices (summarized in the preceding chapters) have triggered great perplexity and confusion in Catholic circles. Conversely, his statements, decisions, and symbolic gestures—which, when considered as a whole, attempt to surrender the Church to modernity—have been warmly received, even with fascination, in secular ambiances and among the world's powers. The media acknowledge this.[504]

The first expressive display of this worldly glee was when the Italian edition of the magazine *Vanity Fair* chose Pope Francis as its 2013 "Man of the Year."[505] He was then chosen "Person of the Year" by *Time* magazine,[506] the newspaper *Le Monde*,[507] and no fewer than eleven Latin American newspapers. Also joining them was *The Advocate*, America's oldest and largest homosexual magazine. Justifying its choice, this publication stated, "Pope Francis's stark change in rhetoric from his two predecessors—both who were at one time or another among *The Advocate*'s annual Phobie Awards—makes what he's done in 2013 all the more daring."[508]

---

504. "The giddy embrace of the secular press makes Francis suspect among traditionalists who fear he buys popularity at the price of a watered-down faith. He has deftly leveraged the media's fascination to draw attention to everything." Nancy Gibbs, "Pope Francis, The Choice," *Time*, Dec. 11, 2013, http://poy.time.com/2013/12/11/pope-francis-the-choice/.

505. "His first hundred days have already put him to the fore in the ranking of world leaders who make history. But the revolution continues." "Vanity Fair elegge papa Francesco 'Uomo dell'anno,'" *Vanity Fair*, Jul. 9, 2013, https://www.vanityfair.it/news/italia/13/07/09/cover-vanity-papa-francesco.

506. The managing editor of *Time* wrote that "in less than a year, he has done something remarkable: he has not changed the words, but he's changed the music" so that, "in a very short time, a vast, global, ecumenical audience has shown a hunger to follow him." Gibbs, "Pope Francis, The Choice."

507. *"Le Monde's* weekly supplement emphasized that at that moment 'it [was] not absurd to speak of 'popemania,' and praised the message of modernity the Argentine pontiff embodied." "França: Le Monde elege o papa Francisco como personalidade do ano de 2013," *Zenit*, Dec. 20, 2013, https://pt.zenit.org /articles/franca-le-monde-elege-o-papa-Francisco-como-personalidade-do-ano-de-2013/.

508. Lucas Grindley, "Person of the Year: Pope Francis," *The Advocate*, Dec. 16, 2013, https://www.advocate.com/year-review/2013/12/16/advocates-person-year-pope-francis. The homosexual magazine added that, "In the same way that President Obama transformed politics with his evolution on LGBT civil rights, a change from the pope could have a lasting effect on religion." Ibid.

Politically, the chorus of praise swelled to a climax after Pope Francis published the Encyclical *Laudato Sì*. Among others, the following world leaders gave it their enthusiastic support:

- Ban Ki-Moon, former secretary general of the U.N.;[509]
- U.S. President Barack Obama;[510]
- French President François Hollande;[511]
- former U.S. Vice-President Al Gore;[512]
- Jean-Claude Juncker, president of the European Commission;[513]
- Karmenu Vella and Miguel Arias Cañete, European commissioners for the Environment and Climate Action (Both went to the Vatican to thank the pope personally for the encyclical.);[514]
- Achim Steiner, executive director of the United Nations Environment Program;[515]

---

509. "I thank deeply Pope Francis for taking such a strong stand on the need for urgent global action. His moral voice is part of a growing chorus of people from all faiths and all sectors of society speaking out for climate action." Ban Ki-Moon, "The Papal Encyclical: A Call for Climate Action," *LinkedIn*, Jun. 18, 2015, https://www.linkedin.com/pulse/papal-encyclical-call-climate-action-ban-ki-moon.

510. "I welcome His Holiness Pope Francis's encyclical, and deeply admire the pope's decision to make the case—clearly, powerfully, and with the full moral authority of his position—for action on global climate change." Danny Wiser, "Obama Calls for World Leaders to Heed Pope Francis's Message," *Catholic Herald*, Jun. 19, 2015, http://www.catholicherald.co.uk/news/2015/06/19/obama-calls-for-world-leaders-to -heed-pope-franciss-message/.

511. "I express my hopes that Pope Francis's particular voice be heard on all continents, and not just by believers." François Hollande, "Message de M. François Hollande, président de la République, sur l'ency-clique du pape François consacrée aux questions écologiques, le 18 Juin 2015," *Discours.Vie-Publique*, Jun. 18, 2015, http://discours.vie-publique.fr/notices/157001654.html.

512. Al Gore responded to a question about *Laudato Sì*: "'I think that Pope Francis is quite an inspiring fig-ure,' Gore said at the Haas School of Business' Dean's Speaker Series at UC Berkeley in early 2015, 'really, a phenomenon. I've been startled by the clarity of the moral force he embodies.'
    'I've said publicly in the last year—I was raised in the Southern Baptist tradition—*I could become a Catholic because of this pope, he is that inspiring to me*.'" "Former VP Al Gore: I Might Become Catholic Be-cause of Pope Francis," *Church POP*, Jul. 28, 2016, https://churchpop.com/2016/07/28/former-vp-al-gore-i -might-become-catholic-because-of-pope-francis/. (Emphasis in the original.)

513. "'We greatly hope that *Laudato Sì* will be an alarm bell that encourages people to confront the prob-lems of our common future,' Juncker stated." Karmenu Vella, "La 'Laudato Sì' dá forza al lavoro comune per cambiare passo," *Avvenire*, Sept. 16, 2015, https://www.avvenire.it/opinioni/pagine/ambiente-gli -euroimpegni-e-impulso-di-francesco.

514. Commissioner Vella also stated, "Many references were made to the papal encyclical during the final discussions on the Sustainable Development Goals which will be approved by the United Nations next week in New York." Ibid.

515. According to Achim Steiner, the encyclical "rings an alarm bell that reverberates not only with Catholics but also with the other inhabitants of the planet." Samuel Bleynie, "Dans le monde entier, des réactions à l'encyclique Laudato Sì du pape François," *La Croix*, Jun. 18, 2015, http://www.la-croix.com/Urbi-et-Orbi /Actualite/Rome/Dans-le-monde-entier-des-reactions-a-l-encyclique-Laudato-si-du-pape-Francois -2015-06-18-1325223.

- Segolène Royal, French minister of Ecology;[516]
- postmodern sociologist Edgar Morin;[517]
- the Europe-Ecology-Greens Party of France, which declared *"Habemus Papam ecologicum!"*;[518]
- Green deputy François de Rugy, president of the French National Assembly;[519] and
- activist and writer Naomi Klein, author of *No Logo*, an alter-globalization reference book translated into twenty-eight languages.[520]

The pope earned new accolades of praise by bringing Muslim families back on his plane from the island of Lesbos. Among those applauding this action were Jean-Claude Juncker,[521] Martin Schultz, president of the European

516. Ségolène Royal stated to *La Croix*: "Yes to [the encyclical's] condemnation of speculation and the race for short-term profits, because they have greatly contributed to the explosion in our greenhouse gas emissions and the explosion of inequalities." Emmanuelle Réju, "Ségolène Royal: 'Défendre la nature, c'est aussi défendre la dignité des personnes,'" *La Croix*, Jun. 18, 2015, http://www.la-croix.com/Religion/Segolene-Royal-Defendre-la-nature-cest-aussi-defendre-la-dignite-des-personnes-2015-06-18-1325240.

517. "The encyclical *Laudato Sì* is perhaps the first act of an appeal for a new civilization." Antoine Peillon and Isabelle de Gaulmyn, "Edgar Morin: 'L'encyclique Laudato Sì est peut-être l'acte 1 d'un a"ppel pour une nouvelle civilisation,'" *La Croix*, Jun. 21, 2015, http://www.la-croix.com/Religion/Actualite/Edgar-Morin-L-encyclique-Laudato-Si-est-peut-etre-l-acte-1-d-un-appel-pour-une-nouvelle-civilisation-2015-06-21-1326175.

518. In an official communiqué, the Greens declared, "Habemus papam ecologicum! . . . Rejection of consumerism, apology for sobriety, denunciation of the powers of money, legitimate questioning of progress and in particular of GMOs, recognition of the ecological debt owed by the countries of the North to those of the South. All, just months before the Paris climate conference. This is a considerable commitment that should lead to an ambitious, binding, and international climate agreement." Julien Bayou, Sandrine Rousseau, spokespersons, "Habemus papam ecologicum," *Europe Écologie Les Verts*, https://eelv.fr/newsletter_archive/habemus-papam-ecologicum-2/. See Emmanuelle Réju, "Les écologistes en accord sur (presque) tout avec le pape François," *La Croix*, Jun. 19, 2015, http://www.la-croix.com/Actualite/France/Les-ecologistes-en-accord-sur-presque-tout-avec-le-pape-Francois-2015-06-19-1325729.

519. "I am amazed to see to what extent the encyclical converges with what we have been saying for many years," said the current president of the French National Assembly. Ibid.

520. Naomi Klein stated to *La Croix*: "Unlikely and surprising alliances are woven, for example, between me and the Vatican. . . . Trade unions, indigenous communities, confessional and green groups work as closely as ever." About the encyclical she added, "It is addressed also to me as a Jewish feminist from a secular environment." "Naomi Klein prend fait et cause pour l'encyclique du pape," *La Croix*, Jul. 7, 2015, http://www.la-croix.com/Urbi-et-Orbi/Actualite/Rome/Naomi-Klein-prend-fait-et-cause-pour-l-encyclique-du-pape-2015-07-02-1330439.

521. In 2016, the city of Aix-la-Chapelle awarded Pope Francis its famous Charlemagne Prize which honors individuals who have stood out in their commitment to European unification. The presidents of the European Commission, Council, and Parliament went to the Vatican for the solemn occasion. In his speech, Jean-Claude Juncker stated, "Holy Father, when you take in refugees in the Vatican, you fill our hearts with new and fresh courage. You personify the idea that solidarity and compassion are not just fine-sounding words but values that require us, time and again, to take a stand and act. This is why you have far more confidence in us, the heirs of the Enlightenment, than we have in ourselves—and rightly so." Jean-Claude Juncker, "Speech by President Jean-Claude Juncker at the Award Ceremony of the Charlemagne Prize to Pope Francis," *European Commission*, May 6, 2016, http://europa.eu/rapid/press-release_SPEECH-16-1681_en.htm.

Parliament,[522] and Jean-Luc Mélenchon, leader of the French far-left party La France Insoumise [Indomitable France].[523]

The pope's statements on Europe's multicultural roots earned him further encomiums from the French Communist Party's secretary-general, Pierre Laurent, in the closing speech of the party's 37th Congress.[524]

Pope Francis's criticisms of capitalism and support for the Left's agenda and popular movements earned him praise from their leading champions. Among them were:

- Hillary Clinton;[525]
- Bernie Sanders;[526]
- French senator Marie-Noëlle Lienemann—a leader of the Socialist Party's left wing;[527]

---

522. "The European Parliament will be receiving the man who at this moment in history is probably a reference point not just for Catholics but for so many people; he is someone who gives direction in an age in which many people feel disoriented." Liz Dodd, "European Parliament Head Commends Pope Francis," *The Tablet*, Oct. 31, 2014, http://www.thetablet.co.uk/news/1344/0/european-parliament-head-commends-pope-francis.

523. When the pope visited the European Parliament, the failed presidential candidate came to the rostrum to protest the visit in the name of secularism, but he wrote the Apostolic Nuncio in Paris praising *Laudato Sì*. Upon learning of the papal gesture after his visit to Lesbos, he published on his Facebook page and blog an article titled, "Long live the pope!" In it, he stated: "I ardently salute the pope's gesture. Besides all the reasons to act and to struggle, one is stronger than all. The pope's gesture makes it shine in the eyes of the dark present: We are all the same humanity!" Jean-Luc Mélenchon, "Vive le pape!" *Melenchon*, Apr. 17, 2016, http://melenchon.fr/2016/04/17/vive-le-pape/. On the sidelines of the 37th Congress of the French Communist Party (his ally), and aware of Bernie Sanders's visit to the Vatican he told Paris's *Le Figaro*: "I too would like to stay at the Santa Marta residence and meet the pope; I have things to tell him." Sophie de Ravinel, "Jean-Luc Mélenchon souhaite rencontrer le pape," *Le Figaro*, Jun. 8, 2016, http://www.lefigaro.fr/politique/le-scan/2016/06/08/25001-20160608ARTFIG00219-jean-luc-melenchon-souhaite-rencontrer-le-pape.php.

524. See ibid.

525. During the presidential campaign, in her speech at the famous Al Smith dinner, she stated, "You certainly don't need to be Catholic to be inspired by the humility and heart of the Holy Father, Pope Francis. Or to embrace his message . . . his calls to reduce inequality, his warnings about climate change, his appeal that we build bridges, not walls." Hillary Clinton, "Read the Transcript of Hillary Clinton's Speech at the Al Smith Dinner," *Time*, Oct. 21, 2016, http://time.com/4539979/read-transcript-hillary-clinton-speech-al-smith-dinner/.

526. In the middle of his presidential campaign, after participating in a Vatican symposium organized by the Pontifical Academy of Social Sciences and having a brief meeting with the pope, U.S. Senator Bernie Sanders stated, "I just wanted to let him know how appreciative I was and the extraordinary role he's playing throughout the world in raising consciousness about massive levels of income and wealth inequality." Elizabeth Landers and Faith Karimi, "Bernie Sanders Says He Met Pope Francis During Visit to Vatican City," *CNN*, Apr. 16, 2016, http://edition.cnn.com/2016/04/16/politics/bernie-sanders-pope-francis-vatican-visit/index.html.

527. "Senator Marie-Noëlle Lienemann . . . gave a resounding tribute to Pope Francis on Saturday, that he 'promotes humanistic values against the commodification' and gives 'priority to generosity and the human.' . . . I often ironize saying that he will be the last anti-capitalist. . . . It is very important that the head of the Catholic Church promote humanistic values against commodification, which reminds us that we are in solidarity, that we are brothers." "Marie-Noëlle Lienemann (PS) rend hommage au pape François," *L'Obs*, Nov. 2, 2016, http://tempsreel.nouvelobs.com/politique/20131102.AFP0782/marie-noelle-lienemann-ps-rend-hommage-au-pape-francois.html.

- Pablo Iglesias,[528] leader of Spain's Podemos party; and,
- the Italian ex-prime minister and former high-ranking communist leader Massimo D'Alema, who stated, "At this moment, the main leader of the left is the pope, even because the left is sick."[529]

The listing of supportive Latin American Marxist leaders is long. For example, Venezuela's Nicolás Maduro commented on *Evangelii Gaudium* saying: "They are documents [*sic*] which, for us in the Bolivarian revolution . . . come into natural harmony with the whole spiritual and ethical legacy and patrimony of our commander Hugo Chávez."[530] In turn, when *Laudato Sì* was published, the Venezuelan dictator solemnly declared on national radio and television: "From Venezuela, we salute this papal encyclical and assume its concepts for the construction of a new human ecologism, which, in Venezuela, we call eco-socialism."[531]

Funding provided by billionaire George Soros's Open Society Foundation to American NGOs is worthy of special mention. The effort sought to influence U.S. Catholic circles by using bishops and laity to build the "critical mass" needed to support Pope Francis's priorities. *WikiLeaks* published an e-mail sent by People Improving Communities by Organizing (PICO)—a Soros-funded organization[532]—to John Podesta, chairman of Hillary Clinton's presidential campaign. Reporting on a Vatican meeting, the e-mail stated, "Pope Francis, as a leader of global stature, will challenge the 'idolatry of the marketplace' in the U.S. and offer a clarion call to change the policies that promote exclusion and

---

528. Pablo Iglesias wrote an article for the newspaper *20 minutos* titled, "If the Mass is celebrated by Pope Francis." He emphasized that the course adopted by the Pontiff is not that of popes John Paul II and Benedict XVI. He further emphasized that, in *Evangelii Gaudium*, Francis "denounces ideologies 'that defend the absolute autonomy of markets and financial speculation' as causing inequality.... This makes the pope and his Church indispensable allies of those who defend social justice." He concluded, "*What is truly important is that Catholics and everyone else can see and hear Francis more often*. And if the Mass is celebrated by Francis, perhaps also the secretary-general of *Podemos* should attend and take some notes." Pablo Iglesias y Héctor Illueca, "Si la misa la oficiara el Papa Francisco," *20 minutos*, Mar. 28, 2017, http://www.20minutos.es/opiniones/pablo-iglesias-hecor-illueca-tribuna-misa-oficiaria-papa-Francis-2996635/#xtor=AD-15&xts=467263. (Emphasis in the original.)

529. "Massimo D'Alema candida papa Francesco: 'Lui è il miglior leader della sinistra,'" *Libero Quotidiano*, Jan. 24, 2018, http://tv.liberoquotidiano.it/video/politica/13302149/papa-francesco-massimo-d-alema-pontefice-miglior-leader-sinistra.html.

530. "Maduro: 'El Papa Francisco está en sintonía con el legado de Chávez,'" *El Mundo*, Jan. 22, 2014, http://www.elmundo.es/america/2014/01/22/52dfb8a0e2704e994a8b4570.html.

531. "Venezuela asume carta encíclica del Papa Francisco para la construcción del ecosocialismo," *AVN*, Jun. 18, 2015, http://avn.info.ve/contenido/venezuela-asume-carta-enc%C3%ADclica-del-papa-Francis-para-construcci%C3%B3n-del-ecosocialismo.

532. See John-Henry Westen, "Breaking: Leaked E-mails Show George Soros Paid $650K to Influence Bishops During Pope's U.S. Visit," *LifeSiteNews*, Aug. 23, 2016, https://www.lifesitenews.com/news/breaking-leaked-e-mails-show-george-soros-paid-to-influence-bishops-during.

indifference to those most marginalized."[533] Months later, in a letter greeting the Regional Meeting of Popular Movements held in Modesto, California, Francis publicly praised PICO, one of the meeting's sponsors.[534]

Equally disturbing is the support of papal initiatives by multimillion-dollar foundations that promote an openly anti-Christian agenda, and warm cheers for his pontificate by leaders and institutions publicly linked to Freemasonry. Vatican analyst Marco Tosatti denounced this surprising fact in his blog, *Stilum Curiæ*, in an article titled, "Freemasonry's Extraordinary Love for the Pontiff: A Study Unveils a Historic First."[535] It lists sixty-two documented cases of statements by notorious Freemasons in leading newspapers and articles published in Masonic magazines available to the public. All of them praise Pope Francis for his teaching and attitudes.[536]

A proverb distilled from centuries-old experience states: "Tell me who your friends are, and I will tell you who you are." In the absence of other evidence, this cannot be considered an absolute criterion, lest one fall into rash judgment. However, it undoubtedly serves as circumstantial evidence, supporting the existing direct evidence. Applause by the leaders of modernity for Pope Francis's statements and initiatives clearly show the public that the present Successor of Peter is promoting an unprecedented revolution within the Catholic Church and in Her relations with the modern world.

That is why, as a lay Catholic whose specific vocation is the *consecratio*

533. George Neumayr, "An Excerpt From George Neumayr's New Book, 'The Political Pope,'" *The American Spectator*, May 3, 2017, https://spectator.org/the-unholy-alliance-between-george-soros-and-pope-francis/.

534. "I would also like to highlight the work done by the PICO National Network and the organizations promoting this meeting. I learned that PICO stands for 'People Improving Communities through Organizing.' What a great synthesis of the mission of popular movements: to work locally, side by side with your neighbors, organizing among yourselves, to make your communities thrive." Francis, "Popular Movements in Modesto."

535. See Marco Tosatti, "L'amore strordinario della massoneria per il pontefice. Uno studio documenta una storica 'prima volta,'" *Stilum Curiæ*, Apr. 9, 2017, http://www.marcotosatti.com/2017/04/09/lamore-straordinario-della-massoneria-per-il-pontefice-uno-studio-documenta-una-storica-prima-volta/.

536. An expressive example of this sympathy is a comment made by the 1st Senior Warden of Seattle's St. John's Lodge no. 9 in the October 2015 issue of that lodge's magazine: "I found the address to the joint session of Congress by Pope Francis very Masonic in nature. He spoke from a universal truth and understanding of God's love for the earth and humanity. His message was nonpartisan and nonsectarian. Pope Francis understands that, if we destroy mother earth, we destroy ourselves. He spoke directly to the leaders of the world about the interconnectedness of all life. He pleaded with us to foster and promote the common good of all mankind. Seems like a Masonic message to me." Anonymous, "Why Do Freemasons Love Pope Francis? Part III," *OnePeterFive*, May 11, 2017, no. 47, https://onepeterfive.com/freemasons-love-pope-francis-part-iii/.

On the role of Masonry in the revolutionary process, see Leo XIII, Encyclical *Humanum Genus*; Corrêa de Oliveira, *Revolution and Counter-Revolution*, pt. 1, ch. 6, §6. "The Agents of the Revolution: Masonry and Other Secret Forces."

mundi,[537] that is, "ordering [temporal affairs] according to the plan of God,"[538] I must ask, "Do Catholics have an obligation to follow the wrong road? Or, on the contrary, is it licit for them to resist guidelines and teachings that lead them astray?"

537. Pius XII, "Speech to Participants in the Second World Congress of the Lay Apostolate," Oct. 5, 1957, http://w2.vatican.va/content/pius-xii/fr/speeches/1957/documents/hf_p-xii_spe_19571005 _apostolato-laici.html.

538. Second Vatican Council, Dogmatic Constitution *Lumen Gentium*, Nov. 21, 1964, no. 31, http://www.vatican.va/archive/hist_councils/ii_vatican_council/documents/vat-ii_const _19641121_lumen-gentium_en.html.

CHAPTER 10
It Is Licit to Resist

Faced with this perplexing situation and following Saint Paul's example (see Gal. 2:11), it is licit to resist. This is not a matter of questioning papal authority since a Catholic's love and veneration should only grow by taking this attitude. Love for the papacy leads the faithful to resist gestures, statements, and politico-pastoral strategies that clash with the depositum fidei *and Church Tradition.*

While it is true that no pope can infallibly teach heresy, a pope can err when not making use of the charism of infallibility or when addressing those things not covered by the charism. In such cases of error, the faithful can and should resist for the sake of Truth and the Church.

Every Catholic who truly loves the Church has great respect and love for the papacy, the Sacred Hierarchy, and the ecclesiastical magisterium. This spiritual bond makes it unimaginable or at least difficult for him to admit that the Church's hierarchy could ever err even in disciplinary matters. This psychological attitude was reinforced by the renewed prestige the papacy acquired with the proclamation of the dogmas on the papal primacy of jurisdiction and infallibility in the Constitution *Pastor Aeternus* of the First Vatican Council, promulgated by Pius IX.

Since the Second Vatican Council, the most notable episodes in the Church's crisis were the revolt of progressive prelates and theologians against traditionally-oriented papal documents such as the Encyclicals *Humanae Vitae* and *Veritatis Splendor*. However, the conservative backlash to that rebellion unwittingly accentuated an erroneous position that had been creeping into the mindset of some of the best Catholics throughout the twentieth century. That error consisted in criticizing progressives not so much for turning away from traditional teaching but for attacking the magisterium of the reigning pope. Accordingly, these conservatives subconsciously held that consistency with the teaching of Scripture and Tradition was no longer the primary rule of orthodoxy. Instead, orthodoxy was equated with present-day teaching, as if magisterial recency were the ultimate rule of faith.

Some have dubbed this deviation "magisterialism."[539] It inevitably led to a form of magisterial positivism analogous to legal positivism. The latter maintains that the law is law not because it is good and just, but because it was promulgated by competent authority. Similarly, magisterial positivism holds

---

539. Chad Ripperger, FSSP, "Operative Point of View: A Scholar Examines the Root Cause of Present Tensions Within the Ranks of Faithful Catholics," *Christian Order*, Mar. 2001, http://www.christianorder.com/features /features_2001/features_mar01.html.

that since today's magisterium is the supreme rule, then what matters is the teaching of the reigning pontiff and the bishops who follow him, regardless if it is supported by Tradition or not. "Whatever the current magisterium says is always what is 'orthodox.'"[540]

Consequently, the magisterial innovations implied in Pope Francis's paradigm shift have given rise to a paradoxical situation. Conservatives affected by "magisterialism" were paralyzed at the very thought of having to disagree with the reigning pope. On the other hand, the old unorthodox rebels cheered and became loud defenders of the papal magisterium.

Indeed, prelates, theologians, and intellectuals favorable to the Church's *ralliement* with modernity—i.e., with the anti-Christian Revolution—argue that the faithful are obliged *in conscience* to follow Pope Francis in the course he has been charting for the Barque of Peter. They claim it is illicit to disagree with his teachings or resist his direction and guidelines.

To drive their point home further, leading representatives of the progressive bloc and others close to Pope Francis assert that the changes implemented to allow "remarried" divorcees to receive Holy Communion stem from a direct action of the Holy Spirit. Therefore, opposing the pope in this matter is tantamount to fighting against God Himself.

Is It Preferable to Be "Deceived With the Pope Than Being Right Against Him"?

The views of Msgr. Pio Vito Pinto, dean of the Roman Rota, are an egregious example of this liberal overreach. In an interview with *Religión Confidencial*, he stated that the faithful who express doubts about *Amoris Laetitia* are questioning "two synods of bishops on marriage and the family. Not just one synod, but two! One ordinary and another extraordinary. One cannot doubt the action of the Holy Spirit!"[541] Hence, this progressive bloc claims opposition to such reforms can only come from egocentrism,[542] a selfish defense of

---

540. Ibid. In part, magisterial positivism was favored by the custom of post-Vatican II popes to support their teachings on Council texts and post-conciliar magisterial documents, in addition to Scripture. Pope Francis has taken this practice to an extreme, with a preference for quoting his own magisterium.

541. "Decano de la Rota Romana: Con otro papa, los cuatro cardenales que le han escrito podrían perder su cardinalato," *Religión Confidencial*, Nov. 29, 2016, http://www.religionconfidencial.com/vaticano/Decano-Rota-Romana-Papa-cardenalato_0_2828717124.html.

542. On Feb. 12, 2015, in his personal blog, Cardinal Donald Wuerl, archbishop of Washington, wrote: "One of the things I have learned . . . is that on closer examination there is a common thread that runs through all of these dissenters. *They disagree with the pope because he does not agree with them and therefore does not follow their position.* Dissent is perhaps something we will always have, lamentable as it is, but we will also always have Peter and his successor as the rock and touchstone of both our faith and our unity." Donald Wuerl, "The Pope, Touchstone of Faith and Unity," *Cardinal Donald Wuerl's Blog*, Feb. 12, 2015, http://cardinalsblog.adw.org/2015/02/pope-touchstone-faith-unity/. (My emphasis.)

old privileges,[543] or simply fear of leaving one's comfort zone, fear of change.[544]

Thus, progressive champions demand full adherence to the new magisterium making no distinctions between the papal teachings' different degrees of solemnity and the varying proper assent due to each one. For example, referring to opponents of the current pontiff's direction, Cardinal Donald Wuerl stated in an interview, "The Church 'with and under Peter' moves forward. There are always people who are unhappy with something that is going on in the Church, but the touchstone of authentic Catholicism is adherence to the teaching of the pope. The rock is Peter, the touchstone is Peter and, as the Holy Father said, it's the guarantee of unity.... They're [the popes] the touchstones of the authenticity of the faith."[545]

Cardinal Oscar Rodríguez Maradiaga is archbishop of Tegucigalpa and secretary of the Council of Nine for the reform of the Curia. In the book he launched in Italy in 2017, he explicitly criticized one of the cardinal signatories of the *dubia* on *Amoris Laetitia*. For the Honduran prelate, the person of the pope and the Church magisterium are one and the same thing: "He [Cardinal Burke] is not the magisterium; the Holy Father is the magisterium, and it is he who teaches the whole church. The other just expresses his own ideas, which deserve no further comment. These are the words of a poor man [*sic*]."[546]

Responding to a question about resistance to Pope Francis on the right, He added, without proper distinctions:

> At the end of the day, the other "papabili" cardinals, whom others
> wanted to elect, lost, while the one whom the Lord wanted was

---

543. In a recent book-interview, Cardinal Maradiaga referred to Cardinal Burke, saying: "[He] is a deluded man who wanted power and instead he lost it. He thought he was the top authority in the United States." Oscar Rodríguez Maradiaga, *Only the Gospel is Revolutionary: The Church in the Reform of Pope Francis*, (Collegeville, Minn.: Liturgical Press, 2018) 40–1.

544. Asked what could be the reasons for opposition to Pope Francis, Cardinal Donald Wuerl answered, "It comes when the Holy Father takes on a structure that includes all the institutions that are a part of the Holy See like the Secretariat of State, dicasteries, congregations and asks if this ought not to be looked at to see if it's really functioning the way it should. As soon as you touch any of these, you touch personal interests.... because of the natural instinct to say, 'We have always done it this way, why do we have to change?'... Then there are some whom [*sic*] I think just feel very uncomfortable; everything was quite secure and safe and now that's being challenged. They're being asked to look at even the way they go about doing some of the routine things, and Francis is calling them to look and see if that is really the best way." Gerard O'Connell, "Cardinal Wuerl: Pope Francis Has Reconnected the Church With Vatican II," *America*, Mar. 6, 2017, https://www.americamagazine.org/faith/2017/03/06/cardinal-wuerl-pope-francis-has-reconnected-church-vatican-ii.

545. Gerard O'Connell, "Cardinal Wuerl Calls Out Pope's Opponents," *America*, Oct. 18, 2015, https://www.americamagazine.org/content/dispatches/cardinal-wuerl-calls-out-popes-opponents.

546. Maradiaga, *Only the Gospel is Revolutionary*, 41.

elected.[547] Dissent is logical and understandable; we cannot all think
in the same way. But it is Peter who guides the Church, and therefore,
if we have faith, we must respect the choices and style of this pope
who came from the far side of the world. If they speak of finding some
"heresy" in Francis's words, they are badly mistaken, because they
are seeing things from a human point of view and not from God's.[548]

Cardinal Maradiaga continues, saying, that unconditional loyalty to the oc-
cupant of the Chair of Peter is necessary: "I believe that for a servant of the
church what is indispensable is loyalty to Peter, who today goes by the name
of Francis. Before him, we had Benedict XVI, and before Benedict there was
John Paul II, and so on. What Jesus asks of me is to be loyal to Peter. Those who
do not act this way seek only popularity."[549]

The Capuchin Fragkiskos Papamanolis, bishop emeritus of Syros, Santorini,
and Crete, and former president of the minuscule Greek Bishops' Conference,
was blatantly offensive. He said the cardinals who presented the *dubia* were
guilty of the sin of scandal. In his open letter to them, he asked if they had not
also committed "the sin of heresy (and apostasy? This is actually how schisms
begin in the Church). It is clear in your document that in practice you do not
believe in the pope's supreme magisterial authority, reinforced by two synods
of bishops from all over the world. One sees that the Holy Spirit inspires only
you, not the Vicar of Christ and not even the bishops gathered in Synod."[550]

---

547. In 1997, asked by Bavarian television whether the Holy Spirit elects the pope, Cardinal Ratzinger answered: "I would not say so, in the sense that the Holy Spirit picks out the pope . . . I would say that the Spirit
does not exactly take control of the affair, but rather like a good educator, as it were, leaves us much space,
much freedom, without entirely abandoning us. Thus the Spirit's role should be understood in a much more
elastic sense, not that he dictates the candidate for whom one must vote. Probably the only assurance he of-
fers is that the thing cannot be totally ruined." James Martin, SJ, "Does the Holy Spirit Choose the Pope?"
Time, Mar. 11, 2013, http://ideas.time.com/2013/03/11/does-the-holy-spirit-choose-the-pope/. In the specific case of Cardinal Jorge Mario Bergoglio the revelations by Jürgen Mettepenningen and Karim Schelkens
in their biography of Cardinal Godfried Daneels made manifest the existence of strong interference by a so-
called "Sankt Gallen mafia" in the 2013 conclave and strong interference by very human factors that could
hardly be associated with the Holy Spirit. Karim Schelkens stated, "Without the least doubt, Bergoglio's election was prepared at Sankt-Gallen. And the main lines of the program that the pope is carrying out are those
that Daneels & Co. began to discuss more than ten years ago." "'Godfried Danneels was al jaren in de weer
als king maker van paus Franciscus,'" *Knack*, Sept. 23, 2015, http://www.knack.be/nieuws/mensen/godfried
-danneels-was-al-jaren-in-de-weer-als-king-maker-van-paus-franciscus/article-longread-607599.html.
Later, these journalists clarified their story, stating they had merely said that, "the 'election of Bergoglio cor-
responded with the aims of St. Gallen.'" Edward Pentin, "Cardinal Danneels' Biographers Retract Comments
on St. Gallen Group," *National Catholic Register*, Sept. 26, 2015, http://www.ncregister.com/blog/edward
-pentin/st.-gallen-group-not-a-lobby-group-say-authors.

548. Maradiaga, *Only the Gospel is Revolutionary*, 82.

549. Ibid., 83.

550. Fragkisskos Papamanolis, "Lettera aperta ai 4 cardinali," *Settimananews*, Nov. 23, 2016,
http://www.settimananews.it/vescovi/lettera-aperta-ai-4-cardinali/.

For progressives today, any dissent from Pope Francis in anything, even in a matter as earthly as immigration would not seem licit. In his book, journalist Laurent Dandrieu presented the case of Fr. Christian Venard, a military chaplain who, after shocking papal statements equating Islamic violence with alleged Catholic violence, wrote an article titled, "Pope Francis and 'Catholic Violence': Stupefaction, Reflection, and Reverence."[551] A week later, he felt obliged to write a second one titled, "I Prefer Being Wrong With the Pope Than Being Right Without Him: The Need to Follow the Holy Father in All Circumstances."[552] The only exception he made was regarding sin.

Theologian Ashley Beck is a professor of Catholic social doctrine at St. Mary's University in southeast London. He wrote an article that further exemplified this unconditional acceptance improperly imposed by liberals: "While the Church does allow for divergent viewpoints on some issues (*Laudato Sì*, 61), we are simply not free to dissent from the teaching of this encyclical, any more than we are free to dissent from Catholic teaching about other moral issues."[553]

What to think of all this? Are these progressive assessments doctrinally acceptable? Are they factually objective and fair? Is "being wrong with the pope" really better "than being right without him" as the French military chaplain wrote? Is the Holy Spirit asking Catholics to renounce reason? Or, on the contrary, does He want them to remain steadfast in the Faith's perennial and unchangeable truths, nourishing themselves with the *sensus fidei*, so that they can resist ecclesiastical authorities if necessary?

---

551. Christian Venard, "Le pape François et la 'violence catholique': Stupéfaction, réflexion et révérence," *Aleteia*, Aug. 2, 2016, https://fr.aleteia.org/2016/08/02/le-pape-francois-et-la-violence-catholique -stupefaction-reflexion-et-reverence/.

552. Christian Venard, "'Je préfère me tromper en suivant le pape que d'avoir raison contre lui': De la nécessité de suivre le Saint-Père en toute circonstance," *Aleteia*, Mar. 23, 2016, https://fr.aleteia.org/2016/08/12 /je-prefere-me-tromper-en-suivant-le-pape-que-davoir-raison-contre-lui/.

   Taking this position to an extreme, Massimo Introvigne, in an essay titled, "The reality of Catholic fundamentalism," condemned the publication by the Instituto Plinio Corrêa de Oliveira of a critique of *Amoris Laetitia* that, while recognizing that it is part of the non-infallible magisterium, refused assent to those affirmations within it that contradict Catholic doctrine. Introvigne claimed that the critique grouped the Instituto among fundamentalists. What would be the main error of that alleged fundamentalism? The Italian sociologist states, "Unlike other founders of religions, Jesus did not write books, he left nothing in writing. . . . Mohammed left the Book to be followed, Jesus left the Church: 'He who listens to you, listens to Me' (Luke 10:13). He left people. Who could and can meet each other. Hence I know that I am Catholic if I follow the person of the pope, not a hypothetical, more or less fossilized text," identified with Tradition. Massimo Introvigne, "La realtà del fondamentalismo cattolico," *La Nuova Europa*, Sept. 13, 2016, 12, http://www.lanuovaeuropa.org/articoli/dossier/la-realt%C3%A0-del-fondamentalismo-cattolico.

553. Ashley Beck, "No Catholic Is Free to Dissent From the Teaching of Laudato Sì," *Catholic Herald*, Jun. 18, 2015, http://www.catholicherald.co.uk/commentandblogs/2015/06/19/no-catholic-is-free-to -dissent-from-the-teaching-of-laudato-si/.

The Holy Spirit Was Not Promised for the Preaching of a New Doctrine
It does not take a master in ecclesiology to understand that papal authority and infallibility have limits and that the duty of obedience to the pope and bishops is not absolute across the board. A balanced position can be summed up in the following truths, which form part of the intellectual and spiritual patrimony of every well-instructed Catholic.

Catholics know by faith that the pope is the head of the visible Church. He is the Successor of Peter, who received the keys of the Kingdom. Our Lord Jesus Christ deliberately and publicly gave him this authority. This explains, not only the faithful's love for the pope (the "sweet Christ on earth," as Saint Catherine of Siena said[554]) but also the obedience that Catholics render to his teachings and decisions as universal Doctor and Shepherd of Christ's flock. This notwithstanding, as Bishop Schneider opportunely and concisely recalled in an interview with *Rorate Cœli*, "The Church is not the private property of the pope. The pope cannot say 'I am the Church,' as did the French king Louis XIV, who said: '*L'État c'est moi.*' ['I am the State.'] The pope is only the Vicar, not the successor of Christ."[555]

In fact, the first duty of the pope—whose supreme ministry is to "strengthen [his] brethren" in the faith (C Luke 22:32)—is to keep, interpret, and proclaim the Word of Christ to the world unchanged (see Deut. 4:2). As Saint Paul the Apostle wrote, "But even if we or an angel from heaven should preach a gospel to you other than that which we have preached to you, let him be anathema" (C Gal. 1:8). For this reason, in defining papal infallibility, the First Vatican Council solemnly stated in the constitution *Pastor Aeternus*: "For the Holy Spirit was promised to the successors of Peter not so that they might, by his revelation, make known some new doctrine, but that, by his assistance, they might religiously guard and faithfully expound the revelation or deposit of faith transmitted by the apostles."[556]

There is no doubt that the breath of the Holy Spirit shall "renew the face of the earth" (Ps. 103:30) and lead the Church to the fullness of truth (see John 16:13). He will do so using the Church's living magisterium, especially papal

---

554. Maria Antonietta Falchi Pellegrini, "St. Catherine and the Priests: A Message for the Church of the Third Millennium," May 17, 2000, accessed Jul. 27, 2018, http://www.vatican.va/roman_curia /congregations/cclergy/documents/jub_preti_20000517_falchi_en.html.

555. "Exclusive: Bishop Athanasius Schneider Interview With Rorate Caeli," *Rorate Cœli*, Feb. 1, 2016, https://rorate-caeli.blogspot.com/2016/02/exclusive-bishop-athanasius-schneider.html. [Publisher's Note: The phrase attributed to Louis XIV may be apocryphal. No contemporary record that the French king said this exists. First recorded use is from 1834, 119 years after the monarch's death.]

556. First Vatican Council, *Pastor Aeternus*, Jul. 18, 1870, session 4, ch. 4, in Norman P. Tanner, SJ, ed., *Decrees of the Ecumenical Councils* (Washington: Georgetown University Press, 1990), 2:816, https://www.ewtn.com/faith/teachings/papae1.htm.

magisterium, to mediate and make current Her unchangeable divine teaching. However, the Holy Spirit does not do this by teaching new truths. Instead, He helps the Church delve deeper into those same revealed words that never pass away (see Matt. 24:35). Therefore, the magisterium does not contain or propose any novelty. Rather, it reiterates and deepens in new ways the perennial truth contained in Scriptures and Tradition: *non nova sed nove* (Not new things, but in a new way). Accordingly, in the exercise of the magisterium, there can never be even the slightest shadow of contradiction between old and new truths since the truths contained in the deposit of faith are unchangeable. Progress and enrichment in their understanding must be "in the same doctrine, in the same sense, and in the same meaning."[557] Catholic truth would not subsist, and there would be no true Tradition if a contradiction were found between a new teaching or discipline and that handed down from time immemorial.[558]

Occasions When It Is Legitimate to Prudentially Suspend One's Assent
Infallible teaching—which can never contradict the deposit of faith entrusted to the Church—is guaranteed to the Church hierarchy only in two situations:

a) solemn (*ex cathedra*—"from the chair") declarations by the pope or by a council summoned and approved by the pope; and,

b) the universal ordinary teaching of the bishops in union with the pope,[559] i.e., in what has been taught "everywhere, always, by all."[560]

---

557. "But some one will say, perhaps, shall there, then, be no progress in Christ's Church? Certainly; all possible progress. For what being is there, so envious of men, so full of hatred to God, who would seek to forbid it? Yet on condition that it be real progress, not alteration of the faith. For progress requires that the subject be enlarged in itself, alteration, that it be transformed into something else. The intelligence, then, the knowledge, the wisdom, as well of individuals as of all, as well of one man as of the whole Church, ought, in the course of ages and centuries, to increase and make much and vigorous progress; but yet only in its own kind; that is to say, *in the same doctrine, in the same sense, and in the same meaning.*" St. Vincent of Lerins, *Commonitory: For the Antiquity and Universality of the Catholic Faith Against the Profane Novelties of All Heresies*, ch. 23, no. 54.

558. That is why it is absurd for the current Superior General of the Society of Jesus, Fr. Sosa Abascal, to claim that it is necessary to "contextualize" Jesus's words about the indissolubility of marriage since "at that time no one had a recorder to record the words." Indeed, from the earliest days of the Church the words of Our Lord were accepted "in the same sense and in the same meaning." Giuseppe Rusconi, "Gesuiti/Padre Sosa: Parole di Gesu'? Da contestualizzare!" *Rossoporpora*, Feb. 18, 2017, http://www.rossoporpora.org/rubriche/interviste-a-personalita/672-gesuiti-padre-sosa-parole-di-gesu-da-contestualizzare.html.

559. The Constitution *Dei Filius* of the First Vatican Council reads: "Further, by divine and Catholic faith, all those things must be believed which are contained in the written word of God and in tradition, and those which are proposed by the Church, *either in a solemn pronouncement or in her ordinary and universal teaching power, to be believed as divinely revealed.*" First Vatican Council, *Dei Filius*, ch. 3. (My emphasis.)

560. *Commonitory* of St. Vincent of Lerins:
[5.] Therefore, it is very necessary, on account of so great intricacies of such various error[s], that the rule for the right understanding of the prophets and apostles should be framed in accordance with the standard of Ecclesiastical and Catholic interpretation.

Therefore, everyday teachings or authentic magisterium that have no antiquity and contain novelties are not endowed with the charisma of infallibility.
They do not constitute a *proximate rule of faith*, which admits no doubt. They
should not be given an *assent of faith*, but only *religious assent* (sometimes
called *religious submission*) *of will and intellect.*[561]

However, when there is contradiction between a novel teaching and the traditional magisterium, or when a teaching or directive is clearly contrary to reason (as seen in the question of unbridled immigration and the radical
ecological agenda), a Catholic is not obliged to err with the pope.[562] On the contrary, it is perfectly legitimate to suspend prudential assent[563] and even present
a "fraternal correction."[564] What Msgr. Brunero Gherardini, dean of the Faculty

---

[6.] Moreover, in the Catholic Church itself, all possible care must be taken, that we hold that faith which
has been believed everywhere, always, by all. For that is truly and in the strictest sense Catholic, which, as
the name itself and the reason of the thing declare, comprehends all universally. This rule we shall observe if
we follow universality, antiquity, consent. We shall follow universality if we confess that one faith to be true,
which the whole Church throughout the world confesses; antiquity, if we in no wise depart from those interpretations which it is manifest were notoriously held by our holy ancestors and fathers; consent, in like manner, if in antiquity itself we adhere to the consentient definitions and determinations of all, or at the least of
almost all priests and doctors. *Commonitory*, ch. 2, nos. 5–6.

561. The renowned Jesuit theologian Domenico Palmieri (1829–1909) wrote:
    Secondly, (to the Roman Pontiff's ordinary magisterium) is also due certain *religious assent when nothing
    prudently leads (suadeat) to a suspension of assent.* I explain these terms. We do not say that an assent of
    Catholic faith is due, for the Church does not propose here a doctrine to be professed (*tenenda*). We do not
    say that a formal assent of divine faith is due, for that assent is due to the infallible proposition said to be
    such and such, and in our hypothesis, that proposition does not exist. *We do not say that it is a metaphysi-
    cally certain assent, for since the certainty of infallibility does not exist, error does not seem impossible and thus
    one sees that the opposite may be true. If that knowledge exists, there can be no place for metaphysical cer-
    tainty. So we say that the assent is morally certain if, as a consequence, motives appear—whether true or false,
    but derived from a non-culpable error—that lead us to conclude otherwise (as to the matter taught), we say
    that assent is not due since in these circumstances the will does not act imprudently upon suspending assent.*"
    Domenico Palmieri, SJ, *Tractatus de Romano Pontifice* (Prati: Giachetti, 1891), 719–20, Latin to Portuguese
    trans. Daniel P. Pinheiro, in "Assentimento ao magistério, (Parte Final: Doutrina Comum dos Teólogos e
    Bibliografia)," *Scutum Fidei*, Feb. 20, 2013, https://scutumfidei.org/2013/02/20/assentimento-ao
    -magisterio-parte-final-doutrina-comum-dos-teologos-e-bibliografia/.

562. In the article "Can There Be Errors in Documents of the Magisterium?" (*Catolicismo*, July 1969), Arnaldo V. Xavier da Silveira, based on leading theologians, demonstrates the thesis that "the First Vatican
Council . . . established the *four conditions* under which the pope is infallible. Thus, it is easy to understand
that, *in principle*, when such conditions are not fulfilled, there can be error in a papal document.
    "In other words, we could say that the simple fact that the documents of the magisterium are divided
into infallible and non-infallible ones leaves open, in thesis, the possibility of error in any of the non-infallible ones." Arnaldo Vidigal Xavier da Silveira, *Can Documents of the Magisterium of the Church Contain Errors? Can the Catholic Faithful Resist Them?* (Spring Grove, Penn.: The American Society for the Defense of
Tradition, Family and Property, 2015), 113, http://www.tfp.org/DocumentsMagisterium.

563. See Palmieri in footnote 561 above.

564. Roberto de Mattei, "The Irrevocable Duties of Cardinals of the Holy Roman Church," trans. Francesca
Romana, *Rorate Cæli*, Dec. 16, 2016, https://rorate-caeli.blogspot.com/2016/12/de-mattei-irrevocable-du-
ties-of.html. In his article, the professor recalls that, besides honors and privileges, cardinals have precise
obligations. "Among these responsibilities there is that of fraternally correcting the pope when he com-
mits an error in the governing of the Church, as happened in 1813, when Pius VII signed the ill-fated

of Theology at the Lateran University for many years, wrote with his usual in-
sight about Church magisterium in general, also applies to the pope's teaching,
gestures, and attitudes:

> The magisterium is not a *super-church* that would impose its judg-
> ments and behaviors on the Church herself, nor a privileged caste
> above the people of God, a kind of *strong power* which one ought to
> obey, period....
> Very often, the instrument is made into an [independent] value
> as such and used to cut off all discussion at its origin as if it were
> above the Church and did not have before it the enormous weight
> of Tradition to embrace, interpret, and retransmit in its integrity
> and fidelity.[565]

Public Resistance to Erroneous Teachings Is Legitimate

Moreover, in serious cases, it is legitimate to publicly resist shepherds and even
the pope:

- When private resistance or mere obsequious silence is not sufficient for the faithful to remain steadfast in the Faith (see 1 Pet. 5:9);
- for protecting the Faith of the Church;
- and for defending what little Christianity remains in countries
in which the faithful are citizens.

Treaty of Fontainbleau with Napoleon, or in 1934 when the Cardinal Dean, Gennaro Granito di Belmonte,
admonished Pius XI , on behalf of the Sacred College, for the rash use he made of the Holy See's finances."

In an interview with the *National Catholic Register*, Cardinal Burke stated, "There is, in the Tradition of
the Church, the practice of correction of the Roman Pontiff. It is something that is clearly quite rare. But if
there is no response to these questions [the dubia], then I would say that it would be a question of taking
a formal act of correction of a serious error....

"It is the duty in such cases, and historically it has happened, of cardinals and bishops to make clear
that the pope is teaching error and to ask him to correct it." Edward Pentin, "Cardinal Burke on Amoris
Laetitia Dubia: 'Tremendous Division' Warrants Action," *National Catholic Register*, Nov. 15, 2016,
http://www.ncregister.com/daily-news/cardinal-burke-on-amoris-laetitia-dubia-tremendous
-division-warrants-action.

565. Brunero Gherardini, "Chiesa-tradizione-magistero," published as "Mons. Gherardini sull'importanza e i limiti del magistero autentico," *Disputationes Theologicae*, Dec. 7, 2011,
http://disputationes-theologicae.blogspot.fr/2011/12/mons-gherardini-sullimportanza-e-i.html.

The danger of this "instrumentalization" of the magisterium to introduce novelties was predicted by
another leading figure of the Roman school, Msgr. Pietro Parente, later a cardinal, in an article published
on February 10, 1942, in *L'Osservatore Romano*. In his study, Msgr. Parente denounced "the strange identi-
fication of Tradition (source of Revelation) with the living magisterium of the Church (custodian and in-
terpreter of the Divine Word)." Pietro Parente, "Supr. S. Congr. S. Officii Decretum 4 febr.
1942—Annotationes," *Periodica de Re Morali, Canonica, Liturgica* 31 (Feb. 1942): 187 [originally published
as "Nuove tendenze teologiche," *L'Osservatore Romano*, Feb. 9–10, 1942]. In fact, if Tradition and magisterium are the same thing, Tradition ceases to be an unchanging deposit of faith and begins to vary according to the teaching of the reigning pope.

Numerous authorities explicitly acknowledge the legitimacy of public resistance to erroneous decisions or teachings by shepherds, including the sov-
ereign pontiff. Arnaldo Xavier da Silveira amply quotes them in his study
titled, "Public Resistance to Decisions by the Ecclesiastical Authority." This
analysis was first published in the August 1969 issue of the Brazilian monthly
Catolicismo.[566] The first of the great authors quoted is none other than Saint
Thomas Aquinas.[567] Others are Saint Robert Bellarmine,[568] Suarez,[569] Vitoria,[570]

---

566. See Xavier da Silveira, *Can Documents of the Magisterium Contain Errors?*, 127–46.

567. "If the faith were endangered, a subject ought to rebuke his prelate even publicly. Hence Paul, who
was Peter's subject, rebuked him in public, on account of the imminent danger of scandal concerning
faith, and, as the gloss of Augustine says on Galatians 2:11, "Peter gave an example to superiors, that if at
any time they should happen to stray from the straight path, they should not disdain to be reproved by
their subjects." St. Thomas Aquinas, *Summa Theologiæ*, II–II, q. 33, a. 4, r. 2.
  In his commentary on the Epistle to the Galatians, studying the episode in which St. Paul resisted St.
Peter to his face, St. Thomas wrote: "The occasion of the rebuke was not slight, but just and useful,
namely, the danger to the Gospel teaching. . . . *The manner of the rebuke was fitting, i.e. public and plain.*
Hence he says, 'I said to Cephas,' i.e. to Peter, 'before them all,' because that dissimulation posed a danger
to all. 'Them that sin, reprove before all' (1 Tim. 5:20). This is to be understood of public sins and not of
private ones, in which the procedures of fraternal charity ought to be observed." St. Thomas Aquinas,
Commentary on Saint Paul's Epistle to the Galatians, ch. 2, lect. 3. (My emphasis.) Earlier in the same chapter, St. Thomas wrote: "[To the] prelates, indeed, an example of humility [was given] that they not disdain
corrections from those who are lower and subject to them; subjects have an example of zeal and freedom,
that they fear not to correct their prelates, particularly if their crime is public and verges upon danger to
the multitude." Ibid.

568. "Just as it is lawful to resist a Pontiff invading a body, so it is licit to resist him invading souls, or disturbing a state, and much more if he tried to destroy the Church. I say, it is lawful to resist him, by not
doing what he commands, and by blocking him, lest he should carry out his will; still, it is not lawful to
judge or punish or even depose him, because he is nothing other than a superior." St. Robert Bellarmine,
De Controversiis, On the Roman Pontiff, trans. Ryan Grant (Charleston, S.C.: Mediatrix Press, 2015) vol. 1,
bk 2, ch. 29, p. 303.

569. "If [the pope] lays down an order contrary to right customs *one does not have to obey him*; if he tries to
do something manifestly opposed to justice and to the common good, *it would be licit to resist him*; if he
attacks by force, he could be repelled by force, with the moderation characteristic of a just defense (*cum
moderamine inculpatæ tutelæ*)." Francisco Suarez, *De fide*, vol. 12, disp. 10, sect. 6, no. 16, quoted in Xavier
da Silveira, *Can Documents of the Magisterium Contain Errors?*, 134. (My emphasis.)

570. Cajetan, in the same work in which he defends the superiority of the pope over the Council, says in chap.
  XXVII: "Then, *one must resist to his face a pope who publicly destroys the Church*, for example not wishing to
  confer ecclesiastical benefices except for money or in exchange for services; and one must deny, with all
  obedience and respect, the possession of such benefices to those who have bought them." And Sylvester
  (Prierias), at the word *Papa*, §4, asks: "What must one do when the pope, by his evil customs, destroys the
  Church?" And in §15: "What must one do if the pope wishes, without cause, to abrogate positive Law?" To
  this, he responds: "He would certainly sin; *one should not permit him to carry on like this, nor should one obey
  him in that which is evil; but one should resist him with a courteous rebuke*." Therefore, if he wished to hand
  over all the treasure of the Church or the patrimony of Saint Peter to his family, if he wished to destroy the
  Church, or other similar things, *one should not permit him to act in this way, rather one would be obliged to
  resist him*. The reason for this is that he does not have power to destroy; it being clear therefore that if he
  does, it is licit to resist him. From all of this it follows that, if the pope, by his orders and his acts, destroys
  the Church, *one can resist him and impede the execution of his commands*. . . .
    A second proof of the thesis. According to natural law, it is licit to repel violence with violence. Now,

Cornelius a Lapide,[571] Wernz-Vidal,[572] and Peinador.[573]

Some of these eminent writers seem to state that only *obsequious silence* is legitimate, not public resistance. Xavier da Silveira's study shows that those authors were analyzing merely *ordinary* cases, not *extraordinary* ones, in which there is:

- "a proximate danger for the faith" (Saint Thomas). . . .
- [or] "an aggression against souls" (Saint Robert Bellarmine) or a "public scandal" (see Cornelius a Lapide) in a doctrinal matter. . . .
- To sustain the contrary would be to ignore the fundamental role of Faith in Christian life.[574]

Thus, Xavier da Silveira concludes that public resistance applies to both doctrinal teachings and disciplinary decisions.

The right to be faithful to the Gospel in matters of Faith and morals and the freedom of conscience to follow one's reasoned convictions in contingent matters[575] are all the more indispensable as Pope Francis's paradigm shift opens Church gates to a flood of errors from the anti-Christian Revolution.

---

with such orders and dispensations, *the pope does violence*, because he acts against the law, as was proven above. *Then, it is licit to resist him.* As Cajetan observes, we do not affirm all this in the sense that someone has the right to be judge of the pope or have authority over him, but rather in the sense that it is licit to defend oneself. Anyone, indeed, has the right to resist an unjust act, to try to impede it and to defend himself. Franciscus de Vitoria, OP, *Obras de Francisco de Vitoria*, 486–7, quoted in Xavier da Silveira, *Can Documents of the Magisterium Contain Errors?*, 133–4. (My emphasis.)

571. That superiors can be rebuked, with humility and charity, by their subjects, in order that the truth be defended, is what Saint Augustine (Epist. 19), Saint Cyprian, Saint Gregory, Saint Thomas, and the others cited above declare on the basis of this passage (Gal. 2:11). They clearly teach that Saint Peter, being superior was reprimanded by Saint Paul. . . . Rightly, then, did Saint Gregory say (Homil. 18 in Ezech.): "Peter held his tongue in order that, being the first in the apostolic hierarchy, he would be also the first in humility." And Saint Augustine wrote (Epist. 19 ad Hieronymum): "Teaching that the superiors should not refuse to let themselves be reprimanded by their subjects, Saint Peter left to posterity an example more unusual and more holy than that which Saint Paul left on teaching that, in defense of the truth, and with charity it is given *to the juniors to have the boldness to resist their elders without fear*." Cornelius a Lapide, vol. 18, *ad. Gal.* 2:11, quoted in Xavier da Silveira, *Can Documents of the Magisterium Contain Errors?*, 135. (My emphasis.)

572. "The just means to be employed against a bad pope are, according to Suarez (*Defensio fidei catholicae*, bk. 4, ch. 6, nos. 17–8): the more abundant help of the grace of God; the special protection of one's guardian Angel; the prayer of the Church universal; *admonition or fraternal correction in secret or even in public; as well as legitimate defense against aggression whether it be physical or moral.*" Wernz-Vidal, *Ius can.*, 2:436, quoted in *Can Documents of the Magisterium Contain Error?*, 136. (My emphasis.)

573. "'A subject also can be obliged to the fraternal correction of his superior.' (*S. Theol.*, II–II, 33, 4). For the superior also can be spiritually needy, and there is nothing to prevent that he be liberated from such need by one of his subjects. Nevertheless, 'in a correction by which subjects reprehend their prelates, it behooves them to act in an appropriate manner, that is, not with insolence and asperity, but with meekness and reverence' (*S. Theol.*, ibid.). Therefore, in general the superior must always be admonished privately. 'Keep in mind however that, when there is a proximate danger for the faith, prelates must be censured even publicly, by their subjects.' (*S. Theol.*, II–II, 33, 4, 2)" Antonius Peinador, *Cursus brevior theol. mor.*, tom. 2, 1:287, quoted in *Can Documents of the Magisterium Contain Errors?*, 136.

574. Xavier da Silveira, *Can Documents of the Magisterium Contain Errors?*, 144–5.

575. See *Summa Theologiæ*, II–I, q. 94, a. 4.

The changes advocated by the pope during these five years amount to coercion over the rightly formed consciences of millions of Catholics. Indeed, the faithful are urged by the highest authorities of the Catholic Church to accept:
- a new faith that does not correspond, in some essential points, to the perennial teachings of Our Lord Jesus Christ;
- the errors of the agnostic and relativist philosophy of modernity and the anti-Christian revolution at its core; and,
- political and socioeconomic solutions and scientific hypotheses that do not rise to the level of studied conclusions attained after mature and objective reflection.

This coercion over souls is seen further as Pope Francis often seeks to discredit attitudes of fidelity to Gospel commands. Doing so, he uses offensive images and epithets that resound well with the mainstream media, whipping up witch hunts against Catholics who dissent from his papacy's orientation.

Pope Francis refrains from naming those who criticize and oppose his pastoral changes and the ideas that undergird them. However, he seems to take pleasure in stigmatizing them. Some of his insults include: "Fundamentalists," "rigid Christians," "Christian hypocrites," "closed hearts," "legalistic slave," "restorationists," "casuistic intellectuals," "accountant of the Spirit," "Pelagians," "Dark Christians," "Spiritualistic pietist," "doctors of the law," and "Reactionaries!"[576]

Bishop Schneider aptly comments on the Family Synod debates:

> During the great Arian crisis in the IV century, the defenders of the Divinity of the Son of God were labeled "intransigent" and "traditionalist" as well. Saint Athanasius was even excommunicated by Pope Liberius, and the pope justified this with the argument that Athanasius was not in communion with the Oriental bishops who were mostly heretics or semi-heretics. Saint Basil the Great stated in that situation the following: "Only one sin is nowadays severely punished: the attentive observance of the traditions of our Fathers. For that reason, the good ones are thrown out of their places and brought to the desert" (*Ep. 243*). To tell the truth, [Bishop Schneider continues,] the bishops who support holy Communion for "remarried divorcees" are the new Pharisees and Scribes, for they despise God's commandment, thus contributing

---

576. "Pope Francis's Bumper Book of Insults," accessed Jul. 27, 2018, http://popefrancisbookofinsults.blogspot.com/. A recent convert to the Catholic Faith, living in Brighton, U.K., runs a blog on current Church affairs. He decided to compile these epithets and published them online as *Pope Francis's Little Book of Insults*. The compilation's success was such that he detached it from his blog and gave it its own website. The collection is now called, *Pope Francis's Bumper Book of Insults*. It is updated regularly.

to have the "divorced and remarried" continue in adultery body and soul (Matt. 15:19), because they want an externally "clean" solution where they too are seen as "clean" in the eyes of the powerful [the media, public opinion].[577]

The Right to Resist Becomes a Duty When the Common Good Is at Stake

In the Gospel, Our Lord teaches, "If one strike thee on thy right cheek, turn to him also the other." "Pray for them that persecute and calumniate you" (Matt. 5:39, 44).

Considered individually, I am sure that millions of perplexed Catholics accept with resignation the pope's coercion against their moral integrity and reasoned convictions in contingent matters. However, they can and sometimes must speak out when his attacks endanger not just their faith, but that of millions of weaker faithful and the very survival of their nations. Faced with the choice of crossing their arms in resignation, and not disagreeing with Pope Francis on the one hand, or resisting his evil pastoral and sociopolitical changes, they may, in good conscience, emulate Saint Paul who "resisted [Saint Peter] to his face because he was in the wrong" (KL Gal. 2:11).

These faithful Catholics can formulate their own reaction by using a model of resistance, which is both firm and imbued with veneration and respect for the supreme pontiff. This model is the "Declaration of Resistance" to Paul VI's policy of *Ostpolitik*. It was written in 1974 by the sorely missed Plinio Corrêa de Oliveira and is titled, "The Vatican Policy of Détente With Communist Governments—Should the TFPs Stand Down? Or Should They Resist?" Its key paragraphs read as follows:

> The bond of obedience to the Successor of Peter, which we will never break, which we love in the most profound depths of our soul, and to which we tribute our highest love, this bond we kiss at the very moment in which, overwhelmed with sorrow, we affirm our position. And on our knees, gazing with veneration at the figure of His Holiness Paul VI, we express all our fidelity to him.
>
> In this filial act, we say to the Pastor of Pastors: Our soul is yours, our life is yours. Order us to do whatever you wish. Only do not order us to do nothing in the face of the assailing Red wolf. To this, our conscience is opposed.[578]

---

577. Athanasius Schneider, "Against Pharisees," *Polonia Christiana* 41 (Nov.–Dec. 2014), http://www.pch24.pl/against-pharisees,31907,i.html.

578. Plinio Corrêa de Oliveira, "The Vatican Policy of Détente With Communist Governments: Should the TFPs Stand Down? Or Should They Resist?" Feb. 18, 1975, http://www.tfp.org/vatican-policy-detente-communist-governments-tfps-stand-resist/, first published as "A política de distensão do Vaticano com os governos comunistas. Para a TFP: omitir-se? ou resistir?" *Folha de S. Paulo*, Apr. 10, 1974, https://pliniocorreadeoliveira.info/MAN%20-%201974-04-08_Resistencia.htm.

CONCLUSION

As I reach the end of this assessment of Pope Francis's first five years, I must answer the question posed in this book's title. All things considered, it is not rash judgment for me to affirm that his paradigm shift is not an organic development of the Church's traditional teaching. On the contrary, it looks increasingly like an about-face.

Therefore, in the measure that this change does not express the teachings of Our Lord Jesus Christ in their purity and integrity, the faithful may and even should publicly resist its doctrinal innovations and practical applications.

That resistance should be exercised not just regarding the admission of adulterers to the Sacrament of the Holy Eucharist, but in defense of human life when threatened by procured abortion and euthanasia. It should lead the faithful to defend indissoluble marriage and oppose the legal recognition of same-sex unions. It should inspire them to stand for private property and free enterprise against collectivist policies and assaults by so-called popular movements. Catholics should be moved to reject miserabilism, and Indigenism, which are proposed as solutions to a theoretical anthropogenic global warming over which the scientific community is divided. The baptized should be motivated to uphold their Christian identity and national culture in the face of the migration crisis. Consequently, it should lead them to reject the West's Islamization, the philosophical and spiritual relativism of a multiculturalist utopia, and the Vatican's *Ostpolitik* with anti-Christian regimes that persecute Catholics.

Catholics must, therefore, enter a *state of resistance*[579] and remain so until the true Catholic paradigm becomes again the compass that guides, inspires, and vivifies the whole life of the Church.

A question, however, remains: How should the faithful deal with pastors who subscribe to and implement the Bergoglian paradigm shift? How should they relate to its promoter, the shepherd of shepherds, himself?

The question is similar to that posed by Fr. Nicola Bux in the title of his 2010 book on the new rite of the Mass, *How to Go to Mass and Not Lose Your Faith*. He used an intentionally provocative title because of the liturgy's ambiguities and the abuses that accompany its celebration.

Catholics must ask themselves: How should they maintain relations with paradigm shift shepherds, at all levels, without losing their faith?

It seems indispensable to avoid two simplistic and opposite solutions. One

---

579. See American TFP, "TFP Statement on Pope Francis's 'Paradigm Shift': Resist as Saint Paul Teaches," Jul. 17, 2108, *TFP.org*, http://www.tfp.org/tfp-statement-on-pope-francis-paradigm-shift-resist-as-saint-paul-teaches/.

would be to say, "After all, the pope is the representative of Christ and the bishops are the successors of the Apostles. They are the living magisterium. Who am I to judge? If the pope and the bishops who support him are mistaken, it is their problem." The other would be, "All this is clearly heresy; therefore, the man promoting it cannot be pope." One would thus embrace sedevacantism and dispense oneself from resisting a superior because his authority is no longer recognized.

These false alternatives must be rejected. The faithful must recognize Pope Francis as the Vicar of Christ on earth and the diocesan bishops as successors of the Apostles. Notwithstanding this recognition, Catholics must "resist them to the face," as Saint Paul did with the first pope.

This balanced and courageous position takes into account the wise words of a great seventeenth-century canonist, Fr. Paul Laymann, SJ, who stated, "As long as the pope is tolerated by the Church and publicly acknowledged as the universal shepherd, he continues to really possess the power of the papacy in such a way that all his decrees have no less strength and authority than they would have if he were a true believer, as Baez and Suarez rightly explain."[580]

This middle way avoids both pitfalls. Plinio Corrêa de Oliveira once suggested it to the Chilean TFP's leaders, as a conclusion for their book, *The Church of Silence in Chile*. This explosive 1976 best seller denounced nearly all of the Chilean hierarchy for having collaborated with Communism in bringing about the country's destruction.[581]

---

580. Paul Laymann, SJ, *Theologia moralis* (Venice: n.p., 1683), tom. 1, bk. 2, tr. 1, ch. 7, 153, https://archive.org/details/bub_gb_cNcQB5d8hqoC. In the same vein, the eighteenth-century Dominican Charles Billuart wrote: "Christ, by a special dispensation, for the common good and tranquility of the Church continues to give jurisdiction even to a heretical pope until the Church declares him to be manifestly heretical." Caroli Renati Billuart, OP, *Tractatus de fide et regulis fidei: D. Th. a Q. 1 ad 16*, vol. 1, *Summa S. Thomæ, Cursus theologiæ, secunda secundæ* (Liège: S.S.E., 1751), diss. 4 ("Dissertation on Vices Opposed to Faith"), a.3 ("On Heresy"), 128, https://books.google.com/books?id=FZBcAAAAcAAJ.

581. [Publisher's Note: Between 1966 and 1976, the Chilean hierarchy, led by the archbishop of Santiago, Cardinal Raul Silva Henríquez, openly favored President Salvador Allende's rise to power with a public statement, arguing that it was morally licit for a Catholic to vote for a Marxist candidate. After Allende's rise to power, the cardinal celebrated, holding a *Te Deum* service in the Cathedral.

During the thousand days it was in power, the communist regime brought Chile to the same situation of oppression and misery that Venezuela suffers today. Despite this, the bishops gave their full support to the government and its structural and political reforms, including the nationalization of all education, even Catholic schools.

Even when the civilian population took to the streets demanding a military intervention to save the country from Communism, and both Parliament and the independent body responsible for verifying public accounts declared that the Allende administration had broken the law, Cardinal Silva Henríquez kept up intense contacts with the Communist Party, trying to make a deal that would prevent the regime's downfall. In the end, however, Salvador Allende's intransigence made his fall inevitable. He committed suicide in the presidential palace, using the AK-47 he received as a gift from Fidel Castro.

During the subsequent military regime, Cardinal Silva Henríquez and the bishops of Chile were the main force opposing the successful program of economic and social reconstruction based on private property and free enterprise that General Augusto Pinochet's cabinet promoted. Echoing a policy

The Brazilian TFP founder's proposal seems all the more valid today. Indeed, a large number of bishops, and the Holy See itself, are helping to topple not just private property, as Salvador Allende's Chile did, but other non-negotiable values as well. Moreover, they labor to subvert the Church's sacramental discipline and, directly or indirectly, Catholic morals and the Faith itself.

The Catholic leader proposed this middle way in answer to the following question:

> Having set forth our attitude of resistance, we turn our attention once again to our spiritual life as Catholics. . . .
>
> Are we obliged, according to sound doctrine, to go to those [demolishing] pastors and priests . . . to receive the teachings of the Church from their lips and to receive the sacraments from their hands?[582]

Plinio Corrêa de Oliveira replied:

> In this respect, it is necessary to point out that:
>
> a) In order for there to be a full ecclesiastical filiation . . . there must be in the spiritual relations between sheep and shepherd, as between son and father, a minimum level of mutual confidence and harmony.
>
> b) Given the extension and importance that these pastors and priests have assigned to the destructive action . . . in the concrete order there are no conditions for the *habitual* exercise of those relations. We cannot see how such an exercise could fail to bring with it a proximate risk for the Faith and *grave* scandals for the good.
>
> c) This being so, and *save for* better judgment, we affirm that the

---

launched by President Jimmy Carter, the cardinal and bishops did this under the pretext of upholding human rights. However, they showed concern only for the pseudo-rights of subversives. They had none for the legitimate rights of the population.

Based on over 200 documents, the book *The Church of Silence in Chile* was an *exposé* of the Chilean hierarchy's collusion with the failed communist revolution and its subversive groups. In its conclusion, it asked how the Catholic faithful should interact with shepherds promoting the country's destruction. It suggested that, while remaining united to Holy Church, the faithful should interrupt their ordinary Church life with the demolishing shepherds. See, The Chilean Society for the Defense of Tradition, Family, and Property, *The Church of Silence in Chile: The TFP Proclaims the Whole Truth* (Cleveland: Lumen Mariae, 1976), 352–8.

As noted, this proposed course of action was the brainchild of Plinio Corrêa de Oliveira. Having first suggested it for the Chilean TFP's book, the founder of the Brazilian TFP did the same for the Uruguayan TFP's work titled, *Leftism in the Church: "Fellow-traveler" of communism in the long adventure of failures and metamorphoses.* He also used it in his own book in Brazil titled, *The Church in the face of the escalating communist threat: An appeal to the silent bishops.*]

582. Chilean TFP, *Church of Silence*, 352.

cessation of ecclesiastical relations[583] with such bishops and priests
is a right of conscience of Catholics who judge it to be unbearable,
that is to say, harmful for the Faith itself and the life of piety, and scandalous for the faithful people.[584]

A reader may wonder: Does the interruption of a Catholic's ordinary Church
life with the demolishing shepherds not amount to schism, even though their
authority and jurisdiction remain fully recognized?

For the reader's peace of mind, I note that the rights that support unjustly
coerced faithful are analogous to those enjoyed by a good wife who is psychologically attacked by an abusive husband. It is comparable to those of children
toward a bad father. Without abandoning the family home, mother and children may legitimately move to an isolated part of the house. In doing this, they
make use of their right of self-defense against the father's evil ways. Their with-
drawing from routine family life does not mean they reject the indissoluble
conjugal and filial ties that bind them to husband and father. Nor are they re-
miss in their duty of fidelity to him by avoiding regular contact. On the contrary, their removal may stir the father to examine his conscience. It may bring
him to repentance. That would mean a return to ordinary family life for all.

This analogy is not a stretch. Indeed, Saint Paul teaches in the Epistle to
the Ephesians, "The husband is the head of the wife, as Christ is the head of
the Church. He is the savior of his body" (Eph. 5:23). Later on, the Fathers
of the Church and medieval canonists used this mystical marriage
metaphor.[585] Thus, the episcopal ring is a symbol of this mystical marriage
between a bishop and his diocese. If the metaphor evokes the faithful's duty
of fidelity and submission—that of "the wife"—it also esteems their position,
either by reiterating their rights or emphasizing the duties of the bishop,

---

583. [Publisher's Note: In the Italian original, the word is *convivenza*, meaning, literally, living together.]

584. Ibid., 352–3. Naturally, the proposal to interrupt ordinary Church life with the demolishing shepherds
should not be put into practice in a universal manner, since "d) . . . it is in the nature of this process [of de-
struction] that its peculiarities do not develop in a manner absolutely simultaneous throughout the entire
country. On the contrary, it is a bit more advanced in one place and a bit more retarded in another" (Ibid.,
353). To transpose the problem to today, I could say, for example, that regarding giving Holy Communion to
civilly "remarried" divorcees, the situation in Germany is not that of neighboring Poland or Africa. Plinio
Corrêa de Oliveira continues: "It is also necessary to consider the case of some ecclesiastics whose commitment to the process of destruction exists, but in a limited way and to a very tenuous degree" (Ibid.).
From the combination of these two circumstances, the reasoning concludes that, "Accordingly, **it is understandable that some of the faithful frequent the churches of the shepherds and priests whom we de-
nounce, and that others refuse to do so** and separate themselves from all *habitual* spiritual and religious
relation with such ecclesiastics, even relating to the sacramental life" (Ibid). (The bold is mine.)

585. The metaphor was used by Sts. Cyprian, Ephrem, Ambrose, and Gregory the Great. It became frequent among medieval canonists starting with Huguccio, around 1190. See Laurent Fontbaustier, *La déposition du pape hérétique: Une origine du constitutionnalisme?* (Paris: Mare & Martin, 2016), 53–65.

who represents—"the husband." *A fortiori*, the metaphor can be applied to the relations between the universal Church and a pope.

However, an old adage says that "every analogy limps." With a marriage's consummation, the bond uniting a Catholic couple becomes absolutely indissoluble. The mystical marriage between a bishop and his diocese, however, is dissolved by his resignation or transfer to another diocese.[586] In the case of the universal Church, it is dissolved by a pope's resigning. *Mutatis mutandis*, this does not prevent the analogy from being valid for the "wife"—that is, a diocesan community or the universal Church. When a Catholic community is the victim of abuse by the "husband"—be it the bishop or the pope—it can legitimately seek to defend itself.

Except for the indissolubility difference, the situations are analogous. Moreover, the rights of a wife who feels obliged to separate from her husband go even further. Indeed, an abused wife has the right to stop living under her husband's roof. She can move to another dwelling, or force her straying consort to do so. Reiterating the Church's millennial legislation, the 1983 *Code of Canon Law* establishes that "Spouses have the duty and right to preserve conjugal living unless a legitimate cause excuses them" (Can. 1151). In addition to unforgiven and uncondoned adultery (Can. 1152), a couple may legitimately separate "with the bond remaining," "if either of the spouses causes grave mental or physical danger to the other spouse or to the offspring or otherwise renders common life too difficult" (Can. 1153 §1).[587] Such separation may be decreed by the local ordinary or, "if there is danger in delay," a spouse can take measures "on his or her own authority" (Ibid). "In all cases, when the cause for the separation ceases, conjugal living must be restored. . . ." (Can. 1153 §2).[588]

Legal separation "with the bond remaining" is an institution that survives in

---

586. Cardinal Bernard Gantin, prefect of the Congregation of Bishops from 1984 to 1998, was adamantly opposed to careerism in the current practice of transferring bishops from a secondary to a more important diocese. In an interview with *30 Giorni*, he stated:, "Let us be clear: The relationship between a bishop and a diocese is also depicted as a marriage and a marriage, according to the spirit of the Gospel, is indissoluble. The new bishop must not make other personal plans. There may well be serious reasons, very serious reasons for a decision by the authorities that the bishop should go from one family, so to speak, to another. In making this decision, the authorities take numerous factors into consideration. They do not include an eventual desire by a bishop to change see." Sandro Magister, "The Scourge of Divorce Between Bishop and Diocese," trans. Matthew Sherry, *L'Espresso–Settimo Cielo*, Jun. 6, 2013, http://chiesa.espresso.repubblica.it/articolo/1350531bdc4.html?eng=y.

587. The 1917 *Pio-Benedictine Code* developed the legitimate causes for interrupting life in common a bit more: "If one spouse gives his name to a non-Catholic sect; if he raises the children non-Catholic; if he leads a criminal or disgraceful life; if one creates grave danger to the soul or body of the other; if, by cruelty, one renders common life too difficult; these reasons and others of their sort are for the other spouse completely legitimate reasons for leaving" (Can. 1131 §1). Edward N. Peters, cur., *The 1917 or Pio-Benedictine Code of Canon Law* (San Francisco: Ignatius, 2001), 388–9.

588. *Code of Canon Law*, http://www.vatican.va/archive/ENG1104/__P45.HTM.

the laws of many countries with Christian roots. It only loosens a bit the conjugal bond by waiving cohabitation. All other marriage duties remain, notably those of fidelity and the obligation to provide succor in case of need.

This separation "with the bond remaining," which is so peaceably accepted by canon and civil law, represents a far more drastic measure than the one I suggest. My proposal is a simple suspension of the ordinary interaction. It is the equivalent of living in separate quarters, though still under the same roof, from shepherds whose flock feels psychologically abused by their efforts to impose an unacceptable paradigm shift in the Church's teaching, discipline, and life.

This well-balanced resistance is what characterizes my proposal as a middle way. In other words, it preserves intact the bond of fidelity that unites the faithful to their legitimate shepherds. On the other hand, however, it takes the needed prudential measures to safeguard the integrity of one's faith. All the while, it shows charity toward the weak by preventing them from becoming scandalized with continued normal relations with prelates who are self-destroying the Church.

I proffer these analyses and the proposal to resist and interrupt ordinary Church life with demolishing shepherds as a simple layman. Although I accompany attentively the great doctrinal questions raised by the clash between the Church and today's anti-Christian revolution, I am guided only by the *sensus fidei* and my reason illuminated by the Faith. I have completed no advanced studies in dogmatic and moral theology or canon law. Accordingly, I present these analyses and proposal alike for the consideration of faithful shepherds wishing to resist the paradigm shift in the Church. They are open to the scholarly critique of canonists, philosophers, and historians. I wish to share them with the leaders of Catholic organizations who are not willing to abandon the struggle for the Gospel's eternal principles in today's society.

Some fear that the virtual division within the Church fostered by the paradigm shift may lead to a formal split. If it happens—God forbid!—then Catholics faithful to their baptismal vows should cling to the perennial teaching of the Church's traditional magisterium. They should hearken to the shepherds who transmit it unchanged. They should do this in the hope that the Holy Spirit will lead the straying shepherds back to the right path. However, they should avoid anxiety over the canonical status of the wayward shepherds. This is a complex and delicate theological and canonical issue that is well beyond the grasp and competence of the average faithful. Even among specialists, it has aroused much controversy.

In the present confusion, which threatens to worsen very soon, one thing is sure: Catholics faithful to their baptism will never break the sacred bond of love, veneration, and obedience that unites them to the Successor of Peter and the successors of the Apostles. This is true even when these may eventually op-press them in their attempt to demolish the Church. If in the abuse of their power and seeking to coerce the faithful into accepting their deviations those prelates condemn them for their fidelity to the Gospel and for legitimately resisting abusive authority, it is those shepherds, not the faithful, who will be responsible for the rupture and its consequences before God, the rights of the Church, and history. Saint Athanasius is a case in point. Although he was a victim of the abuse of power, he remains a star in the Church's firmament forever.

Even in such extreme circumstances, without mitigating their legitimate position of resistance, the faithful should continue to pray for the conversion of those straying shepherds. Thus would they imitate the actions of a good mother and her children in the face of an abusive husband and father with whom they have ceased to have daily interaction. These would pray in the hope that their conjugal and family life would be restored as soon as the cause for their separation has ended.

* * *

I close this assessment of Pope Francis's first five years by reiterating my unshakable faith and unalterable fidelity to the Roman Pontiff's primacy of universal jurisdiction and his *ex cathedra* infallibility, as well as to the truth of the Faith on the indefectibility of the Church as contained in Holy Writ and proclaimed by the ordinary universal magisterium. The indefectibility of the One, Holy, Roman Catholic Church is the supernatural property that guarantees the perpetuity and immutability of Her essential elements—the Faith, sacraments, and sacred hierarchy. It is founded on the promise of Our Lord and confirmed in the closing verse of the Gospel of Saint Matthew: "Behold, I am with you all days, even to the consummation of the world" (Matt. 28:20).

The words that Sister Lúcia, one of the Fatima seers, addressed to the late Cardinal Carlo Caffarra, first president of the John Paul II Institute for Studies on Family and Marriage, further reinforce my confidence in the Church's indefectibility. The cardinal had written her, announcing that he had consecrated the Institute's work to the Immaculate Heart of Mary. His Eminence explained her response in an interview, saying: "I received a very long letter. . . . In it we find written: 'the decisive battle between the Lord and the kingdom of Satan will be about marriage and the family.' 'Do not be afraid,' she added, 'because anyone who works for the sanctity of marriage and the family will always be fought and opposed in every way, because this is the decisive issue.' And then she concluded: 'However, Our Lady has already crushed [the devil's] head.'"[589]

---

589. Diane Montagna, "Fatima Visionary to Cardinal: 'Final Battle Between God and Satan Will Be Over Marriage and Family,'" *Aleteia.org*, Jan. 17, 2017, https://aleteia.org/2017/01/17/fatima-visionary-to-cardinal-final-battle-between-god-and-satan-will-be-over-marriage-and-family/.

"The future belongs to God," Plinio Corrêa de Oliveira wrote, and, full of holy optimism, he added:

> As we look at some brethren in the Faith, we are even faced with a great deal of sorrow and apprehension. In the heat of battle, it is possible and even likely that we will have terrible disappointments. However, it is quite certain that the Holy Spirit continues to stir up in the Church admirable and indomitable spiritual energies of faith, purity, obedience, and dedication, which in due time will once again cover the Christian name with glory.
>
> The twentieth century will be not only the century of the great struggle but especially the century of the immense triumph.[590]

I finish these lines, therefore, confident of Mary Most Holy's approaching intervention to solve the present crisis of self-destruction in the Church. I do this, inspired only out of love for the papacy, and with the desire to see it shine again with renewed splendor.

"Lord, that your kingdom may come, may the reign of Mary come!"

---

590. Plinio Corrêa de Oliveira, "O século da guerra, da morte e do pecado," *Catolicismo*, no. 2 (Feb. 1951) 6, http://www.pliniocorreadeoliveira.info/1951_002_CAT_O_s%C3%A9culo_da_guerra.htm.

BIBLIOGRAPHY

I. Papal Documents

Benedict XVI.
(Addresses, Messages, and Speeches—chronological order)
———. "To the Members of the European People's Party on the Occasion of the Study Days on Europe." Mar. 30, 2006. http://w2.vatican.va/content/benedict-xvi /en/speeches/2006/march/documents/hf_ben-xvi_spe_20060330_eu -parliamentarians.html.
———. "For the 97th World Day of Migrants and Refugees (2011): 'One Human Family.'" Sept. 27, 2010. http://w2.vatican.va/content/benedict-xvi/en/messages /migration/documents/hf_ben-xvi_mes_20100927_world-migrants-day.html.
———. "To Participants in the General Assembly of *Caritas Internationalis*." May 27, 2011. http://w2.vatican.va/content/benedict-xvi/en/speeches/2011/may /documents/hf_ben-xvi_spe_20110527_caritas.html.

(Papal Documents—alphabetical order)
———. *Caritas in Veritate* (Encyclical). Jun. 29, 2009. http://w2.vatican.va/content/benedict-xvi/en/encyclicals/documents /hf_ben-xvi_enc_20090629_caritas-in-veritate.html.
———. *Sacramentum Caritatis* (Post-Synodal Apostolic Exhortation). Feb. 22, 2007. http://w2.vatican.va/content/benedict-xvi/en/apost_exhortations /documents/hf_ben-xvi_exh_20070222_sacramentum-caritatis.html.

Francis.
(Addresses and Speeches—chronological order)
———. "Meeting With the World of Labor and Industry: Address of Pope Francis." Jul. 5, 2014. https://w2.vatican.va/content/francesco/en/speeches/2014/july /documents/papa-francesco_20140705_molise-mondo-del-lavoro.html.
———. "Address of Pope Francis: Private Visit of the Holy Father to Caserta for a Meeting With the Evangelical Pastor Giovanni Traettino." Jul. 28, 2014. https://w2.vatican.va/content/francesco/en/speeches/2014/july/documents /papa-francesco_20140728_caserta-pastore-traettino.html.
———. "Address of Pope Francis to the Participants in the World Meeting of Popular Movements." Oct. 28, 2014. http://w2.vatican.va/content/francesco/en/speeches /2014/october/documents/papa-francesco_20141028_incontro-mondiale -movimenti-popolari.html.
———. "Address of Pope Francis to the Council of Europe." Nov. 25, 2014. http://w2.vatican.va/content/francesco/en/speeches/2014/november /documents/papa-francesco_20141125_strasburgo-consiglio-europa.html.
———. "Pope's Audience With Children of 'The Peace Factory.'" *Zenit*. May 12, 2015. https://zenit.org/articles/pope-s-audience-with-children-of-the-peace-factory/.

———. "Address of the Holy Father—Participation at the Second World Meeting of Popular Movements." Jul. 9, 2015. http://w2.vatican.va/content/francesco/en/speeches/2015/july/documents/papa-francesco_20150709_bolivia-movimenti-popolari.html.

———. "Address of the Holy Father: Meeting With the Members of the General Assembly of the United Nations Organization." Sept. 25, 2015. http://w2.vatican.va/content/francesco/en/speeches/2015/september/documents/papa-francesco_20150925_onu-visita.html.

———. "Address of His Holiness Pope Francis—Conclusion of the Synod of Bishops." Oct. 24, 2015. http://w2.vatican.va/content/francesco/en/speeches/2015/october/documents/papa-francesco_20151024_sinodo-conclusione-lavori.html.

———. "Responses of the Holy Father to the Questions of Three Members of the Evangelical Lutheran Community of Rome." Nov. 15, 2015. https://w2.vatican.va/content/francesco/en/speeches/2015/november/documents/papa-francesco_20151115_chiesa-evangelica-luterana.html.

———. "Address of His Holiness Pope Francis: Conferral of the Charlemagne Prize." May 6, 2016. http://w2.vatican.va/content/francesco/en/speeches/2016/may/documents/papa-francesco_20160506_premio-carlo-magno.html.

———. "Address of His Holiness Pope Francis to Participants in the Pilgrimage of Lutherans." Oct. 13, 2016. https://w2.vatican.va/content/francesco/en/speeches/2016/october/documents/papa-francesco_20161013_pellegrinaggio-luterani.html.

———. "Address of His Holiness Pope Francis to Participants in the 3rd World Meeting of Popular Movements." Nov. 5, 2016. http://w2.vatican.va/content/francesco/en/speeches/2016/november/documents/papa-francesco_20161105_movimenti-popolari.html.

———. "Address of His Holiness Pope Francis to Participants of the III Global Meeting of the Indigenous Peoples' Forum of the International Fund for Agricultural Development." Feb. 15, 2017. https://w2.vatican.va/content/francesco/en/speeches/2017/february/documents/papa-francesco_20170215_popoli-indigeni.html.

———. "Greeting of the Holy Father: Blessing of the Candles—Pilgrimage of His Holiness Pope Francis to the Shrine of Our Lady of Fatima." May 12, 2017. https://w2.vatican.va/content/francesco/en/speeches/2017/may/documents/papa-francesco_20170512_benedizione-candele-fatima.html.

———. "Address of His Holiness Pope Francis to Participants in the Meeting Promoted by the Pontifical Council for Promoting the New Evangelization." Oct. 11, 2017. http://w2.vatican.va/content/francesco/en/speeches/2017/october/documents/papa-francesco_20171011_convegno-nuova-evangelizzazione.html.

———. "Address of His Holiness Pope Francis to the Members of the Diplomatic Corps Accredited to the Holy See for the Traditional Exchange of New Year Greetings." Jan. 8, 2018. http://w2.vatican.va/content/francesco/en/speeches/2018/january/documents/papa-francesco_20180108_corpo-diplomatico.html.

———. "Address of the Holy Father: Meeting With Indigenous People of Amazonia."
Jan. 19, 2018. http://w2.vatican.va/content/francesco/en/speeches/2018
/january/documents/papa-francesco_20180119_peru-puertomaldonado
-popoliamazzonia.html.

(Angelus and Regina Caeli—chronological order)
———. "Angelus." Mar. 17, 2013. http://w2.vatican.va/content/francesco/en
/angelus/2013/documents/papa-francesco_angelus_20130317.html.
———. "Regina Cæli." Mar. 28, 2016. http://w2.vatican.va/content/francesco/en
/angelus/2016/documents/papa-francesco_regina-coeli_20160328.html.

(Forewords, and Other Non-traditional Papal Writings)
———. "Il papa: 'La Chiesa missionaria non si chiuda in se stessa.'" *Corriere Della
Sera.* Oct. 19, 2015. http://www.corriere.it/cronache/15_ottobre_19/papa
-francesco-la-chiesa-missionaria-non-si-chiuda-se-stessa-2973aab8-7620
-11e5-9086-b57baad6b3f4.shtml.

(General Audiences—chronological order)
———. "General Audience." Jun. 22, 2016.
http://w2.vatican.va/content/francesco/en/audiences/2016/documents
/papa-francesco_20160622_udienza-generale.html.
———. "General Audience." Jun. 21, 2017.
http://w2.vatican.va/content/francesco/en/audiences/2017/documents
/papa-francesco_20170621_udienza-generale.html.
———. "General Audience." Sept. 27, 2017.
https://w2.vatican.va/content/francesco/en/audiences/2017/documents
/papa-francesco_20170927_udienza-generale.html.

(Homilies—chronological order)
———. "Jesus Excludes No One: Morning Meditation in the Chapel of Domus Sanctae
Marthae." May 8, 2013. http://w2.vatican.va/content/francesco/en/cotidie
/2013/documents/papa-francesco-cotidie_20130508_non-exclusion.html.
———. Galvan, Kelen. "Papa diz que para evangelizar, cristãos devem construir pontes
e não muros." *Canção Nova–Notícias.* May 8, 2013. https://noticias.cancaonova.com
/especiais/pontificado/Francis/papa-diz-que-para-evangelizar-cristaos-devem
-construir-pontes-e-nao-muros/.
———. "Homily of His Holiness Pope Francis: Holy Mass With Representatives of the
Indigenous Communities of Chiapas." Feb. 15, 2016. http://w2.vatican.va/content
/francesco/en/homilies/2016/documents/papa-francesco_20160215_omelia
-messico-chiapas.html.
———. "For a Culture of Encounter: Morning Meditation in the Chapel of the Domus
Sanctae Marthae." Sept. 13, 2016. https://w2.vatican.va/content/francesco
/en/cotidie/2016/documents/papa-francesco-cotidie_20160913_for-a-culture
-of-encounter.html.

———. "Homily of His Holiness Pope Francis." Dec. 24, 2017. http://w2.vatican.va/content/francesco/en/homilies/2017/documents /papa-francesco_20171224_omelia-natale.html.

(Interviews)

———. "Full English Text of Pope Francis' Interview With 'Il Messaggero'–Pope Francis: Communism Stole Our Flag." *Zenit*. Jul. 2, 2014. https://zenit.org/articles /full-english-text-of-pope-francis-interview-with-il-messaggero/.

———. **Ambrogetti**, Francesca and Sergio Rubin. *Pope Francis: His Life in His Own Words—Conversations With Jorge Bergoglio*. New York: G. P. Putnam's Sons, 2010, 2013.

———. **Benarroch**, Henrique Cymerman. "Entrevista al Papa Francisco: 'La secesión de una nación hay que tomarla con pinzas.'" *La Vanguardia*. Jun. 12, 2014. http://www.lavanguardia.com/internacional/20140612/54408951579 /entrevista-papa-Francis.html

———. **de Bortoli**, Ferruccio. "Benedetto XVI non è una statua: Partecipa alla vita della Chiesa." *Corriere della Sera*. Mar. 5, 2014. http://www.corriere.it/cronache /14_marzo_04/vi-racconto-mio-primo-anno-papa-90f8a1c4-a3eb-11e3-b352 -9ec6f8a34ecc.shtml.

———. **Denis**, Jean-Pierre. "Conversation politique avec le pape François." *La Vie*. Mar. 2, 2016. http://www.lavie.fr/religion/catholicisme/conversation-politique -avec-le-pape-francois-02-03-2016-71086_16.php.

———. **Goubert**, Guillaume, and Sébastien Maillard. "Le pape François à *La Croix*: 'Un état doit être laïque.'" *La Croix*. May 16, 2016. http://www.la-croix.com /Religion/Pape/Le-pape-Francois-a-La-Croix-Un-Etat-doit-etre-laique-2016 -05-16-1200760526.

———. **Falasca**, Stefania. "L'intervista ad Avvenire. Papa Francesco: Non svendo la dottrina, seguo il Concilio." *Avvenire*. Nov. 17, 2016. https://www.avvenire.it /papa/pagine/giubileo-ecumenismo-concilio-intervista-esclusiva-del-papa -adavvenire.

———. **Piqué**, Elisabetta. "Pope Francis: 'God Has Bestowed on Me a Healthy Dose of Unawareness.'" *La Nación*. Dec. 7, 2014. https://www.lanacion.com.ar/1750350 -pope-francis-god-has-bestowed-on-me-a-healthy-dose-of-unawareness.

———. "The Synod on the Family: 'The Divorced and Remarried Seem Excommunicated.'" *La Nación*. Dec. 7, 2014. https://www.lanacion.com.ar/1750351 -the-synod-on-the-family-the-divorced-and-remarried-seem-excommunicated.

———. **Scalfari**, Eugenio. "The Pope: How the Church Will Change." *La Repubblica*. Oct. 1, 2013. http://www.repubblica.it/cultura/2013/10/01/news/pope_s _conversation_with_scalfari_english-67643118/.

———. ———. "Il Vicario di Cristo e la verità relativa che conduce a Dio." *La Repubblica*. Oct. 28, 2014. http://www.repubblica.it/cultura/2014/10/28/news /il_vicario_di_cristo_e_la_verit_relativa_che_conduce_a_dio-99162795/.

———. ———. "Francesco, papa profeta che incontra la modernità." *La Repubblica*. Jul. 1, 2015. http://www.repubblica.it/cultura/2015/07/01/news /francesco_papa_profeta_che_incontra_la_modernita_-118048516/.

———. ———. "Conservatori e temporalisti lo frenano ma Francesco non si fermerà." *La Repubblica*. Oct. 25, 2015. http://www.repubblica.it/politica/2015/10/25/news /conservatori_e_temporalisti_lo_frenano_ma_francesco_non_si_fermera _-125834299/.

———. ———. "Pope Francis: 'Trump? I Do Not Judge. I Care Only If He Makes the Poor Suffer.'" *La Repubblica*. Nov. 11, 2016. http://www.repubblica.it/vaticano/2016/11/11 /news/pope_francis_trump-151810120/.

———. ———. "Scalfari intervista Francesco: 'Il mio frido al G20 sui migranti.'" *La Repubblica*. Jul. 8, 2017. http://www.repubblica.it/vaticano/2017/07/08/news /scalfari_intervista_francesco_il_mio_grido_al_g20_sui_migranti_-170253225/.

———. **Spadaro, SJ**, Antonio. "A Big Heart Open to God: An Interview With Pope Francis." *America*. Sept. 30, 2013. https://www.americamagazine.org/faith/2013/09/30 /big-heart-open-god-interview-pope-francis.

———. **Tornielli**, Andrea. "Never Be Afraid of Tenderness." *La Stampa–Vatican Insider*. Dec. 15, 2013. http://www.lastampa.it/2013/12/16/vaticaninsider/eng/the-vatican /never-be-afraid-of tenderness-3sMZy95oJWmaNvfq4m1sTN/pagina.html.

———. **Wolton**, Dominique. *Politique et société: Pape François, rencontres avec Dominique Wolton*. Paris: Observatoire, 2017.

(Messages—chronological order)

———. "Message of His Holiness Pope Francis for the World Day of Migrants and Refugees (2014). Aug. 5, 2013. http://w2.vatican.va/content/francesco/en/messages /migration/documents/papa-francesco_20130805_world-migrants-day.html.

———. "Show Mercy to Our Common Home: Message of His Holiness Pope Francis for the Celebration of the World Day of Prayer for the Care of Creation." Sept. 1, 2016. http://w2.vatican.va/content/francesco/en/messages/pont-messages/2016 /documents/papa-francesco_20160901_messaggio-giornata-cura-creato.html.

———. "Message of His Holiness Pope Francis on the Occasion of the World Meetings of Popular Movements in Modesto (California) [16-18 February 2017]." Feb. 10, 2017. http://movimientospopulares.org/es/carta-del-papa-Francis-a -los-movimientos-populares-modesto-california-16-19-feb-2017/.

———. "To the Participants in the European Regional Meeting of the World Medical Association." Nov. 7, 2017. https://w2.vatican.va/content/francesco/en /messages/pont-messages/2017/documents/papa-francesco_20171107 _messaggio-monspaglia.html.

———. "Message of His Holiness Pope Francis for the 104th World Day of Migrants and Refugees 2018." Jan. 14, 2018. http://w2.vatican.va/content/francesco/en /messages/migration/documents/papa-francesco_20170815_world -migrants-day-2018.html.

(Traditional Papal Documents—Alphabetical Order)

———. "A los Obispos de la Conferencia Episcopal Venezolana" (Letter). May 5, 2017. https://w2.vatican.va/content/dam/francesco/pdf/apost_exhortations /documents/papa-francesco_esortazione-ap_20160319_amoris-laetitia_en.pdf.

———. *Amoris Laetitia* (Apostolic Exhortation). Mar. 19, 2016.
https://w2.vatican.va/content/dam/francesco/pdf/apost_exhortations
/documents/papa-francesco_esortazione-ap_20160319_amoris-laetitia_en.pdf.

———. "Carta del Santo Padre Francisco a los Obispos de la Región Pastoral de
Buenos Aires" (Letter). Sept. 5, 2016. http://w2.vatican.va/content/francesco/es
/letters/2016/documents/papa-francesco_20160905_regione-pastorale
-buenos-aires.html

———. *Evangelii Gaudium* (Apostolic Exhortation). Nov. 24, 2013.
http://w2.vatican.va/content/francesco/en/apost_exhortations/documents
/papa-francesco_esortazione-ap_20131124_evangelii-gaudium.html.

———. *Gaudete et Exsultate* (Apostolic Exhortation). Mar. 19, 2018.
https://w2.vatican.va/content/francesco/en/apost_exhortations/documents
/papa-francesco_esortazione-ap_20180319_gaudete-et-exsultate.html.

———. "Joint Declaration of His Holiness Pope Francis With His Holiness Kirill, Patriarch of Moscow and All Russia." Feb. 12, 2016. https://w2.vatican.va/content
/francesco/en/speeches/2016/february/documents/papa-francesco
_20160212_dichiarazione-comune-kirill.html.

———. *Laudato Sì* (Encyclical). May 24, 2015. http://w2.vatican.va/content/francesco
/en/encyclicals/documents/papa-francesco_20150524_enciclica
-laudato-si.html.

———. "Letter of His Holiness Pope Francis to the Christians in the Middle East."
Dec. 21, 2014. http://w2.vatican.va/content/francesco/en/letters/2014
/documents/papa-francesco_20141221_lettera-cristiani-medio-oriente.html.

———. "Letter to a Non-believer: Pope Francis Responds to Dr. Eugenio Scalfari Journalist of the Italian Newspaper 'La Repubblica.'" Sept. 4, 2013.
http://w2.vatican.va/content/francesco/en/letters/2013/documents
/papa-francesco_20130911_eugenio-scalfari.html.

———. *Mitis et Misericors Iesus* (Motu Proprio). Aug. 15, 2015.
https://w2.vatican.va/content/francesco/en/motu_proprio/documents
/papa-francesco-motu-proprio_20150815_mitis-et-misericors-iesus.html

———. *Mitis Iudex Dominus Iesus* (Motu Proprio). Aug. 15, 2015.
https://w2.vatican.va/content/francesco/en/motu_proprio/documents
/papa-francesco-motu-proprio_20150815_mitis-iudex-dominus-iesus.html.

———. *Summa Familiae Cura* (Motu Proprio). Sept. 8, 2017. http://w2.vatican.va
/content/francesco/en/motu_proprio/documents/papa-francesco-motu
-proprio_20170908_summa-familiae-cura.html.

———. *Veritatis Gaudium* (Apostolic Constitution). Dec. 8, 2017.
https://w2.vatican.va/content/francesco/en/apost_constitutions/documents
/papa-francesco_costituzione-ap_20171208_veritatis-gaudium.html

(Trip Press Conferences—chronological order)
———. "In-Flight Press Conference of Pope Francis During the Return Flight: Apostolic Journey to Rio de Janeiro on the Occasion of the XXVIII World Youth Day."
Jul. 28, 2013. http://w2.vatican.va/content/francesco/en/speeches/2013
/july/documents/papa-francesco_20130728_gmg-conferenza-stampa.html.

———. "In-Flight Press Conference of His Holiness Pope Francis From Santiago de Cuba to Washington, D.C." Sept. 22, 2015. http://w2.vatican.va/content/francesco /pt/speeches/2015/september/documents/papa-francesco_20150922 _intervista-santiago-washington.html.

———. "In-Flight Press Conference of His Holiness Pope Francis From Mexico to Rome." Feb. 17, 2016. http://w2.vatican.va/content/francesco/en/speeches/2016/february /documents/papa-francesco_20160217_messico-conferenza-stampa.html.

———. "In-Flight Press Conference of His Holiness Pope Francis From Lesbos to Rome." Apr. 16, 2016. http://w2.vatican.va/content/francesco/en/speeches /2016/april/documents/papa-francesco_20160416_lesvos-volo-ritorno.html.

———. "In-Flight Press Conference of His Holiness Pope Francis From Armenia to Rome." Jun. 26, 2016. https://w2.vatican.va/content/francesco/en/speeches/2016 /june/documents/papa-francesco_20160626_armenia-conferenza-stampa.html.

———. "In-Flight Press Conference of His Holiness Pope Francis From Poland to Rome." Jul. 31, 2016. https://w2.vatican.va/content/francesco/en/speeches/2016 /july/documents/papa-francesco_20160731_polonia-conferenza-stampa.html.

———. "In-Flight Press Conference of His Holiness Pope Francis From Azerbaijan to Rome." Oct. 2, 2016. http://w2.vatican.va/content/francesco/en/speeches /2016/october/documents/papa-francesco_20161002_georgia-azerbaijan -conferenza-stampa.html.

———. "Return Flight Press Conference of His Holiness Pope Francis From Egypt to Rome." Apr. 29, 2017. http://w2.vatican.va/content/francesco/en/speeches/2017 /april/documents/papa-francesco_20170429_egitto-volo.html.

———. "Press Conference of His Holiness Pope Francis on the Return Flight From Colombia to Rome." Sept. 10, 2017. http://w2.vatican.va/content/francesco/en /speeches/2017/september/documents/papa-francesco_20170910 _viaggioapostolico-colombia-voloritorno.html.

(Videos—chronological order)
———. Pope's Worldwide Prayer Network. "Inter-religious Dialogue." *Holy Cross TV.* Jan. 8, 2016. https://www.youtube.com/watch?v=XODAb0ImTKg.

———. "Bergoglio ai presunti rifugiati: Bibbia e corano lo stesso Dio, condividere la propria fede." *YouTube.* Uploaded Aug. 10, 2015. https://youtu.be/BXaqlOj4qIg.

John XXIII. *Pacem in Terris* (Encyclical). Apr. 11, 1963. http://w2.vatican.va/content /john-xxiii/en/encyclicals/documents/hf_j-xxiii_enc_11041963_pacem.html.

John Paul II. *Familiaris Consortio* (Apostolic Exhortation). Nov. 22, 1981. http://w2.vatican.va/content/john-paul-ii/en/apost_exhortations/documents /hf_jp-ii_exh_19811122_familiaris-consortio.html.

———. *Sollicitudo Rei Socialis* (Encyclical). Dec. 30, 1987. http://w2.vatican.va /content/john-paul-ii/en/encyclicals/documents/hf_jp-ii_enc_30121987 _sollicitudo-rei-socialis.html

———. *Centesimus Annus* (Encyclical). May 1, 1991. http://w2.vatican.va/content /john-paul-ii/en/encyclicals/documents/hf_jp-ii_enc_01051991 _centesimus-annus.html.

Leo XIII. *Au milieu des sollicitudes* (Encyclical). Feb. 16, 1892. http://w2.vatican.va /content/leo-xiii/en/encyclicals/documents/hf_l-xiii_enc_16021892 _au-milieu-des-sollicitudes.html.
———. *Humanum Genus* (Encyclical). Apr. 20, 1884. http://w2.vatican.va/content /leo-xiii/en/encyclicals/documents/hf_l-xiii_enc_18840420_humanum-genus.html.
———. *Notre Consolation* (Letter to French bishops). May 3, 1892. https://w2.vatican.va /content/leo-xiii/fr/letters/documents/hf_l-xiii_let_18920503_notre-consolation.html.

Paul VI. "Address of Pope Paul VI During the Last General Meeting of the Second Vatican Council." Dec. 7, 1965. http://w2.vatican.va/content/paul-vi/en /speeches/1965/documents/hf_p-vi_spe_19651207_epilogo-concilio.html.
———. "Discorso di Paolo VI ai membri del Pontificio Seminario Lombardo." Dec. 7, 1968. http://w2.vatican.va/content/paul-vi/it/speeches/1968/december /documents/hf_p-vi_spe_19681207_seminario-lombardo.html.
———. *Octogesima Adveniens* (Apostolic Letter). May 14, 1971. http://w2.vatican.va/content/paul-vi/en/apost_letters/documents/hf _p-vi_apl_19710514_octogesima-adveniens.html.

Pius IX. *Iamdudum Cernimus* (Allocution). Mar. 18, 1861. https://w2.vatican.va /content/pius-ix/it/documents/allocuzione-iamdudum-cernimus-18 -marzo-1861.html.

Pius X. *Notre Charge Apostolique* (Encyclical). Aug. 25, 1910. http://www.papalencyclicals.net/pius10/p10notre.htm.

Pius XI. *Divini Redemptoris* (Encyclical). Mar. 19, 1937. https://w2.vatican.va /content/pius-xi/en/encyclicals/documents/hf_p-xi_enc_19370319_divini -redemptoris.html.

Pius XII. "Allocation to the Union of Men of the Italian Catholic Action." Oct. 12, 1952. https://w2.vatican.va/content/pius-xii/it/speeches/1952/documents /hf_p-xii_spe_19521012_uomini-azione-cattolica.html.
———. "Speech to Participants in the Second World Congress of the Lay Apostolate." Oct. 5, 1957. http://w2.vatican.va/content/pius-xii/fr/speeches/1957 /documents/hf_p-xii_spe_19571005_apostolato-laici.html.

II. Other Holy See Sources

Catechism of the Catholic Church. http://www.vatican.va/archive/ccc_css/archive/catechism/p3s1c2a2.htm.

Congregation for the Doctrine of the Faith. "Doctrinal Note on Some Questions Regarding the Participation of Catholics in Political Life."Nov. 21, 2002. http://www.vatican.va/roman_curia/congregations/cfaith/documents /rc_con_cfaith_doc_20021124_politica_en.html.

———. "Instruction on Certain Aspects of the 'Theology of Liberation." Aug. 6, 1984. http://www.vatican.va/roman_curia/congregations/cfaith/documents /rc_con_cfaith_doc_19840806_theology-liberation_en.html.

———. "Letter to the Bishops of the Catholic Church Concerning the Reception of Holy Communion by the Divorced and Remarried Members of the Faithful." Sept. 14, 1994. http://www.vatican.va/roman_curia/congregations/cfaith /documents/rc_con_cfaith_doc_14091994_rec-holy-comm-by-divorced_en.html.

First Vatican Council. Dogmatic Constitution *Dei Filius*. Apr. 24, 1870. In *Decrees of the Ecumenical Councils*. Edited by Norman P. Tanner, SJ. Washington: Georgetown University Press, 1990. https://www.ewtn.com/library/councils/v1.htm#4.

———. Dogmatic Constitution *Pastor Aeternus*. Jul. 18, 1870. In *Decrees of the Ecumenical Councils*. Edited by Norman P. Tanner, SJ. Washington: Georgetown University Press, 1990. https://www.ewtn.com/faith/teachings/papae1.htm.

Holy See. *Acta Apostolicae Sedis*. Vol. 108, no. 10. http://www.vatican.va/archive/aas/documents/2016/acta-ottobre2016.pdf

———. "On the Outcome Document of the United Nations Summit for the Adoption of the Post-2015 Development Agenda 'Transforming Our World: The 2030 Agenda for Sustainable Development.'" Sept. 1, 2015. https://holyseemission.org /contents//statements/55e60e559a5749.94098476.php.

———. *Code of Canon Law*. Città del Vaticano: Libreria Editrice Vaticana, 2003. http://www.vatican.va/archive/ENG1104/__P45.HTM.

Holy See Press Office. "XIV Ordinary General Assembly of the Synod of Bishops—List of Participants." *Holy See Press Office*. Updated Oct. 5, 2015. http://press.vatican.va /content/salastampa/it/bollettino/pubblico/2015/09/15/0676/01469.html.

———. "Communiqué, 03.05.2018." *Holy See Press Office*. May 3, 2018. http://press.vatican.va/content/salastampa/en/bollettino/pubblico/2018/05 /03/180503e.html.

———. **Burke, dir.**, Greg. "Dichiarazione del direttore della Sala Stampa." *Holy See Press Office*. Jan. 30, 2018. https://press.vatican.va/content/salastampa/it /bollettino/pubblico/2018/01/30/0089/00168.html#ing.

———. **Lombardi, dir.**, Fr. Federico. "Dichiarazione del Direttore della Sala Stampa a nome del Santo Padre." Aug. 7, 2014. https://press.vatican.va/content /salastampa/it/bollettino/pubblico/2014/08/07/0559/01234.html

———. ———. "Statement Regarding a Meeting of Pope Francis and Mrs. Kim Davis at the Nunciature in Washington, DC, 02.10.2015." Oct. 2, 2015. https://press.vatican.va /content/salastampa/it/bollettino/pubblico/2015/10/02/0749/01616.html.

Pontifical Council for Legislative Texts. "Declaration: II. Concerning the Admission to Holy Communion of Faithful Who Are Divorced and Remarried." Jun. 24, 2000. http://www.vatican.va/roman_curia/pontifical_councils/intrptxt/documents /rc_pc_intrptxt_doc_20000706_declaration_en.html.

Pontifical Academy for Life. "Statutes." Accessed Jul. 15, 2018. http://www.academyforlife.va/content/dam/pav/documents/academy_statute.pdf.

Pontifical Academy for Science. "Protect the Earth, Dignify Humanity. The Moral Dimensions of Climate Change and Sustainable Humanity." *Pontifical Academy of Sciences.* Apr. 28, 2015. http://www.casinapioiv.va/content/accademia/en/events /2015/protectearth.html.

Pontifical Council for the Pastoral Care of Migrants and Itinerant People and Pontifical Council Cor Unum. "Welcoming Christ in Refugees and Forcibly Displaced Persons." http://www.pcmigrants.org/documento%20rifugiati%202013/927-INGL.pdf.

Pontifical Council for the Family. *The Meeting Point: Project for Affective and Sexual Formation.* July 19, 2016.

Second Vatican Council. Dogmatic Constitution *Lumen Gentium.* Nov. 21, 1964. http://www.vatican.va/archive/hist_councils/ii_vatican_council/documents /vat-ii_const_19641121_lumen-gentium_en.html.

Synod of Bishops, Fourteenth Ordinary General Assembly (On the Family). "The Vocation and Mission of the Family in the Church and the Contemporary World—*Instrumentum Laboris.*" Jun. 23, 2015. http://www.vatican.va/roman_curia/synod/documents /rc_synod_doc_20150623_instrumentum-xiv-assembly_en.html.
———. "The Vocation and Mission of the Family in the Church and Contemporary World—*Lineamenta.*" Dec. 9, 2014. http://www.vatican.va/roman_curia /synod/documents/rc_synod_doc_20141209_lineamenta-xiv-assembly_en.html.

Synod of Bishops, Third Extraordinary General Assembly (On the Family). "Pastoral Challenges to the Family in the Context of Evangelization—Preparatory Document." Nov. 5, 2013. http://www.vatican.va/roman_curia/synod/documents /rc_synod_doc_20131105_iii-assemblea-sinodo-vescovi_en.html.
———. "*Relatio post disceptationem.*" Oct. 13, 2014. http://catholic-ew.org.uk /Home/News/2014/Synod-2015/Relatio-Post-Disceptationem.

III. Other

Allen, Jr., John L. "Translated Final Interview With Martini." *National Catholic Reporter.* Sept. 4, 2012. https://www.ncronline.org/blogs/ncr-today/translated -final-interview-martini.

Ambrogetti, Francesca and Sergio Rubin. *Pope Francis: His Life in His Own Words—Conversations With Jorge Bergoglio.* New York: G. P. Putnam's Sons, 2010, 2013.

American TFP. "TFP Statement on Pope Francis's "Paradigm Shift": Resist as Saint Paul Teaches." July 17, 2108. *TFP.org.* http://www.tfp.org/tfp-statement-on-pope -francis-paradigm-shift-resist-as-saint-paul-teaches/.

Amig@s MST. "Movimenti di tutto il mondo, unitevi! La lotta di classe secondo i senza terra brasiliani. Stedile al Valle (7 Dicembre 2013) + Video." *Amig@s MST–Italia.* Accessed Jul. 15, 2018. http://www.comitatomst.it/node/1058.

Anonymous. "Why Do Freemasons Love Pope Francis? [In 3 parts]." *OnePeterFive.* Apr. 7, 2017; Apr. 28, 2017; May 11, 2017. https://onepeterfive.com/freemasons -love-pope-francis/.

AVN. "Venezuela asume carta encíclica del Papa Francisco para la construcción del ecosocialismo." *AVN.* Jun. 18, 2015. http://avn.info.ve/contenido/venezuela -asume-carta-enc%C3%ADclica-del-papa-Francis-para-construcci%C3%B3n -del-ecosocialismo.

Aymans, Winfried, ed. *Eleven Cardinals Speak on Marriage and the Family.* San Francisco: Ignatius, 2015.

Baudrillard, Jean, Jacinto Lageira and Alain Brunn. "Modernité." In *Encyclopédie Universalis.* Accessed Jul. 24, 2018. https://www.universalis.fr/encyclopedie/modernite/.

Billuart, OP, Caroli Renati. *Tractatus de fide et regulis fidei: D. Th.* Vol. 1. *Summa S. Thomæ, Cursus Theologiæ, Secunda Secundæ.* Liège: S.S.E., 1751. https://books.google.com/books?id=FZBcAAAAcAAJ.

Boulad, Henri. "Pere Henri Boulad: 'Attentats contre les chrétiens coptes dimanche des ramaux: J'accuse l'islam." *Dreuz.info.* Apr. 19, 2017. http://www.dreuz.info /2017/04/19/pere-henri-boulad-attentats-contre-les-chretiens-coptes -dimanche-des-ramaux-jaccuse-lislam/.

Broglie, Albert de. *Questions de religion et d'histoire.* Paris: Michel Lévy Frères, 1860. https://books.google.com/books?id=9JUTIdKex-QC.

Buenos Aires Region Bishops. "Obispos de la Región Buenos Aires dan criterios pastorales sobre los divorciados en nueva unión." *AICA.* Sept. 13, 2016. http://www.aica.org/25025-obispos-de-la-region-buenos-aires-dan-criterios -pastorales-sobre.html.

Burke, Raymond. "'Amoris Laetitia' and the Constant Teaching and Practice of the Church." *National Catholic Register.* Apr. 12, 2016. http://www.ncregister.com/daily -news/amoris-laetitia-and-the-constant-teaching-and-practice-of-the-church/.

———. "The Remnant Interview of Cardinal Raymond Burke." *The Remnant*. Jan. 9, 2017. https://remnantnewspaper.com/web/index.php/articles/item/2980-the -remnant-interview-of-cardinal-raymond-burke.

Cantalamessa, OFM, Cap., Raniero. "'Be Reconciled to God'–Good Friday Sermon, 2016, in St. Peter's Basilica." *Cantalamessa.org*. Mar. 26, 2016. http://www.cantalamessa.org/?p=3050&lang=en.

Carusi, Stefano. "L'influsso di Lutero dietro la 'tesi Kasper'? Un aspetto del recente sinodo sulla famiglia." *Disputationes Theologicae*. Dec. 21, 2014. http://disputationes -theologicae.blogspot.fr/2014/12/linflusso-di-lutero-dietro-la-tesi.html.

Cavalcoli, Giovanni. "La dipendenza dell'idea dalla realtà nella *Evangelii Gaudium* di papa Francesco." *PATH* (2/2014), 13:287–316. http://www.cultura.va/content /dam/cultura/docs/pdf/accademie/path/2-2014.pdf.

Chilean Society for the Defense of Tradition, Family, and Property. *The Church of Silence in Chile: The TFP Proclaims the Whole Truth*. Cleveland: Lumen Mariae, 1976.

Cole, OP, Basil. "Thomism, Moral Claim and Amoris Laetitia." *Anthropotes* 33 (2017): 313–26. http://www.istitutogp2.it/public/Basil%20Cole%20OP_Anthropotes %202017-1_estratto.pdf.

Corbett, OP, John, et al. "Recent Proposals for the Pastoral Care of the Divorced and Remarried: A Theological Assessment." *Nova et Vetera* 12, no. 3 (Summer 2014): 601–30. http://www.laikos.org/recent-proposals-a-theological-assessment.pdf.

Corrêa de Oliveira, Plinio. *A Igreja ante a escalada da ameaça comunista* [The Church in the face of the escalating communist threat: An appeal to the silent bishops]. Third Edition. São Paulo: Editora Vera Cruz, 1977.
———. "A perfeita alegria" [The perfect joy]. *Folha de S. Paulo*. Jul. 12, 1970. http://www.pliniocorreadeoliveira.info/1970_236_CAT_A_perfeita_alegria.htm.
———. *Indian Tribalism: The Communist-Missionary Ideal for Brazil in the Twenty-First Century*. In *Crusade for a Christian Civilization* 10, no. 4 (Oct.-Dec. 1980). http://www.tfp.org/indian-tribalism-the-communist-missionary-ideal-for -brazil-in-the-twenty-first-century/.
———. *Revolution and Counter-Revolution*. Third English edition. York, Penn.: The American Society for the Defense of Tradition, Family and Property, 1993. http://www.tfp.org/revolution-and-counter-revolution/.
———. "The Vatican Policy of Détente With Communist Governments: Should the TFPs Stand Down? Or Should They Resist?" http://www.tfp.org/vatican-policy -detente-communist-governments-tfps-stand-resist/. First published as "A política de distensão do Vaticano com os governos comunistas. Para a TFP: omitir-se? ou resistir?" *Folha de S. Paulo*. Apr. 10, 1974. https://pliniocorreadeoliveira.info /MAN%20-%201974-04-08_Resistencia.htm.

"Correctio filialis de haeresibus propagatis." Jul. 16, 2017.
    http://www.correctiofilialis.org/wp-content/uploads/2017/08
    /Correctio-filialis_English_1.pdf.

Cupich, Blasé. "Pope Francis's Revolution of Mercy: Amoris Laetitia as a New Para-
    digm of Catholicity." Von Hügel Institute Annual Lecture. Feb. 9, 2018.
    https://www.vhi.st-edmunds.cam.ac.uk/resources-folder/papers
    -presentations/cupich-annual-lecture-2018.

Dandrieu, Laurent. *Église et immigration: Le grand malaise–Le pape et le suicide de la
    civilization européene.* Paris: Renaissance, 2017.

"Declaration of Fidelity to the Church's Unchangeable Teaching on Marriage and to Her
    Uninterrupted Discipline." Accessed Jul. 23, 2018. http://www.filialappeal.org/full.

Delprat, Jean, Solange Ehrler, Michel Romain, and Jacques Xenard. "Estudio de la pren-
    sión." *Encyclopédie Médico-Chirurgicale.* https://fr.scribd.com/document/106460939
    /05-Estudio-de-La-Prension. First published as "Bilan de la préhension." *Encycl.
    Méd. Chir.* Paris: Editions Scientifiques et Médicales Elsevier, 2002. Kinésithérapie-
    Médecine physique-Réadaptation. 26-008-D-20. 2002. 16 p.

Diocesi di Como. "Nota pastorale per l'attuazione del cap. VIII di *Amoris Laetitia:* Ac-
    compagnare, discernere e integrare le fragilità." Feb. 14, 2018.
    https://famigliechiesacomo.files.wordpress.com/2018/02/diocesicomo
    _notapastorale_capviii_al2.pdf.

El Mundo. "Maduro: 'El Papa Francisco está en sintonía con el legado de Chávez.'" *El
    Mundo.* Jan. 22, 2014. http://www.elmundo.es/america/2014/01/22
    /52dfb8a0e2704e994a8b4570.html.

Etienne, Jacques. "Loi et grâce: Le concept de la loi nouvelle dans la *Somme théologi-
    que* de S. Thomas d'Aquin." *Revue théologique de Louvain* 16, no. 1 (1985): 5–22.
    https://www.persee.fr/doc/thlou_0080-2654_1985_num_16_1_2089.

exmusulmanschretiens.fr. "From Former Muslims Who Became Catholics, and Their
    Friends, to His Holiness Pope Francis, About His Attitude Toward Islam." Dec. 24,
    2017. http://exmusulmanschretiens.fr/en/.

"Filial Appeal to His Holiness Pope Francis on the Future of the Family." Accessed Jul. 23,
    2018. https://www.tfpstudentaction.org/assets/imgs/inline/filialpetition-en.pdf.

Fontbaustier, Laurent. *La déposition du pape hérétique: Une origine du constitution-
    nalisme?* Paris: Mare & Martin, 2016.

Gherardini, Brunero. "Chiesa-tradizione-magistero." Published as "Mons. Gherardini sull'importanza e i limiti del magistero autentico." *Disputationes Theologicae.* Dec 7, 2011. http://disputationes-theologicae.blogspot.fr/2011/12/mons -gherardini-sullimportanza-e-i.html.

Grabois, Juan. "Capitalismo popular: La respuesta liberal a la crisis de la sociedad salarial." *Blog de Juan Grabois.* Sept. 1, 2012. http://juangrabois.blogspot.com/.
———. "Capitalismo popular: Una variante salvaje del modelo. Nota en agenda oculta." *La Alameda.* Sept. 10, 2012. https://laalameda.wordpress.com/2012/09/10 /capitalismo-popular-una-variante-salvaje-del-modelo/.
———. "Introducción." In "Documentos: Encuentro Mundial de Movimientos Populares." Accessed Jul. 14, 2018. http://movimientospopulares.org/wp-content/ uploads/2016/10/Documents_castellano_web.pdf.
———. "La economía popular 'surge de la exclusión. No es una expresión de la solidaridad humana.'" *Prudentia Politica.* Oct. 24, 2014. https://prudentiapolitica.blogspot .com/2014/10/la-economia-popular-no-va-ser-nunca.html.

Himes, OFM, Kenneth R., and James A. Coriden. "Notes on Moral Theology 1995: Pastoral Care of the Divorced and Remarried." *Theological Studies* 57 (1996): 97– 123. http://cdn.theologicalstudies.net/57/57.1/57.1.6.pdf.

Houelebecq, Michel. *Submission: A Novel.* Translated by Lorin Stein. New York: Farrar, Straus & Giroux, 2015.

Höver, Gerhard. "'Time Is Greater Than Space': Moral-Theological Reflections on the Post-Synodal Apostolic Exhortation *Amoris Laetitia.*" Translated by Brian McNeil. http://www.academyforlife.va/content/dam/pav/documenti%20pdf/2018/01 _Hoever_pdf.pdf. First published as "'Die zeit ist mehr wert als der raum' moraltheologische überlegungen zum nachsynodalen apostolischen schreiben Amoris Laetitia." *Marriage, Families and Spirituality* 23, no. 1 (2017): 3–18.

Iglesias, Pablo y Héctor Illueca. "Si la misa la oficiara el Papa Francisco." *20 minutos.* Mar. 28, 2017. http://www.20minutos.es/opiniones/pablo-iglesias-hecor-illueca -tribuna-misa-oficiaria-papa-Francis-2996635/#xtor=AD-15&xts=467263.

Juncker, Jean-Claude. "Speech by President Jean-Claude Juncker at the Award Ceremony of the Charlemagne Prize to Pope Francis." *European Commission.* May 6, 2016. http://europa.eu/rapid/press-release_SPEECH-16-1681_en.htm.

Kasper, Walter. "'Amoris Laetitia': Bruch oder aufbruch?" *Stimmen Der Zeit* 11 (Nov. 2016): 723–32. http://www.stimmen-der-zeit.de/zeitschrift/ausgabe/details?k _beitrag=4752128&cnid=13&k_produkt=4754046.

Kazakhstan bishops. Full Text of Kazakhstan Catholic Bishops Statement on Amoris Laetitita." *LifeSiteNews.* Jan. 2, 2018. https://www.lifesitenews.com/news/full -text-of-kazakhstan-catholic-bishops-statement-on-amoris-laetitia.

Ki-Moon, Ban. "Secretary-General's Remarks at Workshop on the Moral Dimensions of Climate Change and Sustainable Development 'Protect the Earth, Dignify Humanity' [As Delivered]." Apr. 28, 2015. https://www.un.org/sg/en/content/sg/statement/2015-04-28/secretary-generals-remarks-workshop-moral-dimensions-climate-change.

Kraus, J. M., ed. *La nuova Chiesa di papa Francesco.* Rome: Moralia, 2013.

Kuhn, Thomas S. *Structure of Scientific Revolutions.* 4th Edition. Chicago: University of Chicago Press, 2012.

Laurentin, René. *Enjeu du deuxième synode: Et contestation dans l'Église.* Paris: Seuil, 1969.

Laymann, SJ, Paul. *Theologia moralis.* Venice: n.p., 1683. https://archive.org/details/bub_gb_cNcQB5d8hqoC.

Libero Quotidiano. "Massimo D'Alema candida papa Francesco: 'Lui è il miglior leader della sinistra." *Libero Quotidiano.* Jan. 24, 2018. http://tv.liberoquotidiano.it/video/politica/13302149/papa-francesco-massimo-d-alema-pontefice-miglior-leader-sinistra.html.

L'Obs. "Marie-Noëlle Lienemann (PS) rend hommage au pape François." *L'Obs.* Nov. 2, 2016. http://tempsreel.nouvelobs.com/politique/20131102.AFP0782/marie-noelle-lienemann-ps-rend-hommage-au-pape-francois.html.

Maddison, Angus. "The West and the Rest in the World Economy: 1000–2030 Maddisonian and Malthusian interpretations." *World Economics* 9, no. 4 (Oct.–Dec. 2008): 75–99. https://www.researchgate.net/publication/237678324

Magister, Sandro. "Another Letter From the Four Cardinals to the Pope. This Too With No Response." *L'Espresso–Settimo Cielo.* Jun. 20, 2017. http://magister.blogautore.espresso.repubblica.it/2017/06/20/another-letter-from-the-four-cardinals-to-the-pope-this-too-with-no-response/.
———. "Thirteen Cardinals Have Written to the Pope. Here's the Letter." Translated by Matthew Sherry. *L'Espresso–Settimo Cielo.* Oct. 12, 2015. http://chiesa.espresso.repubblica.it/articolo/1351154.html.

Martin, SJ, James. "We Need to Build a Bridge Between LGBT Community and the Catholic Church." *America.* Oct. 30, 2016. https://www.americamagazine.org/faith/2016/10/30/james-martin-sj-we-need-build-bridge-between-lgbt-community-and-catholic-church;

Martini, Cardinal Carlo M. and Georg Sporschill. *Night Conversations With Cardinal Martini.* Mahwah, N.J.: Paulist, 2012.

Matt, Michael. "The Remnant Interview of Cardinal Raymond Burke." *The Remnant.*
     Jan. 9, 2017. https://remnantnewspaper.com/web/index.php/articles/item
     /2980-the-remnant-interview-of-cardinal-raymond-burke.

Mattei, Roberto de. *The Crusader of the 20th Century: Plinio Corrêa de Oliveira.*
     Leominster, Herefordshire, U.K.: Gracewing, Fowler Wright, 1995.
——. "L'esortazione post-sinodale Amoris Laetitia: Prime riflessioni su un docu-
     mento catastrofico." *Corrispondenza Romana.* Apr. 13, 2016.
     http://www.corrispondenzaromana.it/lesortazione-post-sinodale-amoris
     -laetitia-prime-riflessioni-su-un-documento-catastrofico/.
——. "The Irrevocable Duties of Cardinals of the Holy Roman Church." Translated
     by Francesca Romana. *Rorate Cæli.* Dec. 16, 2016.
     https://rorate-caeli.blogspot.com/2016/12/de-mattei-irrevocable-duties-of.html.
——. *Le ralliement de Léon XIII: l'échec d'un projet pastoral.* Paris: Cerf, 2016.
——. *The Second Vatican Council: An Unwritten Story.* Translated by Patrick T. Bran-
     nan, SJ, Michael J. Miller, and Kenneth D. Whitehead. Edited by Michael J. Miller.
     Fitzwilliam, NH: Loreto, 2012.

Matzuzzi, Matteo. "Only a Blind Man Can Deny That There's Now in the Church
     Great Confusion." Translated by Juliana Freitag. *Caffarra.it.* Jul. 21, 2018.
     http://www.caffarra.it/eng140117.php.

Mayer, Antônio de Castro. *Carta pastoral sobre problemas do apostolado moderno: Con-
     tendo um catecismo de verdades oportunas que se opõem a erros contemporâneos.* Sec-
     ond Edition. Campos, Brazil: n. p. 1953. https://www.pliniocorreadeoliveira.info
     /Carta%20Pastoral%20sobre%20os%20Erros%20do%20Apostolado%20Moderno.pdf.

McCusker, Matthew. "Key Doctrinal Errors and Ambiguities of Amoris Laetitia. *Voice
     of the Family.* May 7, 2016. http://voiceofthefamily.com/key-doctrinal-errors-and
     -ambiguities-of-amoris-laetitia/.
——. "The Impact of the United Nations' Sustainable Development Goals on Chil-
     dren and the Family, and Their Endorsement by the Holy See." *Voice of the Family.*
     Feb. 3, 2017. http://voiceofthefamily.com/wp-content/uploads/2017/02
     /Impact-of-the-United-Nations-Sustainable-Development-Goals22-2-17.pdf.

Meadows, Donella H., Dennis L. Meadows, Jørgen Randers, and William W. Behrens III.
     The Limits to Growth. New York: Universe, 1972. http://www.donellameadows.org
     /wp-content/userfiles/Limits-to-Growth-digital-scan-version.pdf

Mélenchon, Jean-Luc. "Vive le pape!" *Melenchon.* Apr. 17, 2016.
     http://melenchon.fr/2016/04/17/vive-le-pape/.

Movimientos Populares (Popular Movements). "Quienes somos." *Encuentro Mundial
     de Movimientos Populares.* Accessed Jul. 13, 2018.
     http://movimientospopulares.org/es/emmp-2/.

———. "La tierra y la producción campesina." *Movimientos Populares*. Accessed Jul. 14, 2018. http://movimientospopulares.org/wp-content/uploads/2015/06 /conclusiones-de-los-talleres-EMMP.pdf.

———. "Declaración final Encuentro Mundial Movimientos Populares." *Movimientos Populares*. Accessed Jul. 14, 2018. http://movimientospopulares.org/wp-content /uploads/2014/10/DECLARACION-FINAL-EMMP-rivista-da-Czerney.pdf.

———. "Carta de Santa Cruz." Jul. 9, 2015. *Movimientos Populares*. http://movimientospopulares.org/wp-content/uploads/2015/07/Carta-di -Santa-Cruz-Portoghese.pdf.

———. "Propuestas de acción transformadora que asumimos los Movimientos Populares del Mundo en diálogo con el Papa Francisco." *Movimientos Populares*. Accessed Jul. 14, 2018. http://movimientospopulares.org/es/propuestas-de -accion-transformadora-que-asumimos-los-movimientos-populares-del -mundo-en-dialogo-con-el-papa-Francis/.

———. Síntese de los Movimientos Populares en los tres dias del EMMP." *Movimientos Populares*. Accessed Jul. 15, 2018. http://movimientospopulares.org/espanol/.

———. "Message from Modesto." World Meeting of Popular Movements. Feb. 19, 2017. http://popularmovements.org/news/message-from-modesto/.

OECD. *How Was Life? Global Wellbeing Since 1820*. Edited by Jan Luiten van Zanden, et al. Paris: OECD, 2014. http://www.oecd.org/statistics/how-was-life -9789264214262-en.htm.

O'Connell, Gerard. "Cardinal Wuerl Calls Out Pope's Opponents." *America*. Oct. 18, 2015. https://www.americamagazine.org/content/dispatches/cardinal -wuerl-calls-out-popes-opponents.

———. "Cardinal Wuerl: Pope Francis Has Reconnected the Church With Vatican II." *America*. Mar. 6, 2017. https://www.americamagazine.org/faith/2017/03/06 /cardinal-wuerl-pope-francis-has-reconnected-church-vatican-ii.

———. "Cuba's Raul Castro Tells Pope Francis: 'I Could Become a Catholic Again.'" *America*. May 10, 2015. https://www.americamagazine.org/content/dispatches /cubas-raul-castro-tells-pope-francis-i-could-become-catholic-again.

Pagotto, SSS, Aldo di Cillo, Robert F. Vasa, and Athanasius Schneider. *Preferential Option for the Family: 100 Questions and Answers Relating to the Synod*. Rome: Supplica Filiale, 2015. http://www.tfp.org/images/stories/PDF_files /Preferential_Option_for_the_Family_English.pdf.

Palmieri, SJ, Domenico. *Tractatus de Romano Pontifice*. Prati: Giachetti, 1891.

Parente, Pietro. "Supr. S. Congr. S. Officii Decretum 4 febr. 1942—Annotationes." *Periodica de Re Morali, Canonica, Liturgica* 31 (Feb. 1942): 184–88. Originally published as "Nuove tendenze teologiche." *L'Osservatore Romano*. Feb. 9–10, 1942.

Pentin, Edward. "Cardinal Burke on Amoris Laetitia Dubia: 'Tremendous Division'
Warrants Action." *National Catholic Register*. Nov. 15, 2016.
http://www.ncregister.com/daily-news/cardinal-burke-on-amoris-laetitia
-dubia-tremendous-division-warrants-action.
———. "Full Text and Explanatory Notes of Cardinals' Questions on 'Amoris Laetitia.'" *National Catholic Register*. Nov. 14, 2016. http://www.ncregister.com/blog
/edward-pentin/full-text-and-explanatory-notes-of-cardinals-questions
-on-amoris-laetitia.
———. *The Rigging of a Vatican Synod? An Investigation Into Alleged Manipulation at
the Extraordinary Synod on the Family*. San Francisco: Ignatius, 2015.

Peters, cur., Edward N. *The 1917 or Pio-Benedictine Code of Canon Law*. San Francisco: Ignatius, 2001.

Pierantoni, Claudio. "Josef Seifert, Pure Logic, and the Beginning of the Official Persecution of Orthodoxy Within the Church." *AEMAET* 6, no. 2 (2017): 22–33.
http://www.aemaet.de/index.php/aemaet/article/view/46/pdf_1.

Pinheiro, Daniel P. "Assentimento ao magistério. (Parte final: Doutrina comum dos
teólogos e bibliografia)." *Scutum Fidei*. Feb. 20, 2013. https://scutumfidei.org/2013
/02/20/assentimento-ao-magisterio-parte-final-doutrina-comum-dos
-teologos-e-bibliografia/.

Piqué, Elisabetta. "Pope Francis: 'God Has Bestowed on Me a Healthy Dose of Unawareness.'" *La Nación*. Dec. 7, 2014. https://www.lanacion.com.ar/1750350-
pope-francis-god-has-bestowed-on-me-a-healthy-dose-of-unawareness.
———. "The Synod on the Family: 'The Divorced and Remarried Seem Excommunicated.'"
La Nación. Dec. 7, 2014. https://www.lanacion.com.ar/1750351-the-synod-on-the-
family-the-divorced-and-remarried-seem-excommunicated.

Potterie, Ignace de la. "Men Are Not Born Sons of God. They Become So." *30Days*.
Dec. 2009. http://www.30giorni.it/articoli_id_22029_l3.htm.

Ramonet, Ignacio. "Impressiones de una jornada histórica." *Movimientos Populares*.
Oct. 27–29, 2014. http://movimientospopulares.org/wp-content/uploads
/2014/10/EMMP-Una-jornada-historica-IR.pdf.

Ratzinger, Joseph. *Principles of Catholic Theology: Building Stones for a Fundamental Theology*. Translated by Mary Frances McCarthy, SND. San Francisco: Ignatius, 1987.
———. "Worthiness to Receive Holy Communion: General Principles" (Letter to Cardinal Theodore McCarrick). Accessed Jul. 9, 2018. http://www.ewtn.com/library
/curia/cdfworthycom.htm.

Ripperger, FSSP, Chad. "Operative Point of View: A Scholar Examines the Root Cause of
Present Tensions Within the Ranks of Faithful Catholics." *Christian Order*. Mar. 2001.
http://www.christianorder.com/features/features_2001/features_mar01.html.

Riva, Angelo. "Approfondimento di teologia morale in margine alla nota pastorale per l'attuazione del cap. VIII di Amoris Laetitia." Jan. 30, 2018. https://famigliechiesacomo.files.wordpress.com/2018/02 /approfondimentoteologiamorale_30gennaio2018_donangeloriva.pdf.

Robert Bellarmine, Saint. *De Controversiis, On the Roman Pontiff.* Translated by Ryan Grant. Charleston, S.C.: Mediatrix Press, 2015.

Rodríguez Maradiaga, Óscar. *Only the Gospel is Revolutionary: The Church in the Reform of Pope Francis.* Translated by Demetrio S. Yocum. Collegeville, Minn.: Litrugical Press, 2018.

Sánchez Sorondo, Marcelo. "A Response From the Pontifical Academy of Sciences." *First Things.* Jun. 25, 2015. https://www.firstthings.com/web-exclusives/2015 /06/a-response-from-the-pas.

Santos, João Vitor. "O Papa Francisco e a teologia do povo: Entrevista especial com Juan Carlos Scannone." Translated by André Langer. *Revista IHU Online.* No. 465 (May 18, 2015). http://www.ihuonline.unisinos.br/index.php?option=com _content&view=article&id=5919&secao=465.

Scalese, Giovanni. "Dottrina vs discernimento." *Antiquo Roboro.* Apr. 18, 2017. http://querculanus.blogspot.fr/2017/04/dottrina-vs-discernimento.html.
———. "I postulati di papa Francesco." *Antiquo Roboro.* May 10, 2016. http://querculanus.blogspot.fr/2016/05/i-postulati-di-papa-francesco.html.

Scalfari, Eugenio (Chronological order)
———. "The Pope: How the Church Will Change." *La Repubblica.* Oct. 1, 2013. http://www.repubblica.it/cultura/2013/10/01/news/pope_s_conversation _with_scalfari_english-67643118/.
———. "Il vicario di Cristo e la verità relativa che conduce a Dio." *La Repubblica.* Oct. 28, 2014. http://www.repubblica.it/cultura/2014/10/28/news/il_vicario_di_cristo _e_la_verit_relativa_che_conduce_a_dio-99162795/.
———. "Francesco, papa profeta che incontra la modernità." *La Repubblica.* Jul. 1, 2015. http://www.repubblica.it/cultura/2015/07/01/news/francesco_papa _profeta_che_incontra_la_modernita_-118048516/.
———. "Conservatori e temporalisti lo frenano ma Francesco non si fermerà." *La Repubblica.* Oct. 25, 2015. http://www.repubblica.it/politica/2015/10/25/news /conservatori_e_temporalisti_lo_frenano_ma_francesco_non_si_fermera _-125834299/.
———. "Scalfari intervista Francesco: 'Il mio grido al G20 sui migranti.'" *La Repubblica.* Jul. 8, 2017. http://www.repubblica.it/vaticano/2017/07/08/news /scalfari_intervista_francesco_il_mio_grido_al_g20_sui_migranti_-170253225/.

Schellnhuber, Hans Joachim (John). "Expanding the Democracy Universe." *Center for Humans & Nature.* Accessed Jul. 16, 2018. http://www.humansandnature.org /democracy-hans-joachim-schellnhuber.

Schlegel, Jean-Louis. "Changer l'église en changeant la politique." In *À la gauche du Christ: Les chrétiens de gauche en France de 1945 à nos jours,* edited by Denis Pelletier and Jean-Louis Schelegel, 259–95. Paris: Seuil, 2012.

Schneider, Athanasius. "Against Pharisees." *Polonia Christiana* 41 (Nov.–Dec. 2014). http://www.pch24.pl/against-pharisees,31907,i.html.
———. "Bishop Athanasius Schneider Replies to *The Remnant*'s Open Letter on Amoris Laetitia." *The Remnant.* Jun. 2, 2016. http://remnantnewspaper.com/web /index.php/articles/item/2558-bishop-athanasius-schneider-replies-to-the -remnant-s-open-letter-on-amoris-laetitia.
———. "Official Response of Bishop Athanasius Schneider to Amoris Laetitia." *Rorate Cæli.* Apr. 26, 2016. https://rorate-caeli.blogspot.com/2016/04/official-response -of-bishop-athanasius.html.
———. "Interview With TV-Libertés—'Terres de Mission,' Program no. 10." *TV-Libertés.* Dec. 4, 2016. https://gloria.tv/video/3TPZg1Enfkw9D7qULW8ejhcdY.

Seifert, Josef. "Amoris Laetitia: Joy, Sadness and Hopes." *AEMAET* 5, no. 2 (2016): 160–64. http://www.aemaet.de/index.php/aemaet/article/view/35/pdf.
———. "Does Pure Logic Threaten to Destroy the Entire Moral Doctrine of the Catholic Church?" *AEMAET* 6, no. 2 (2017): 2–9. http://www.aemaet.de/index .php/aemaet/article/view/44/pdf_1.

Servant General, The. "Report and Reflections on the III Extraordinary General Assembly of the Synod of Bishops." *Couples for Christ.* Oct. 24, 2014. http://cfcffl.net/report-and-reflections-on-the-iii-extraordinary-general -assembly-of-the-synod-of-bishops/.

Shaw, Joseph, et al. "The Apostolic Exhortation *Amoris Laetitia*: A Theological Critique." *OnePeterFive.* Accessed Jul. 24, 2018. https://onepeterfive.com/wp-content /uploads/2016/07/45-theologians-censure-AL.pdf.

Solimeo, Luíz S. "Because of Its Grave Errors 'Amoris Laetitia' Should Be Rejected." *TFP.* May 4, 2016. http://www.tfp.org/tfp-home/catholic-perspective /because-of-its-grave-errors-amoris-laetitia-should-be-rejected.html.
———. "Cardinal Cupich's Modernist Concepts." *TFP.org.* Feb. 21, 2018. http://www.tfp.org/cardinal-cupichs-modernist-concepts/.

Sporschill, SJ, Georg, and Federica Radice Fossati Confalonieri. "'Chiesa indietro di 200 anni': L'ultima intervista: 'Perché non si scuote, perché abbiamo paura?'" *Corriere Della Sera.* Sept. 1, 2012. http://www.corriere.it/cronache/12_settembre_02/le -parole-ultima-intervista_cdb2993e-f50b-11e1-9f30-3ee01883d8dd.shtml.

Stédile, João Pedro. "E la terra tremerà." *Adista News.* Jan. 3, 2014.
http://www.adista.it/articolo/53494.
———. "El mundo en crisis: Síntesis del primer dia de trabajo del Encuentro Mundial de Movimientos Populares, Roma, 27 de Octubre, de 2014." *Movimientos Populares.* Accessed Jul. 14, 2018. http://movimientospopulares.org/wp-content /uploads/2014/10/El-Mundo-en-Crisis-EMMP-Joa-Pedro-Stedile.pdf.

Thomas Aquinas, Saint. *Commentary on Saint Paul's Epistle to the Galatians.* Translated by F. R. Larcher, OP. Albany, NY: Magi, 1966. html format by Joseph Kenny, OP. https://dhspriory.org/thomas/SSGalatians.htm.
———. *Summa Theologiæ.* Translated by Fathers of the English Dominican Province. Second, Revised Edition. New York: Benziger Bros., 1920. Revised and edited by Kevin Knight for New Advent. http://www.newadvent.org/summa/.

TFPs (various). *Um homem, uma obra, uma gesta: Homenagem das TFPs a Plinio Corrêa de Oliveira.* São Paulo: Artpress, 1989.
http://www.pliniocorreadeoliveira.info/Gesta_0000Indice.htm.

Turco, Giovanni. "[Da leggere] alcune linee guida per la lettura filosfica del pontificato di Bergoglio." *Radio Spada.* Jun. 25, 2017. https://www.radiospada.org/2017/06/da -leggere-alcune-linee-guida-per-la-lettura-filosofica-del-pontificato-di-bergoglio/. Republished summary of "Axes De Lecture Philosophique De Textes Du Pontificat Actuel." *Courrier de Rome* 593 (Nov. 2016). https://laportelatine.org/publications /presse/courrier_de_rome/2016/1611cdr593.pdf.

Turkson, Peter. "Conferencia de prensa." *Movimientos Populares.* Jul. 6, 2015.
http://movimientospopulares.org/wp-content/uploads/2015/06/press -conference-ESP.pdf.
———. "Conferencia." *Movimientos Populares.* Jul. 7, 2015. http://movimientospopu lares.org/wp-content/uploads/2015/06/2015.07.07-pkat-intro.pdf.

United Nations Sustainable Development Solutions Network. "SDSN and Pontifical Academy of Sciences Assembles Top Mayors to Discuss U.N. Sustainable Development Goals." *UNSDSN.org.* Jul. 17, 2015. http://unsdsn.org/news/2015/07/17 /sdsn-and-pontifical-academy-of-sciences-assembles-top-mayors-to-discuss -un-sustainable-development-goals/.

Uruguayan TFP. *Izquierdismo en la Iglesia: compañero de ruta del comunismo.* Montevideo: Sociedad Uruguaya de Defensa de la Tradición, Familia y Propiedad, 1977.

Vandentorren, MD, Stéphanie, et al. "Mortality in 13 French Cities During the August 2003 Heat Wave." *American Journal of Public Health* 94, no. 9 (Sept. 2004): 1518–20. https://www.ncbi.nlm.nih.gov/pmc/articles/PMC1448485/

Vargas, Iván de. "Entrevista a los autores de libro documento 'Francisco, el Papa manso.'" *Zenit*. Nov. 29, 2013. https://es.zenit.org/articles/entrevista-a-los-autores-de-libro-documento-francisco-el-papa-manso/.

Venezuelan Bishops Conference. "Comunicado de la presidencia de la CEV: 'No reformar la constitución sino cumplirla.'" *Il Sismografo*. May 5, 2017. http://ilsismografo.blogspot.fr/2017/05/venezuela-comunicado-de-la-presidencia.html.

Vignelli, Guido. *A Pastoral Revolution: Six Talismanic Words in the Synodal Debate on the Family*. Spring Grove, Penn.: The American Society for the Defense of Tradition, Family, and Property, 2018. http://www.tfp.org/PastoralRevolution.

Vincent of Lerins, Saint. *Commonitory: For the Antiquity and Universality of the Catholic Faith Against the Profane Novelties of All Heresies*. Translated by C.A. Heurtley. From *Nicene and Post-Nicene Fathers, Second Series*. Vol. 11. Edited by Philip Schaff and Henry Wace. Buffalo, NY: Christian Literature, 1894. Revised and edited for New Advent by Kevin Knight. http://www.newadvent.org/fathers/3506.htm.

Voice of the Family. "Professor Schellnhuber: Climate Science and the 'Population Problem.'" Jun. 26, 2015. http://voiceofthefamily.com/professor-schellnhuber-climate-science-and-the-population-problem/.

Weinandy, OFM, Cap., Thomas G. "July 31, 2017 Letter to the Holy Father." *Crux*. Jul. 31, 2017. https://cruxnow.com/wp-content/uploads/2017/10/Francis-Letter-Final.pdf.

Wimmer, Anian Christoph. "Full Text: Interview With Robert Spaemann on Amoris Laetitia." *Catholic News Agency*. Apr. 29, 2016. https://www.catholicnewsagency.com/news/full-text-interview-with-robert-spaemann-on-amoris-laetitia-10088.

Wolton, Dominique. *Politique et société: Pape François, rencontres avec Dominique Wolton*. Paris: l'Observatoire, 2017.

Xavier da Silveira, Arnaldo Vidigal. *Can Documents of the Magisterium of the Church Contain Errors? Can the Catholic Faithful Resist Them?* Spring Grove, Penn.: The American Society for the Defense of Tradition, Family and Property, 2015. http://www.tfp.org/DocumentsMagisterium.
———. "Notes on *Laudato Sì*." Aug. 3, 2015. http://www.unavox.it/ArtDiversi/DIV1294_Da-Silveira_Note_su_Laudato-si.html.

INDEX

Bibi, Asia, 72
Biggar, Nigel, 17
Billuart, Fr. Charles, 166n580
Bioethical questions, 11n26
Biological sexual identity, 57
Bipolar tensions, 84
Birth control. *See also* Contraception
    abortion as method of, 14
    artificial methods of, 92, 135
    Humanae Vitae in legitimizing, 94–95
Block, Stephanie, 93n338
Boezi, Francesco, 19n61
Boff, Leonardo, 50
Boko Haram, 72
Bongaarts, John, 14
Bonino, Emma, 12–13
Boo, Juan Vicente, 27n82
Boquet, Fr. Shenan, 23
Bortoli, Ferruccio de, 11n25
Bouhassira, Eric E., 18n54
Boulad, Fr. Henri, 74, 75
Bourne, Lisa, 91n327
Brandmüller, Cardinal Walter, 107, 110, 119
Broglie, Albert de, 132
Brown, Judy, 94
Brunn, Alain, 130
Burke, Cardinal Raymond, 107, 114, 116n408, 119, 125, 153n543
Burke, Greg, 47
Bux, Nicola, 165

C
Cafete, Miquel Arias, 144
Caffarra, Cardinal Carlo, 15, 19, 86, 107, 111n394, 113, 119, 120, 125, 171
Cajetan, 160n570
Calabrò, Maria Antonietta, 13n36
Camarotti, Gerson, 31n106
Cambronero, Marcelo López, 27
Cañizares, Cardinal Antonio 92
Cannone, Juan Carlos, 29
Cantalamessa, Fr. Raniero, 78–79
Capitalism, 27, 32
    attacks on, 39

criticisms of, 146
Caram, Lúcia, 92
Carbon dioxide pollution, 51n174
Cardenal, Ernesto, 30n97
Careaga, Esther Ballestrino de, 27, 28
Caritas, 67
Carusi, Stefano, 79n290
Casaroli, Cardinal Ricardo, 16n45, 48, 70n266
Castellano, Danilo, 111n395
Castillo, Ignacio A., 92n334
Castro, Fidel, 39
Castro, Raul, 25
Catani, Federico, 8, 20
Catechism of the Catholic Church, 20, 65, 81, 97
Catherine of Siena, Saint, 156
Catholicism
    end-of-life teaching in, 19–20
    future of, 2–3
    social doctrine in, 2, 28–29, 64
    teachings of, 2
Catholic university teaching, 2
Celli, Archbishop Claudio Maria, 46
Chardin, Fr. Pierre Teilhard de, 56
Charisma, of infallibility, 158
Charlemagne Prize, 145n521
Chavez, Hugo, 40, 147
Chiapas Indians, 54
China, Communism and underground Catholics and, 44–46
Chiodi, Fr. Maurizio, 18, 94, 95
Chretien, Claire, 45n149, 125n437, 127n449
Christian civilization, basic values of, 7
Christianophobia motives, 73
Christian persecution
    religious nature of, 61
    reluctance to talk about, 71–73
Church, future of, 2
The Church of Silence in Chile, 166, 167
Cirinnà, Monica, 22
Class struggle, 31, 37
    Marxism and, 28
Cleemis, Cardinal Baselios, 111n394

Free e-book versions of this work are available at:

English:
www.tfp.org/ParadigmShift

Italian:
www.atfp.it/il-cambio-di-paradigma-di-papa-francesco

Portuguese:
https://ipco.org.br/a-mudanca-de-paradigma